Songs and Sounds of the
Anti-Rent Movement in Upstate New York

SUNY SERIES, AN AMERICAN REGION:
STUDIES IN THE HUDSON VALLEY

THOMAS S. WERMUTH, EDITOR

Songs and Sounds of the Anti-Rent Movement in Upstate New York

Including Twenty-Two New Settings of Period Tunes

NANCY NEWMAN

SUNY
PRESS

Cover Credit: "An Incident of Anti-Rentism" Milne 200 Mural, 1935, by David Lithgow.
Milne Library Preservation Project Photographs, archived in the M. E. Grenander
Special Collections and Archives, University at Albany–SUNY.

Published by State University of New York Press, Albany

Publication of this book was made possible in part by the generous support of the General Fund of the
American Musicological Society, supported in part by the National Endowment for the Humanities
and the Andrew W. Mellon Foundation.

For information, contact State University of New York Press, Albany, NY
www.sunypress.edu

Library of Congress Cataloging-in-Publication Data

Name: Newman, Nancy, author.
Title: Songs and sounds of the anti-rent movement in upstate New York: Including twenty-two new settings of
    period tunes / Nancy Newman.
Description: Albany : State University of New York Press, [2025] | Includes bibliographical references and index.
Identifiers: ISBN 9798855800722 (hardcover : alk. paper) | ISBN 9798855800739 (ebook)
Further information is available at the Library of Congress.

For Matt and Pamela

Lend them an ear and the kingdom will fall
The kingdom will fall for a song.

—Anaïs Mitchell, *Hadestown*, 2010

Contents

Illustrations

Figures

Table

Land Acknowledgment

This is a work about property relations that reach back to the first contact between Indigenous peoples and Europeans. The land I discuss is the traditional homeland of Muhheaconneok, Ho-de-no-sau-nee-ga, and Schaghticoke communities. Many descendants of the Muhheaconneok (Mohican) nation are members of the Stockbridge-Munsee Band today. The Ho-de-no-sau-nee-ga (also known as the Haudenosaunee or Iroquois Confederacy) are an alliance of six distinct nations: Mohawk, Oneida, Onondaga, Cayuga, Seneca, and Tuscarora. I wish to show respect to all Muhheaconneok, Ho-de-no-sau-nee-ga, and Schaghticoke peoples, past and present.

Acknowledgments

A book like this incurs many debts. My first is to Andy Spence, cofounder and former executive director of Old Songs. Ms. Spence is the creator of *Down with the Rent!* and several similarly structured works of folk theater based on regional history and folklife. I had the honor of consulting with Old Songs on their 2017 pageant, *Forward into Light*, which commemorated the centenary of women's suffrage in New York. When I expressed interest in the earlier Anti-Rent show, Andy invited me to her home for a lengthy interview. I am grateful for her generous sharing of regional history and materials.

Little did I know, when watching *Down with the Rent!*, that it would lead me along such a varied and fascinating path. To understand what the Anti-Renters sang about, and how they sang it, I explored property and contract law, the early workers movement, transatlantic social theory, and much else. And like many witnesses to the 2008 recession, my thinking about societal interdependencies evolved. News reports of sheriffs refusing to evict residents during the foreclosure crisis—and again during the pandemic—reverberated uncannily with themes in Old Songs' show. I turned to David Graeber's monumental book, *Debt: The First 5000 Years*, for an understanding of how social relations are coded in the exchange of wealth and services. Debt, after all, was at the heart of the Anti-Rent struggle: what tenants owed landlords, by what means landlords could collect, how obligations might be ameliorated, and the legitimacy of competing claims.

Debt also plays a significant part in the creation of new works. I am deeply indebted to my University at Albany colleague Martha Rozett for her thorough critique of my manuscript at multiple stages of development. Martha's keen understanding of form and rhetoric helped clarify my ideas. Photographer Stephen DiRado (Clark University) graciously offered to edit the many digital images in this book. During several marathon sessions, he magically turned marred, yellowing archival materials into legible sheet music. This book is better for Martha's and Stephen's efforts.

I wish to thank Dean Jeanette Altarriba, University at Albany College of Arts and Sciences, for arranging a year-long sabbatical and subsequent leave to complete a fellowship at the Newberry Library. This book would not exist without such tangible support. My work also benefitted from the expertise of university librarians Deborah LaFond, Kabel Stanwicks, and Jodi Boyle, each of whom located essential resources. Jodi, as supervisory archivist of special collections, facilitated my contact with the descendants of David Lithgow, creator of the book's cover image. I thank Lithgow's great-granddaughter Val Lloyd for graciously allowing reproduction of this bucolic painting.

Two UAlbany graduates contributed meaningfully to this project. Meara McTague shared her extensive knowledge of Anglo-American balladry and folklore. Working alongside Meara in the university library's special collections as COVID restrictions began to ease was a delight. A modest research stipend while I was department chair made it possible to commission singer-songwriter and composer *extraordinaire* Justin Friello. Justin's arrangement and recording of an Anti-Rent political campaign song is discussed in chapter 3. His fantastical treatment of Pamela Barrie's contra-contrafactum of this song continues to amuse.

I am very grateful to my University at Albany colleagues Alejandra Bronfman, Kyra Gaunt, Robert Gluck, Richard Hamm, Bernadette Socha, Barbara Sutton, Eszter Szalczer, Victoria Von Arx, Kate Walat, and Albin Zak for their interest in this work and ongoing support. A bit further afield, musicologists Lydia Hammesley, John Graziano, and Denise Von Glahn offered helpful feedback. Kelly Wisecup's insights on the politics of representation—the power of language to erase or enhance—while we were Newberry Library Fellows exerted a formative influence on my writing.

I will never forget the day that Ellen Dunlap, president of the American Antiquarian Society in Worcester, Massachusetts, gave me her office to conduct research because I had dropped in at a time the reading room was closed. Ellen, Laura Wasowicz, and the AAS staff make using their collections a joy. I must also thank Sam Bessen, Eleanor and Lester Levy Family Curator at Johns Hopkins University. Sam located several pieces of rare sheet music and provided high-quality images at my request. We all owe a debt to the Levy family for their continued support of this valuable, publicly accessible sheet music collection.

I also appreciate the many individuals who took the time to answer questions and send digitized items from their respective institutions. Such efforts are all the more significant when allocations for research services are constrained. My thanks to Joe Festa, librarian at the Fenimore Art Museum; Kathryn Haines, University of Pittsburgh Library System; Tiffany Hore, Vaughan Williams Memorial Library; and Paul Mercer, Elizabeth Jakubowski, and the unnamed staff members who helped me navigate the New York State Library. I also want to acknowledge several who volunteered their expertise: Joanne Kosuda-Warner, Andes Society for History and Culture president; Ray LaFever, Delaware County Historical Association archivist; Voorheesville historian Dennis Sullivan; and the musician George Ward, whose period arrangements and original songs are an important part of Anti-Rent's musical legacy. I especially wish to thank George for permission to quote the chorus of his song, "Old Horns, Proud Horns." His enthusiastic response to learning of my project was, "You have to write that book, because I need to read it!" I hope others feel the same.

It has been a pleasure to work with Richard Carlin and the excellent, expert staff at SUNY Press. Thanks go to Hugh Egan for allowing me to read an advance copy of his introduction to *The Redskins* and Thomas Wermuth for including my book in his series. The anonymous reviewers of the proposal and manuscript made my work better through their thoughtful critiques. Any lacunae and errors that remain represent my limitations.

Finally, there are the incalculable debts owed to the many family members and friends who contributed to and sustained this project. My dear friend Pamela Barrie shared her deep knowledge of printing, poetry, and literature, enthusiastically conveying her own findings on Anti-Rent matters. Pamela also introduced me to Greg Joly and the "togglers" at the Thomas Farm Print Shop, Historic Eastfield Village, Rensselaer County. Discovering the lingering spirit and tangible relics of Anti-

Rentism with Pamela and Greg over several summers has been a great joy. My mother, Adrian, and sisters, Loretta and Susan, are among those who indulgently watched *Dragonwyck* with me. My husband, Matt Malsky, blew the tin horn at Eastfield and accompanied me on numerous field trips to the hilltowns and historical sites where Anti-Rent agitation took place. I am indebted to him for long restorative walks, complex cocktails, technical support, and so much more. Our adult children, Bea and Isaac, and their respective partners, Kalil and Marianne, patiently listened to my progress reports, shared their insights, and punctuated my absorption with news of their own.

Lore about the landlords and their challengers permeates the region I have called home for nearly twenty years. The professional basketball team is named the Albany Patroons. The motto and logo of the local Democratic Socialists of America chapter is derived from the Anti-Rent movement. An artisanal cheesemaker in Rensselaer County calls itself "Four Fat Fowl." Their premiere product is "St. Stephen," an exceedingly rich brie made at their base in Stephentown. Signs and symbols of the Anti-Rent struggle are everywhere, resonating with the issues of our time.

Prelude

An unexpected consequence of Governor Andrew Cuomo's mask mandate to stem the spread of COVID-19 was that it conflicted with New York State law. As Attorney General Letitia James pointed out, the governor's April 15, 2020, executive order contradicted Penal Law 240.35(4), which made "being masked or in any manner disguised by unusual or unnatural attire or facial alteration . . . in a public place with other persons so masked or disguised . . . a criminal violation." Following James's lead, state legislators moved quickly to repeal the provision. As one assemblymember observed, the legal conflict made men of color especially vulnerable to police harassment. "If we are to stop the spread of COVID-19, we must ensure that everyone feels safe wearing a mask in public, without the threat of arrest, prosecution, or worse." The mask mandate was confusing for all New Yorkers, the legislator noted.[1]

Feeling safe in a mask necessitated that state residents overcome 175 years of history. Opera manager Max Maretzek, for example, declined his supporters' offer to hold a series of Fancy Balls for his benefit in 1849, noting that "masks are here prohibited." Having immigrated to New York the previous year, Maretzek knew the rules. Masks were illegal, and in his view costumes without them were pointless. New York galas did not bear "any resemblance to the tumultuous thronging and headlong gaiety of a *bal masque* at Paris," he opined. A New Yorker would dress up, but with "full consciousness of the awkwardness of a novel costume written upon his bared face . . . he moves as stiffly, and dances as awkwardly" as a wooden figure. Only with sufficient alcohol could the partygoer overcome such embarrassment. Eventually, "his limbs begin to be loosened, and he forgets the strangeness of his unwonted attire, under the influence of a flask of Champagne."[2]

From the tragic to the frivolous, masks have long been a volatile issue in the Empire State. Their prohibition dates to 1845, when Governor Silas Wright approved the legislation that formed the basis of anti-mask Penal Law 240.35(4). The original "Act to Prevent Persons Appearing Disguised and Armed" was adopted specifically to suppress the "Calico Indians," Anti-Renters who camouflaged their identities with homemade gowns and garish face coverings. Eventually the prohibition would be amended to allow for masquerade balls of the type Maretzek desired. But it would also be invoked to constrain Ku Klux Klan gatherings and discipline political activists during Mayor Rudy Giuliani's administration and Occupy Wall Street.[3]

The number of people today aware that New York's mask law originates with the upstate Anti-Rent conflict is relatively small. But as the pandemic revealed, the Anti-Rent movement continues to resonate in surprising and profound ways. Its participants expressed their feelings and aspirations musically, rallying themselves and others to their cause. Their antagonists and hecklers would sometimes pen an up-rent lyric, too. It is this story that the present volume tells.

Introduction

Down with the Rent!

Yielding and paying therefor, yearly and every year. . . . Twenty Eight schepples of good clean merchantable Winter Wheat, four fat fowls (to be delivered at the now mansion-house of the said Stephen Van Rensselaer) . . . and [to] perform one day's service with carriage and horses.

—Rensselaerville indenture, 1793[1]

This book had its genesis in a brilliant work of folk theater called *Down with the Rent!: The Anti-Rent Rebellion of New York*. Produced and performed by the traditional music collective Old Songs, the evening-length performance combined narrative and song to tell a riveting historical tale. As a transplant to the region, I was fascinated by the Anti-Renters' story and songs. Following the work's November 2014 premiere, I saw it twice more at the New York State Museum in Albany and Proctors Theatre in Schenectady.

Down with the Rent! commemorates the struggle of upstate tenant farm families to contest the feudal conditions under which they lived during the early 1840s. Their landlords were known by the Dutch American term, *patroon*. Several thousand families lived on the original patroonship, "Rensselaerwyck," which was established by the area's first major European claimant, Killiaen Van Rensselaer, in the seventeenth century. The conflict is not particularly well known outside the Hudson-Mohawk region, but its effects are recognized locally to this day. The glossy six-page program for *Down with the Rent!* included images of more than twenty roadside markers attesting to the Anti-Rent movement's imprint on regional consciousness. Yet the complex circumstances of such long-ago events require explanation; show creator Andy Spence included a glossary and bibliography in the program with terms such as *Leasehold Estates* and *Tin Dinner Horn*.[2]

What did it mean to be "Anti-Rent" in upstate New York during the 1840s? *Down with the Rent!* made it clear that the operative notion of *rent* differed significantly from its modern usage. Current definitions assume periodic payments, typically of cash, for an agreed-upon term. In contrast, the tenant farmers of upstate New York were expected to convey goods and service *in perpetuity* to someone exercising the prerogatives of a manor lord. The excerpt at the head of the chapter from a typical agreement between landlord and tenant indicates something of this strange, archaic situation. The town of Rensselaerville in Albany County was founded by the ninth patroon, Stephen Van

Rensselaer III, to attract farmers to his vast holdings soon after the American Revolution. Instead of selling parcels of land outright, however, he offered them contracts predicated on the feudal property relations of colonial times. Responsibility for taxes belonged to the tenant, but mineral, water, and timber rights were all reserved to the patroon. Van Rensselaer had the right to build roads, mines, and mills anywhere he deemed suitable. Furthermore, the patroon was permitted "free ingress, egress and regress, way and passage" with "horses, cattle, carriages and servants, to, from, in and out of the said hereby granted premises," and numerous other privileges.[3] By the time Stephen III died in 1839, many a farm was operated by descendants who had never had a say in the indenture's contractual obligations. Their rent strike was a rebellion against the demand for their deference and fealty along with wheat and fowl.

The tenant farmers' collective struggle to challenge this system lasted seven years, from Stephen III's death through 1846, when the New York State Constitution was revised to preclude such contracts in the future. Old Songs' *Down with the Rent!* made this struggle vivid through narration of its major events, a bit of sketch humor, and more than twenty songs. Eight singers accompanied themselves and each other on hammered dulcimer, keyboard, violin, guitar, banjo, double bass, and tin horn. The show's mix of period and original songs was thoughtful and rich, with traditional tunes drawn from dance, hymnody, and other genres. The original songs included several by local folk musician George Ward, who set poems written by Anti-Renters to newly created melodies. Several others combined Anti-Rent poetry with preexisting American tunes such as "Sweet Betsy from Pike." Most fascinating to the musicologist in me were the five numbers created by the Anti-Renters themselves, such as the "Halderbarak Quick Step" and "The Land Lord's Lament." Thus began my investigation into a little-known historical backroad where music and social justice intersected, revealing a legendary mountain of song. The five period works presented in *Down with the Rent!* were the iceberg's tip, as later became apparent.

Songs and Sounds of the Anti-Rent Movement in Upstate New York collects thirty musical numbers in a single volume, contextualizing and analyzing their origin and production. It is the first book-length publication primarily devoted to documenting and interpreting the Anti-Rent movement's expressive culture. It is also the first to provide notated scores of the repertory created by the conflict's mid-nineteenth-century contemporaries. *Songs and Sounds* is divided into two parts, combining the features of critical edition and songbook. Part 1, "Critical Perspectives," begins with the movement's origins and central themes, followed by two chapters that discuss the musical numbers as they were created and disseminated during the early 1840s. The final chapter examines aesthetic works and commemorations that perpetuated the Anti-Rent legacy through the twentieth century and beyond. Part 2, "Musical and Lyrical Works," presents the 1840s music and poetry discussed in part 1 in songbook fashion with newly created vocal scores. Twenty-two of the thirty titles are presented with their original poetic text, historic musical source, and new musical setting (see List of Works). My creation of scores was necessitated by the fact that the Anti-Renters' songs were never published as sheet music. Instead, lyrics circulated in newspapers and on broadsides with associated tune titles indicated. Contemporary performers must have relied on oral and rote practices for the songs' realization, as often occurs in vernacular music-making. My hope is that my provision of arrangements for modern users of this volume will enhance our understanding of the lively and substantive role played by music in nineteenth-century social reform.

This foray into vernacular music has left me perplexed about the lack of an accepted term for songs that set new lyrics to preexisting melodies. The practice itself is long-standing and widespread.

Nonetheless, there is no standard term for the resulting creations. The most likely candidates are *contrafactum*, *parody*, and *borrowing*. After much consideration, I settled on the Latin *contrafactum* (plural, *contrafacta*) for these works. Like *parody*, the term originates with music of the late Middle Ages and Renaissance, primarily in association with reworkings of liturgical plainchant. *Parody*, however, has acquired connotations of satire and burlesque, making its use here problematic. The gerund *borrowing* is sometimes used by scholars of nineteenth-century popular music for objects created by fitting new lyrics to familiar tunes. This pervasive practice seemingly became relegated to informal music-making when its free exercise in public was constrained by the revision of copyright law in the early twentieth century. I suspect this is part of the reason that we lack a precise term for such works. With *parody* having the wrong connotation and *borrowing* feeling awkward and obscure, I chose *contrafactum*. The advantage of this anachronism is that it helps draw attention to the special relationship between text and tune expressed through the movement's musical artifacts.

As part 1 elaborates, the association between words and notes in Anti-Rent contrafacta is anything but arbitrary. For each title, I have investigated *why* the association was made: why it seemed appropriate to the creator—who can rarely be fully identified—to connect particular sentiments to particular melodies. The result might be pointed, humorous, rousing, or any number of other effects and messages. My perspective is that the combination of new lyrics and an older tune—which typically has its own lyrics, stylistic features, and generic associations—results in a whole or *gestalt* that is more than the sum of its parts. The assorted elements interact in the production of a unique and novel meaning and experience. At the same time, aesthetic engagement with a particular contrafactum involves a fluid awareness as the performer or listener's comprehension moves between constituent elements. Consider, for example, how the American patriotic song, "My Country, 'Tis of Thee," would have sounded and felt when this reworking of the British anthem "God Save the King" was introduced at a Fourth of July celebration in Boston in 1831. The substitution of "let freedom ring" for the original's closing repetition of "God Save the King" must have been visceral at a time when the War of 1812 was living memory and the United States was still deemed an "experiment." As this example suggests, the goal of *Songs and Sounds* is to recover a vibrant sense of Anti-Rent expressive works through explication of their historical and musical specificity. I believe the exercise is meaningful because the issues at the heart of the movement—monopolies of land, wealth, and power—remain vital today.

Part 1

Critical Perspectives

Chapter 1

Tin Horn Rebellion

For Helderberg had groaned and shook for years,
E'en from the time that Holland hither sent
Her yonkers, boors, and lordly patroons-peers
To hoard up beaver-skins, and wheat and rent . . .

—Henry Rowe Schoolcraft, *Helderbergia*[1]

"New York in the colonial period was like a feudal kingdom," observed Howard Zinn in *A People's History of the United States*.[2] The patroonships that shaped much of the future state had their origin in the early seventeenth century, when Dutch West India Company cofounder Killiaen Van Rensselaer was granted a vast tract of land lining the Hudson River by the Dutch Republic. The patroon system of perpetual fiefs designed by Van Rensselaer persisted through the English political takeover of 1664, transforming its patriarchs into manor lords and patent holders. Millions of acres were soon controlled by a small number of interrelated families, including the Dutch Van Rensselaers and Schuylers and the Scots-English Livingstons.

The colonial period's hereditary titles were effectively abolished after the American Revolution by the new state constitutions. Patriots and veterans, however, were well-rewarded for their loyalty in land grants and retention of certain privileges. Alexander Hamilton, who was married to Elizabeth Schuyler, helped devise a legal instrument so that New York's great landed families could retain their property claims *in perpetuity*. This arrangement was both sales agreement and lease, making the grantee both owner and tenant. A "contract of incomplete sale," it went by assorted names, including *lease in fee* and *quarter lease*.[3] Whatever term was used, the instrument specified annual payment of rent in wheat, fowl, and labor to about twenty families controlling more than two million acres in the Hudson-Mohawk region. Among other stipulations, if tenants wanted to sell their lease, one-quarter of the sale price was owed to the landlord. By the 1840s, more than a quarter-million people—approximately one-twelfth of New York State's population—lived under the patroon system. Among its major beneficiaries was Stephen Van Rensselaer III (1764–1839), who as Killiaen's descendant claimed upward of 750,000 acres (i.e., about 1,200 square miles). For nearly fifty years, "the Good Patroon" collected annual tribute from his Rensselaerwyck tenants, exerting considerable influence

7

on New York State politics and becoming one of the richest men in America. His death in January 1839 sparked several decades of protest and civil disobedience that coalesced into the "largest and most sustained farmers' movement in American history" prior to the Civil War.[4]

The movement's initial confrontation in autumn 1839 is vividly described by Zinn. For several months, Van Rensselaer's heirs had attempted to collect "back rents" from the farmers to pay the family's considerable debt. That September, law officers attempted to serve notice to leaseholders in the Helderberg Mountains west of Albany. "When a deputy arrived in the farming area with writs demanding the rent, farmers suddenly appeared, assembled by the blowing of tin horns. They seized his writs and burned them."[5] In early December, the sheriff came with a *posse comitatus* of five hundred from Albany to pursue Van Rensselaer's interests and quell the rebellion. The posse was similarly met by "shrieking tin horns" as the number of resisting farmers approached two thousand. The sheriff's company retreated, but the "Anti-Rent War" had begun. The tin horn, normally used to call folks to dinner, soon became a powerful and practical symbol of the struggle's vicissitudes. The *New York Herald* sent a correspondent to cover "The Insurrection in Helderbarrack," publishing a series of reports, some of which were versified.[6] An engraving emblazoning the front page of the morning edition on December 16, 1839, impressed the matter on readers.

Figure 1.1. "The Insurrection in Helderbarrack," *Morning Herald* (New York, NY), December 16, 1839. From the digital collection, *Chronicling America: Historic American Newspapers*. Courtesy of the Library of Congress.

The following year, an anonymous piece of sheet music was published by the New York City firm of Hewitt & Jaques. Titled "Halderbarak Quick Step," the two-page piano piece includes a section designated "The Gathering" for "Tin Horn Solo" (plate 5). The "Halderbarak Quick Step" is the only instrumental composition associated with the conflict. Texts with tunes, however, played an important role in mobilizing sentiment as the tenant farmers pursued their cause. Dozens of contrafacta were written. In creating new lyrics fitted to preexisting tunes, authors drew on musical genres such as vernacular ballads, temperance and minstrel tunes, and political campaign songs. Contrafacta lyrics appeared alongside much poetry in periodicals ranging from New York City's mainstream press to protest organs such as the *Albany Freeholder* and *Young America*.

The acoustic landscape was filled with more than song and oratory, however. With tenant farms spread across considerable territory, sound came to play an outsize role in the Anti-Rent cause. Tin horns were used to warn, summon, and intimidate, like the "rough-musicking" of charivari. Some farmers used masks and cotton dresses as disguises in confrontations with local authorities. They invoked the Revolutionary Era Boston Tea Party by calling themselves "Calico Indians." They also disguised their voices to confound informants wherever the opposition—deemed *up-renters*—was suspected to have infiltrated. "Tin horn rebellion" became one of the conflict's several mottos. An important chronicle of this history, *Tin Horns and Calico: A Decisive Episode in the Emergence of Democracy*, was published by the journalist Henry Christman in 1945. Thirty years later, the cover of the bicentennial edition alerted readers to "The Thrilling Unsung Story of an American Revolt Against Serfdom."[7] As we will see, this book was crucial in demonstrating that the Anti-Rent struggle was, indeed, sung.

The Anti-Rent Imaginary: Themes and Context

The expressive culture of this struggle—its regional soundscape and national impact—was at its most intense from 1839 to 1846. The topical works that emerged during this period range from early satirical versifications to the rally songs and stoic meditations of later years. Consideration of the songs' chronological appearance in historical context illuminates their role in the "Anti-Rent imaginary." Literary scholar Roger Hecht coined this term to encapsulate "the cultural work poetry performed for the movement." By examining such aesthetic objects, we can ascertain "how the farmers understood the Anti-Rent conflict and how they imagined themselves in relation to the conflict and to the landlords."[8] I have expanded Hecht's characterization of the Anti-Rent imaginary to include music and other features of the aural environment. "Critical Perspectives" follows such expressions into the twenty-first century to consider the ongoing projection of the Anti-Rent imaginary.

The reconstruction of Anti-Rent songs in part 2 was necessitated by the lack of contemporary artifacts. A barrier to current understanding of music's role during the Anti-Rent conflict has been the separation of lyrics and melodies in widely disparate sources. As with many vernacular practices, the works were not recognized and preserved as a cohesive repertory by their practitioners. In the case of Anti-Rent expressive culture, this difficulty was already recognized and regretted more than a century ago. In 1912, regional folklorist Emelyn Gardner was told by an elderly informant that "in former years he had known many songs pertaining to the Anti-Rent troubles, but that he had forgotten them and knew of no place where they could be obtained."[9] I address this lacuna by gathering the poetry and corresponding tunes into one volume. Of the twenty-two contrafacta identified, only one—"Bill Snyder"—has previously been published with its intended tune (i.e., "Old Dan Tucker"; see plate 7). To date, it is also the only one that has been professionally recorded and distributed. Pete Seeger and Ed Renehan included a rendition on their 1976 Folkways album of Hudson Valley songs.[10]

In addition to reconstructed contrafacta, part 2 includes seven texts that reference song and music through vocabulary terms or structure but fail to identify an intended tune.[11] A sampling of such works is presented here for its topicality and aural associations despite the lack of musical specificity. It is not impossible that future research will unearth the works' intended settings.

For the twenty-two explicit contrafacta, sixteen distinct tunes are indicated. Scots ballads are an important musical inspiration. Five poetic works are set to Robert Burns's rendition of "Bruce's Address," and several others are associated with Walter Scott's collection *Minstrelsy of the Scottish Border*. Three contrafacta are set to the American minstrel tune "Old Dan Tucker" and another to "The Boatman's Dance." Five—like the minstrel tunes—were closely tied to stage performance, ranging from solo acts to legitimate theater. They include "Rosin the Beau," "Hail to the Chief," and "A Life on the Ocean Wave." The remaining contrafacta are drawn from diverse and often overlapping categories of popular and traditional music, often circulating more or less concurrently within temperance, abolition, and political movements. For this edition, I have relied on versions of the designated tunes available to the Anti-Renters through contemporary published sources wherever possible. This does not preclude the tunes' circulation through oral transmission, as my discussion of individual songs makes clear.

Each plate for the contrafacta in part 2 designates a set of items: a transcription of the complete text, a preexisting musical score in facsimile, and my setting of the contrafactum's initial verse to the preexisting melody indicated. In creating these new musical settings, I have adapted Ruth Crawford Seeger's "model tune" approach. Crawford Seeger developed this strategy for the purpose of publishing transcriptions of phonograph recordings of American folksong. Such works contain a tremendous number of variants across successive verses, related songs, and different performers' renditions. Crawford Seeger recognized that all variants are important for scientific study. But to create practical transcriptions of the repertory, she focused on *the tune of one single stanza of one song as sung in one performance* (emphasis in the original). Her choice of tune and stanza as representative was guided by "majority usage" as the tune was sung from first to last verse. In this book, I use published music potentially available to Anti-Renters and their contemporaries as a "model tune" and fit the lyrics' initial stanza closely to it. The complete lyrics of each contrafactum—some with translations of dialect—are transcribed separately. Users of this edition are encouraged to engage the practices of oral transmission to create their own variants. As Crawford Seeger said, "The writing down of oral tradition should be of such a character that it may foster rather than work against that tradition."[12]

Detailed discussion of the musical works in chapters 2 and 3 shed light on their contemporary use and significance. Their chronological presentation is based on publication dates or the clues offered by internal evidence. This approach allows each one to be discussed in order of its appearance and function in the Anti-Rent movement's progress and setbacks. As we will see, each creative effort was a response to a major event or development; its impetus and occasion are summarized and its meaning interpreted. The musical sources for some are still well known, but many are obscure. In recovering the lyrics' musical associations, these chapters offer a complex portrait of the rich sonic environment that affected and reflected the experience of a significant portion of New York's population. Furthermore, this body of song provides insight into the role vernacular music played in one of the nineteenth century's major social reform movements. Its contextualization enhances our knowledge of how different traditional and theatrical musics, including diverse immigrant and religious repertories, shaped the evolution of American popular song, especially where the latter was used as a form of protest.

My treatment of the repertory's historical background is highly indebted to two major scholarly examinations of the Anti-Rent movement that appeared about twenty years ago. Reeve Huston's *Land and Freedom: Rural Society, Popular Protest, and Party Politics in Antebellum New York* examines the relationship between land distribution and ideology as expressed by owners and laborers of different socioeconomic strata. Charles McCurdy's *The Anti-Rent Era in New York Law and Politics* probes the interrelated workings of the legal system, political partisanship, and "social forces" to shed light on the ideas and institutions that limited the potential of democracy during the nineteenth century.[13] Both historians pioneered new ways of thinking about the struggle and its ramifications.

Another especially important secondary source for this project was Henry Christman's monumental *Tin Horns and Calico*. A native son and professional journalist, Christman told the Anti-Rent story in riveting and persuasive prose. He was also close enough to events to interview descendants who could piece together "with bit by bit recollection the songs and ballads of the Anti-Renters, songs familiar to many ears" when they were young. *Tin Horns and Calico* concludes with more than a dozen poems, three of which have tunes indicated. Most were reprinted from newspapers; others were handed down by word of mouth in "remembered quatrains."[14] Two significant primary sources for my expansion of Christman's foundational sampling of contrafacta are the *Albany Freeholder* and the *Working Man's Advocate*, later titled *Young America*. These serials are the nineteenth-century equivalent of the "alternative press," reporting and analyzing events and ideas not well-covered by mainstream newspapers. The American Antiquarian Society and New York State Library are particularly important in conserving these rare materials, as well as a few broadsides containing contrafacta. Unfortunately, the condition of the State Library's microfilm for the *Albany Freeholder* and the *Anti-Renter* is very poor, and access to the print editions is highly restricted. To date, neither the alternative nor the mainstream Albany newspapers of this period have been fully digitized. Perhaps more songs will become evident when these materials are more readily accessible and searchable.

A discussion of the circumstances and issues that led to the Anti-Rent conflict is provided in the final two sections of this chapter. "This Land is Your Land" begins with the situation for major landholders in upstate New York as the new nation transitioned from colony to republic after the American Revolution. Before we turn to that discussion, however, an overview of the subsequent chapters offers a glimpse of what lies ahead in *Songs and Sounds of the Anti-Rent Movement*.

Chapter 2, "A Movement Takes Shape, 1839–1844," addresses the developments of these years and a dozen musical works. The chapter picks up where the present one's account of the Van Rensselaer family leaves off: with the death of the Good Patroon in January 1839. Saddled with the family debt, his heirs pursue the estate's tenants for back rents. A failed attempt to negotiate with

Stephen Van Rensselaer IV leads some farmers to write their own Declaration of Independence and declare a rent strike. Confrontations that autumn result in the governor's intervention, the movement's first aesthetic works, and its sole instrumental composition. In 1841, further conflict with law officers leads some Anti-Renters to don disguises. The Calico Indians' appropriation of Native American imagery and symbolic action is discussed in conjunction with the related theme of land appropriation. By 1842, Rensselaerwyck tenants are allied with farmers in neighboring Schoharie County. The movement's first newspaper, the *Helderberg Advocate*, circulates for about two years until a court case brought by the Livingston family forces its suspension. In early 1844, the newly formed National Reform Association (NRA) in New York City creates an alliance with the Anti-Renters upstate through the activities of the recently immigrated Thomas Ainge Devyr. The NRA's weekly, the *Working Man's Advocate*, publishes contrafacta expressing the common interests of urban and rural laborers.

Throughout these years, the Anti-Renters made numerous appeals to the state legislature for relief. By spring 1844, they had experienced severe legal setbacks. The tenants are repeatedly limited to private settlement with the landlords as the sanctity of contracts is invoked. In response to the legal system's intransigence, the movement spreads to eight additional counties. Aspirations are articulated and sung at Fourth of July gatherings, and "lecturers" help transform the struggle from a localized skirmish to a "well-organized revolt against leasehold tenure throughout the eastern part of the state."[15] By the end of the year, several Anti-Rent leaders were in jail.

Chapter 3, "Climax and Denouement, 1845–1846," begins with the mask law of January 1845, which made the wearing of disguises illegal. A dozen contrafacta appeared during this year, reflecting the intensity of the Anti-Renters' collective resistance. The staging of a British melodrama, *The Rent Day*, capitalized on local sentiment just as Herman Melville returned home from overseas. His novel *Pierre: Or, The Ambiguities*, critiqued the landholding class a half-dozen years later. In August 1845, an undersheriff's death in Delaware County and the subsequent arrest of hundreds of men deterred the farmers' physical resistance to land agents and law officers. Two Anti-Renters were sentenced to death; their verdicts were commuted to life imprisonment just a week before the fateful date. Several others received life sentences. The Anti-Renters' increased influence in electoral politics led to the prisoners' pardon when a new governor took office in 1847. Several of the half-dozen songs of 1846 had encouraged solidarity at the ballot box; the final one mocks the landlords' response to major legislative changes to the tune of "Oh Dear, What Can the Matter Be." The Anti-Rent movement played an important role in the abolishment of distress—the sale of a family's goods to satisfy debt—and revision of the state constitution, which was amended to preclude new feudal leases. Perpetual leases were still valid, however, shifting the theater of action back to the Van Rensselaers. The family soon sold off its remaining landholdings to investors, leading to sporadic conflict among private parties for several decades.

A major up-rent literary trilogy, James Fenimore Cooper's "Littlepage Manuscripts," appeared as the Anti-Rent episode reached its climax. Chapter 4 begins with Cooper's work and other examples of "feudal nostalgia," namely Oliver Shaw's "Rensselaer Waltz" and Thomas Cole's paintings of the Manor House. Cooper idealized the role of the landlord class in New York's development. With the "Littlepage Manuscripts," he attempted to justify the landlords' way of life and "expose the nefarious designs of the antirenters."[16] The trilogy's final installment—insensitively named *The Redskins*—juxtaposes authentic Native American Indians with the false "Injin" disguises of the Anti-Renters. Native American imagery also pervades Henry Rowe Schoolcraft's lengthy 1855 poem *Helderbergia*. Each chapter of part 1 begins with a few lines from this obscure tome, which is discussed in chapter 4 along with other examples of the Anti-Rent movement's "Living Memory and Legacy."

Perhaps because the tenants' seven-year agitation led to just partial success, the Anti-Rent spirit "lived on in the movement's songs" and the stories told to descendants about community resistance to hegemonic forces.[17] Interest surged around the movement's centenary. Christman's *Tin Horns and Calico* had its counterpart among historians in David Maldwyn Ellis's 1946 *Landlords and Farmers in the Hudson-Mohawk Region, 1790–1850*, another foundational study. Expressive treatments around the centennial include Vivian Fine's 1941 piano solo *Tin-horn Rebellion* and the painted mural on the State University of New York campus in Albany reproduced on the book cover. Another wall mural was installed in the United States post office in the town of Delhi. As the Delaware County seat, Delhi was the site of the Calico Indians' final suppression after the tragic events of August 1845. The striking WPA-style mural reflected the lingering intensity of past conflict. Also marking the centennial was Anya Seton's 1944 novel *Dragonwyck*, a gothic horror story set among the Hudson Valley's patroon families and tenant farmers. Seton's bestseller was quickly made into a Hollywood film featuring the young Vincent Price as manor lord Nicholas Van Ryn. The film was released in 1946 with music by the prolific Alfred Newman (no relation). Among the cues is a haunting set piece representing the patroons' insularity.

Descendants and locals have periodically dramatized the Anti-Rent episode in regional public commemorations. An elaborate Centennial Pageant took place on Labor Day, 1945, in the Delaware County town of Andes. In 1958, Camp Woodland director Norman Studer staged an original musical play depicting the Anti-Rent struggle at the Folk Festival of the Catskills. Several school plays and community theater productions were mounted from the 1970s through the 1990s in the Albany area. Local folksinger George Ward provided much of the musical continuity for these shows, as well as for Old Songs' twenty-first century production, *Down with the Rent!* It is a testament to the movement's persistence in regional memory that the show was performed a dozen times from 2014 to 2016 at nine different venues. As I describe in the introduction, this example of Old Songs' folk theater was the impetus for this project.

Such periodic commemorations and re-presentations are a reminder of the essential relationship between land—the means of survival—and self-determination. Just as the Anti-Renters' emergent sense of social justice remains instructive, their expressive culture retains more than antiquarian interest. It is not impossible for real estate empires and other monopolies concentrating wealth and power in the hands of a few to threaten democracy even today. The remainder of this chapter discusses the Anti-Rent movement's historical background and several major strategies of resistance.

This Land Is Your Land

The patroon or "manor" system persisted after the Revolutionary War because the patroon families were handsomely rewarded for supporting the cause and highly involved in shaping the new state. "Tory landholders saw their acres confiscated, but patriotic families such as the Van Rensselaers kept their holdings intact," observed Ellis.[18] Although New York State abolished entails and primogeniture in 1782, vested property agreements were allowed to persist. As a result, a unique social system predicated on a closely interrelated aristocracy dominated the Hudson-Mohawk region. A concise illustration of typical family relations can be traced in just a few steps. Stephen Van Rensselaer III's great-grandfather was Philip Livingston, second lord of the 160,000-acre Livingston Manor during the colonial period. His grandfather, also named Philip, signed the Declaration of Independence. Van Rensselaer married Margaret Schuyler, whose sister Elizabeth was Alexander Hamilton's wife. The sisters' father was Revolutionary General Philip Schuyler, and their mother was Catherine Van Rensselaer. Catherine's mother, Engeltje (Angelica), was a Livingston. Family properties were variously commingled through marriage, divided through inheritance, and enlarged through speculation as land became increasingly commodified after the Revolution. Men in patroon and manor families occupied influential political offices at both state and national levels in the early republic.[19]

Stephen Van Rensselaer III inherited the family's colossal estate as a child and took administrative control when he turned twenty-one in 1785. Rensselaerwyck extended twenty-four miles along the Hudson River and twenty-four miles east and west from its banks, covering nearly the entirety of Albany and Rensselaer counties. In 1786, Stephen III's brother-in-law Hamilton recommended that he offer tenants a lease in fee so that the patroon's interest in the land could be retained.[20] Hamilton knew the benefits of possession. His grandfather in Scotland (for whom he was named) was a laird whose "family estate was so huge that it encompassed not just [the town of] Stevenston but half the arable land in the parish."[21] From 1789 to 1795, Hamilton served as the nation's first Secretary of the Treasury—the office charged with land distribution for the new republic.

While Stephen III contemplated the novel lease in fee, the New York State Legislature passed the "Act Concerning Tenures." The 1787 law provided a basis for landholding in the new state by declaring that lands granted in the people's name "shall be and remain *allodial* and not *feudal*" (emphasis in the original).[22] This meant that property was to be sold outright and title transferred to the new owner, breaking the chain of hereditary claims and persistent obligations. In other words, property hereafter would be "alienated in fee simple." The 1787 Act was an important step in the transformation of land into a commodity freely bought and sold (i.e., "alienated") without ongoing restrictions. Upstate landholders, recognizing that the new system was not in their long-term interest, astutely adopted the lease in fee, which guaranteed them rent, feudal privileges, and reservations on alienation. For the latter, a quarter of the sale price was typically demanded. This feature was doubly advantageous for the landlord because it discouraged tenants from leaving but generated considerable profit if they did. In contrast to New England's Yankee farmers, who held clear title to their land, tenants under the manor system were subject to multiple covenants and limitations for its use. And the landlord gained all the tenant family's improvements to the land if they departed.

Stephen III was eager to develop the manor when he came of age and began advertising for occupants. European-American settlement along the Hudson River had been sporadic since Killiaen's time, when it was a largely unfulfilled condition of his land grant from the Dutch government. The population increased slowly through the colonial period; when Stephen III assumed control, there were fewer than six hundred tenants. To attract farmers, he offered seven years of free occupancy on newly apportioned 160-acre lots. Hundreds of families, "some from the old Dutch and German settlements and some from the hills of New England," soon took up the offer.[23] (Given that the patroon families were slaveholders at the time, it is unlikely that many of the tenants were people of color.[24]) By 1800, Rensselaerwyck had more than three thousand tenants on half a million acres, an extraordinary increase.

The number of tenant families remained roughly the same during Stephen III's later decades, however. This stagnation is partly attributable to what happened when the new arrivals visited the patroon at the end of seven years. The contracts proffered later became the subject of much legal dispute and quite a few poems. An especially poignant tale appears in "Dere vos a Time" (plate 23), a ballad describing a young, illiterate couple's naïve agreement to the terms presented.

> The landlord asked us if we'd have a lease, we said we would,
> And then he wrote us one he did, and said that it was good.
> . . . .
> There were a hundred other words that were so very long,
> If he had not said that they were right, we'd thought that they were wrong.

So many contracts of this type were issued that a printed template was created, as seen in the Rensselaerville indenture cited in the introduction. Space was left for names, dates, the property survey, and a few other variables to be added by hand. The document's long words made the tenant responsible for paying all taxes and assessments levied by governmental authorities. All timber, mineral, and water rights, as well as the right to erect mines, mills, buildings, and roads anywhere on the property were reserved to the patroon. The annual rent, due at the patroon's home in early January, was typically ten to fifteen bushels of "good clean" winter wheat per hundred acres, four fat fowl, and a day's labor with team of horses or oxen. The grantor had the right to auction off the tenant's belongings and repossess the property if the rent went unpaid in whole or in part for twenty-eight days or for breach of any condition or covenant. Patroon and tenant agreed that the contract's term was "for ever" for them and their "heirs and assigns."[25]

Leases on Livingston Manor in southern Columbia County contained covenants similar to the Van Rensselaer contracts, with one important difference. Rather than being *in perpetuity*, they typically ran for two to three lives. Depending on the timing, this difference had positive or negative ramifications for the tenant. Renegotiation could be devastating for a successive generation with few options other than to capitulate to the landlord's terms or leave, relinquishing all improvements and as much as one-third the sale price.[26] On the other hand, tenants whose leases came due after 1846, when legislation precluded feudal privileges in new agreements, negotiated with landlords on terms different from the past. This was not the case for holders of a Rensselaerwyck indenture, however.

Whether the lease was *in perpetuity* or for multiple lives, the annual rent circa 1800 was generally manageable once a new farm was established. On average, ten acres per year could be cleared by industrious occupants. And as long as the soil was fertile and wheat prices remained high, relations were relatively harmonious. Landlords profited from multiple aspects of their integrated operations, selling lumber to tenants, milling tenants' grain, collecting rent, and engaging personal service. Even at modest calculations, thirty thousand bushels of wheat and twelve thousand fowl were due Stephen III annually. As Anti-Rent advocate Thomas Devyr described, the "granaries were groaning under that 'merchantable winter wheat'" and the fat fowl were "a drug in the market."[27]

In addition to agricultural commodities, the Van Rensselaers had nearly year-round access to the labor of ten men daily.

The Hudson-Mohawk region's feudal relations were predicated on long-standing beliefs in human hierarchies still operative during the early republic. Acceptance of the manor system meant "participation in a theatre of benevolence and deference," as Huston observes. The annual rent was more than mere payment; it carried the symbolism of feudal tribute long after the Revolution. Landlords continued to dole out leniency and generosity in exchange for tenants' loyalty and subordination. Stephen III was so adept at positioning himself that he came to be called the "Good Patroon." His example was widely imitated by his peers. "Great and middling landlords throughout the leasehold district followed Van Rensselaer's example in rationalizing rent collection and making shrewd use of lenience to encourage payment."[28] The precarious balance between beneficent patriarchy and deferential dependency was disturbed, however, by the economic turmoil that followed the Panic of 1819. Debt-laden landlords pursued tenants in arrears with vigor, while the latter grappled with poor soil, population pressures, and increased market competition for their grain, wool, and dairy products. The shift toward a more commercially based, capital-intensive agriculture dramatically changed social relationships, including the landlords' grip on voter loyalty. The Panic of 1837 and lingering economic depression intensified farmers' desire for independence, ownership of their improvements, and clear title to the land they worked. Yet, the Anti-Renters' rejection of the old ideology seems to have surprised some members of the landholding class. Cooper expressed incredulity in his preface to *The Redskins*: "The notion that every husbandman is to be a Freeholder, is as Utopian in practice, as it would be to expect that all men were to be on the same level in fortune, condition, education and habits. As such a state of things as the last never yet did exist, it was probably never designed by divine wisdom that it should exist."[29] For the Anti-Rent cause to gain momentum, the prevailing order of things had to be challenged.

Over the course of his long life, Stephen Van Rensselaer III supported churches and schools, served as New York's lieutenant governor and representative in Congress, presided over the Erie Canal Board, and cofounded the New York State Board of Agriculture to disseminate improved farming techniques. Yet, despite his good works—or maybe because of them—he died with at least $311,000 in debt. It is no small wonder that tenant rent owed to the patroon was calculated by his heirs and executors to cover that amount.[30]

Strategies and Challenges

After the Good Patroon's death, tenants and their allies attempted a wide range of tactics to address their situation. The farmers' initial challenge to the demand for back rent by his son, Stephen Van Rensselaer IV, evolved into a general strike against paying the annual tribute. Within a few years, opposition within Rensselaerwyck ignited simmering grievances on other estates. Tenants in the surrounding counties, which had their own history of conflict, were drawn into the collective struggle. Periodic protests on the Livingston Manor and Schuyler-Rensselaer holdings in Columbia County during the 1790s, for example, included tactics and circumstances that would be echoed in the 1840s: title challenges, distress sale disruptions, "Indian" disguises, and a sheriff's death.[31] Bodily resistance, ideological agitation, legal action, and political partisanship would all play a role in the Anti-Rent movement. They would all leave a trace on its poetry and music, too.

A steady stream of petitions and legal claims contesting the patroon system were assembled by tenants, their lawyers, and allies from 1839 to 1846. One important strategy involved title challenges. The Anti-Renters searched document archives in Albany, New York City, Amsterdam, and London to ascertain the authenticity of titles and the exact privileges imparted.[32] They questioned the precise boundaries of land grants, the validity of negotiations with—and compensation to—Native Americans, whether the original grant's conditions (such as settlement) had been fulfilled, and the vagaries of descent. Tracing paper titles involved an historical trail dating back hundreds of years, even before Killiaen Van Rensselaer's initial claims. One key legal issue involved the thirteenth-century statute known as *Quia Emptores*.

When Britain assumed control from the Dutch in 1664, the bulk of its laws were installed across colonial New York. A possible exception was the Parliamentary statute *Quia Emptores*, signed by Edward I in 1290. After this date, no new manors could be created in England, but whether the law applied in its colonies was another matter. Certainly, New York's colonial governors had ignored *Quia Emptores* and established new manors. But were descendants of the appointed lords due loyalty, service, and agricultural goods under the state constitution after the Revolution? Surprisingly, the answer seems to have been "yes." New York State's 1787 "Act Concerning Tenures" allowed such tribute to continue in agreements made before its adoption. Section V states that this Act shall not "take away or discharge, any rents certain, or other services" due "any mean [mesne] lord, or other private person, or the fealty or distresses incident thereunto."[33] In other words, agreements approved by colonial administrators and the crown could persist under statehood. McCurdy concludes that as a result, "a form of landholding Parliament had strangled half a millennium earlier still existed in New York State. It meant that in one respect, at least, republican New York was more feudal than monarchical England."[34] Perhaps this helps explain why the traditional tune known as "Bruce's Address," which dates to the period of Edward I, became the most frequently used melody for Anti-Rent contrafacta. The question of *Quia Emptores* continued to be relevant after the 1846 revision of New York's constitution because the Van Rensselaers' perpetual leases were allowed to persist.[35] It would be revisited periodically by New York's judiciary and legislature and continues to shape the vocabulary of property law today.

Other challenges mounted by the Anti-Renters pertained to specific conditions of the lease in fee. Quarter sales were especially galling; reservations on alienation were decried as antithetical to republican principles. Like the lease's labor requirement, quarter sales kept the tenant in "fealty to a superior lord" and therefore lacking "the independence required for republican citizenship."[36] Anti-Rent sympathizers also noted the patroon gained the entire sale price if the property turned over four times and would retain title even then. The *Albany Evening Journal* wondered whether such a practice "is either just, or honest, or to be endured."[37]

Clearly, the lease in fee's instantiation of feudal relations was anachronistic. However, a landmark case decided by the New York State Supreme Court in 1820 put it on a modern foundation. The court ruled that restraints on alienation in Rhinebeck Patent contracts—written during the colonial era—were enforceable. The lease in fee's terms were valid because they were based on freedom of contract between parties of equal status. In the absence of fraud or coercion, tenants and landlords had "a right to bargain as they please."[38] The New York court's reconceptualization of the lease in fee put landlords in a powerful position because the US Constitution's contract clause prohibited the states from intervening in such agreements. Article 1, section 10 declares that no state shall pass any law "impairing the Obligation of Contracts." In 1843, the US Supreme Court reaffirmed the contract clause's restrictions on state intervention. The decision was a setback for the Anti-Renters; only the parties to a contract could alter the rights and remedies of its terms.

Despite periodic disappointments, the tenant farmers persevered in their pursuit of juridical and legislative redress. They knew that change could and did happen with the support of sympathetic lawmakers and politicians. For example, debtor's prison had been abolished in 1832 under the principle that the remedy of imprisonment—the state's responsibility—was not part of contractual obligations between private parties. The Anti-Renters would achieve a related victory when the "Act to Abolish Distress for Rent" became New York State law in 1846. *Distress* or *distraint* was the seizure of a debtor's possessions in lieu of payment, a common law holdover that caused much hardship. The first Calico Indian appearances in 1841 occurred in response to distress sales, scheduled auctions held by law officers and landlords' agents. If the Anti-Renters were successful, no buyers came forward for the family's chattel and goods.

The Anti-Renters' attempts to constrain distress actions through legislation took place during a larger national debate concerning debtor protection following the Panic of 1837. "Between 1837 and 1843 American society was passing through the deep hollow of a great economic cycle, and the air became heavy with doubt and distress," observed historian Samuel Rezneck.[39] His final term carries a double meaning; distraint caused families tremendous anxiety and economic hardship. In 1842, New York State adopted legislation allowing the debtor to retain $150 in personal property when a distress action was taken. This would enable artisans to keep their tools and farmers to retain implements and livestock. The exemption went into effect the following year, a tremendous relief for tenants in arrears. However, the state supreme court ruled in 1844 that the statute did not apply to contracts made before its passage. Landlords renewed their claims, and the Calico Indians mounted greater resistance.

It is worth pointing out that distress sales affected the entire family. Under the prevailing system of coverture, nearly everything possessed by a married woman was her husband's property—and thus liable to be sold to satisfy creditors. Coverture was another holdover of English common law in the United States. Under the doctrine of marital unity, it perpetuated the legal fiction that "husband and wife were one person—the husband." The wife was without an autonomous legal identity, as Norma Basch documents in her study of marriage and property law in nineteenth-century New York. Basch explicitly links the dire economic situation around 1840, which affected all socioeconomic levels, to the passage of debtor exemptions that "carried the possibility of saving some of the family's assets" from creditors.[40] Passage of the "Act to Abolish Distress for Rent" in May 1846 helped achieve this goal by putting an end to public auctions of household possessions to satisfy arrears. At the New York Constitutional Convention that summer, Anti-Rent sympathizers advanced a proposal that would insulate a married woman's property from her husband's debt. Although the initiative failed, it was an important step toward the preservation of family resources. In *Songs and Sounds of the Anti-Rent Movement*, I try to foreground the manor system's detrimental impact on families and households. Although signatories to the lease in fee were typically adult males, the contract bound more than those individuals.

While the question of distress worked its course, Anti-Renters pursued complementary tactics of resistance. Some disputed that agreements made by subsistence farmers—in some cases by previous generations—were truly freedom of contract between equal parties. Others argued that the lease in fee hindered the public good. They challenged landlords' reservations on water, mineral, and timber usage, which limited the development of natural resources in the public interest. They argued that the state's tax burden should be shared by landlords and not fall exclusively on tenants, a claim dating back to at least 1835. And they asked New York State to invoke eminent domain. Early in the conflict, tenants had hoped that state-appointed commissioners would compel landlords to sell. When that failed, tenants requested that the state seize all leasehold land by eminent domain, compensate the landlords equitably, and then sell to the tenants on reasonable terms.[41] Although the state was currently acquiring land through eminent domain for the railroads, it declined taking land from one private party to give to another in the tenants' case.

The taxation question led to a second May 1846 victory when New York adopted the "Act to Equalize Taxation" and landlords became responsible for taxes on income from leases.[42] The state constitutional convention later that year had an even greater impact. The resulting revised constitution prohibited the creation of new feudal tenures and limited the rental of agricultural lands to a twelve-year term. Landowners could no longer retain reservations on alienations and other covenants. Over time, more land would become allodial, a goal of the 1787 "Act Concerning Tenures." For farmers with leases in lives, the 1846 revision put future negotiations on a new footing. Some landlords sold outright to them or agreed to leases in years. Others refused to sell, leaving tenants little choice but to capitulate to the terms offered or abandon improvements they had made. McCurdy notes that well into the late 1870s there were reports of farmers "who burned down their houses and threw down their fences rather than allow the fruits of their labor" to be appropriated by the landowner.[43] The situation for Van Rensselaer tenants in 1846 was perhaps more dire than for those with multi-live leases. Like the 1787 Act, the revised constitution allowed leases held *in perpetuity* to remain in force. The exception to the abolishment of feudal tenures was "all rents and services certain, which at any time heretofore have been lawfully created or reserved."[44] This brought the arena of Anti-Rent resistance back to Rensselaerwyck, and the chapter of collective action across the region to a close.

Despite the Anti-Renters' best arguments and the election of sympathetic lawmakers, their quest to invalidate landlords' claims was only partially successful. This was the movement's great paradox. "The amazing thing about the Anti-Rent story is that nobody defended the lease in fee after the rent strike began," observes McCurdy. Four consecutive governors condemned it, numerous legislative committees denounced it, "a generation of appellate judges hated it, and virtually all the organs of public opinion scorned it." Yet nearly a decade of litigation "in which the state judiciary recast New York's law of real property" was insufficient to abolish the lease in fee categorically.[45] The manor system was just too entrenched to fail. What remained were private disputes between the landlords' heirs and assignees, some of which persisted for decades. Two thousand lawsuits, initiated by Rensselaerwyck purchaser Walter Church, clogged the courts through the late nineteenth century. Spectacular evictions—the landlord's remaining remedy—occurred periodically. These are just some of the developments that have kept regional memory of the Anti-Rent movement alive across generations.

Chapter 2

A Movement Takes Shape, 1839–1844

Thus oped the war. To hear the farmer's side,
A congress met; the sheriff to elude,
They chose the hour of midnight in a forest wide . . .

—H. R. Schoolcraft, *Helderbergia*[1]

The Conflict Begins

Stephen Van Rensselaer III's 1839 will followed the logic of primogeniture while dodging its legal prohibition. Rensselaerwyck was divided between the oldest sons of his two wives, neatly bisected by the Hudson River. Stephen IV received the land west of the river; his brother William received the land to the east. In order to claim their inheritance of the West and East Manors, however, the brothers were obligated to settle their father's debts through collection of back rents from the 3,063 farm families residing there. The Good Patroon's lenience had helped keep tenants' simmering resentment in check during his lifetime. But his sons Stephen IV and William needed an influx of cash to settle more than $300,000 in debt, and the farmers had no evidence of past rents being forgiven. In effect, Stephen III's will "called for the systematic impoverishment of people whose loyalty, even devotion, he had cultivated assiduously for more than fifty years."[2]

In spring 1839, Stephen IV published notices in the Helderberg hilltowns demanding back rents be paid. Farmers held meetings in five townships—Rensselaerville, Knox, Westerlo, New Scotland, and Berne—to formulate a response. Each region selected a representative to meet with the new patroon. They visited the manor office at the Rensselaer mansion in Albany on May 22, but Stephen IV refused to see them in person. A week later, he rejected their written proposal to modernize the leases and renewed his demand for back rents.[3]

On the Fourth of July, tenants held their first mass meeting and rally in Berne. The gathering, which now included farmers from the township of Guilderland, resulted in the "Anti-

21

Renters' Declaration of Independence." Echoing the spirit of the American Revolution, the authors refused "unconditional submission to the will of one man, elevated by an aristocratic law, [and] emanating from a foreign monarchy." They proposed that Stephen IV, after proving his title, cast aside "the day's services, fowls, quarter sales, [and] all reservations and restrictions contained in the old leases."[4] The representatives insisted, as they had in May, that the wheat rent be converted to a reasonable cash basis and that farmers have the option of purchasing the land they worked with fee simple mortgages.

The Anti-Renters deemed their condition *voluntary slavery*, a characterization with which Governor William Henry Seward would soon agree. Tenants declared they could "no longer endure the infamy of thus tamely entailing upon future generations such wretchedness and unhallowed bondage" in their Declaration of Independence. Allusions to slavery appear in many contrafacta with metaphorical and topical associations. New York, which had taken a gradualist approach to abolition, finally ended the legal ownership of people on July 4, 1827. The curtailment of all male African Americans' voting rights in anticipation of this date was instructive. Revisions to the state constitution in 1821, which extended universal suffrage to white men, added a substantial property requirement for Black males that would persist until after the Civil War. Rights could be lost as well as gained.

Undaunted by the tenants' Fourth of July declaration, Stephen IV convinced the Albany County sheriff to continue advancing his property claims. Beginning in late August, Sheriff Artcher and his deputies attempted to serve writs of *fieri facias*, a prelude to distress and eviction, to dozens of West Manor farmers. The law officers repeatedly encountered collective resistance to the papers' delivery. Intimidation tactics included the threat of tar and feathers and burning official documents. In October, the sheriff and his team were rebuffed by a crowd estimated at seventy to one hundred. The officers returned in late November to confront three hundred people, many of whom followed the men for eight miles, "blowing their horns and vociferously crying out 'down with the rent.'"[5]

In response, Sheriff Artcher assembled a *posse comitatus* of five hundred in Albany on December 2 to quell the resistance. As described in chapter 1, the confrontation that day became the Anti-Rent War's first major conflict and led to its first versifications. The situation did not quiet down until mid-month. After Artcher's *posse* was rebuffed, he asked Governor Seward for the state's assistance. A week later, the sheriff was allowed to summon the military companies of Albany and Rensselaer Counties and have others in readiness. The armed, uniformed troops were met by thousands of Anti-Renters as they marched into the Helderberg hills on December 10. Nevertheless, the state's spectacular show of force led to the tenants' capitulation within a few days. Sheriff Artcher resumed serving papers, which now included arrest warrants. Meanwhile, the governor urged tenant farmers to address their grievances "by application to the Courts of Justice and to the Legislature."[6] Although he had maintained "law and order" as requested, Seward made his sympathies for the Anti-Renters clear. His annual state address that January advocated for land reform: manorial tenures are "inconsistent with existing institutions, and have become odious to those who hold under them. They are unfavorable to agricultural improvement, and inconsistent with the prosperity of the districts."[7] The ramifications of Governor Seward's position, balancing vested property rights and republican principles, would play out over the next half-dozen years.

Initial Expressions, December 1839

The first Anti-Rent poetry came from the offices of the *New York Herald*. Reports of the December 1839 conflict between upstate patroons and their tenants had quickly reached *Herald* editor James Gordon Bennett. A small notice appeared in the morning paper on December 2. On December 10, the daily reported the governor's requisition of 1,500 New Yorkers should they be needed to quell the rebellion. Bennett sent a correspondent upstate the same day to investigate "The Small Potato War." He soon published several articles and four long, satirical poems that likened the conflict to the border wars of his native Scotland. Three, entitled "Border Ballads—The Wars of Hilderbarrack," appeared on the front page December 16 under the image seen in figure 1.1. Several of the poems have musical associations (plates 1–4). "The Route of Reidsville" was linked to the traditional tune "True Thomas." "The Bloody Battle at Clarksville Ale House" was clearly modelled on Walter Scott's "The Battle of Pentland Hills." And "Marcy's March," a reference to former New York State Governor William Marcy, was a parody of the already brazen "Lesley's March."

The flippant tone of the *Herald's* verse was typical, as its pioneering editor aimed to entertain as much as to inform. He may have also been influenced by the satirical *Albany Microscope*, which published a front-page account and engraving, replete with tin horn.[8] Initially, Bennett presented the farmers' dilemma sympathetically and their responses as peaceful resistance in the *Herald's* reports and editorials. This would soon change, as the editor became antagonistic to the Anti-Renters, land reform, and abolition.[9] But in December 1839, the *Herald* printed detailed accounts of Killiaen Van Rensselaer's maneuvers to obtain title, his family's historical prerogatives as landlords, and the current heirs' intractability. Bennett noted cynically that banks, merchants, and financiers had been allowed to suspend debt payments during the Panic of 1837, causing great hardship and turmoil. "But for the ignorant, big-breeched Dutchmen of the hills of Helldebarrech, to suspend paying their rents is clearly a great crime to the noble Van Rensselaers, and a great violation of the laws of the land."[10] The paper predicted that the local conflict would have an impact on the state's future elections, "and through that will probably decide the next election for President" (December 13). As a matter of fact, the next cycle unseated incumbent and local son Martin Van Buren, a major defeat for the Democrats.

Bennett also cast "this little speck of trouble" in Albany County in terms of the history and literature of his birthplace. The widely read journalist had immigrated from Scotland to the United States twenty years earlier, working for various newspapers before founding the *New York Herald* in 1835.[11] Bennett first linked the Anti-Rent conflict "in the hills of Hollibeck" to Scotland with the explicit invocation of "Bruce's Address to his troops at Bannockburn" in a single stanza (December 10, 1839).

> Now's the day and now's the hour;
> See the pigs and poultry lower;
> See approach the Patroon's power,
>   Small potatoes we!

Without mentioning Robert Burns, Bennett called forth the poet in the mind of many readers. Burn's poem begins, "Scots wha' hae," and these words are frequently used for its title. Bennett's parody was based on the poem's second stanza, which corresponds to the second half of the well-known tune:

Now's the day and now's the hour;
See the front of battle low'r;
See approach proud Edward's pow'r,
       Chains and Slavery.[12]

The melody Burns used for "Bruce's Address" would form the basis of at least five multiverse contrafacta as the Anti-Rent conflict persisted. For now, it is worth pointing out that Bennett's short, mocking lyric neatly encapsulated the situation. With the authorities' assistance, the Van Rensselaers were prepared to seize the farmers' possessions—pigs, poultry, potatoes—and auction them off if the rent was not paid.

A few days later, the *Herald*'s correspondent and "secretary"—identified only as Ariel— compared the farmers' gatherings to the "Cameronians or borderers, in Scotland, in the olden time," invoking the radical faction of Presbyterian Covenanters led by Richard Cameron, who had resisted unification with England in the early eighteenth century (December 14, 1839). Ariel then alluded to the late medieval bard, "Thomas the Rhymer," long associated with prophecies regarding sovereignty and land disputes. Thomas the Rhymer was sometimes called "True Thomas" for his inability to tell a lie. His legend had been elaborated in the several editions of Sir Walter Scott's *Minstrelsy of the Scottish Border* published internationally since 1802. Whatever Ariel's identity, the *Herald*'s editor was well-acquainted with Scott's work. After college, Bennett had traveled extensively throughout Scotland, "visiting many national shrines and especially the places described by Sir Walter Scott."[13] References to Cameron's followers and Thomas the Rhymer were among the several ways the *Herald* cast the Helderbergs in Scotland's light.

Ariel's prose account of developments since the various Albany and other county "soldiers" arrived was accompanied by a lengthy poem, "The Route of Reidsville," about the December 2 confrontation with the sheriff's posse.[14] Plate 1a is a transcription of the entire poem, including transliteration of its three dialect verses. The fifteen-verse satire depicts the hillcrest sixteen miles southwest of Albany (with an altitude ascent of 1,300 feet) where the posse was rebuffed by about 2,000 tenants. The initial verse sets the scene: "On Reidsville hill a fray began / At Clark's Ale house it ended." The sheriff had retreated to the tavern at Clarksville, about four miles downhill from Reidsville, where his forces regrouped before making the trek back to Albany. Ariel's account was sent from the very same tavern. Although the *Herald* does not give explicit indication of a tune for "The Route of Reidsville," it leads readers to associate it with "True Thomas." The mocking ballad could easily be sung to the eight-bar modal melody in plate 1b.

Notation for the "ancient tune" known variously as "True Thomas" and "Thomas the Rhymer" appeared in the 1839 American edition of Walter Scott's anthology.[15] The initial motive of this catchy plagal melody on G begins each of its four short phrases. In the late nineteenth century, "Thomas Rymer" was designated ballad 37 in Francis Child's collection, *The English and Scottish Popular Ballads.*[16] Bertrand Bronson, who systematically paired the Child ballad texts with their traditional melodies in the twentieth century, recognized Scott's "True Thomas" as representative of a large tune-family that "can be followed back to the sixteenth century with ease, and doubtless a good deal further."[17] The modal classification of "True Thomas" is ambiguous due to the fleeting appearance of scale degree 6 (E-flat), which appears only as a passing tone in the last bar. Bronson's second variant (in *Traditional Tunes of the Child Ballads*) omits scale degree 6 entirely. He designates such pitch collections "Aeolian or Dorian/Aeolian, that is, hexatonic with minor third and seventh but lacking [the] sixth" scale degree.[18] The modal contours of "True Thomas" create tension with the keyboard arrangement provided in Scott's 1839 edition. The melody's harmonization with the natural form of G minor results in a somewhat uneasy mix of modal and modern practices not untypical of such accompaniments.

Contemporary readers of "The Route of Reidsville" needed just a short leap of imagination to call forth this enduring tune, whose four short phrases fit the poem's four-line stanzas well. "The Route of Reidsville" is in ballad meter, alternating lines of 8–6–8–6 syllables flexibly. While several verses mock the farmers' Dutch dialect, the sharpest words are directed at the former governor, William Marcy, and "Prince John" Van Buren, the president's son, for their participation in the Albany sheriff's posse.[19] Much was made, in the *Herald*'s prose and verse, of the posse's dissolute behavior in the Helderberg hills. A swipe was taken at Governor Seward, whom Bennett imperiously called "Small Potatoes." Plate 1c sets the contrafactum's first verse to the ancient tune published by Scott.

"'Twixt Helderbergh and New York Town"

"The Route of Reidsville" turned out to be mere prelude. An editorial column announced the *New York Herald* would publish *several* new ballads "on the events of the war, which, in the year of our Lord 2225, will be read and prized as much as Sir Walter Scott's 'Minstrelsy of the Scottish Border Wars'" (December 14). The facetious prediction was followed two days later by a splashy front page featuring a "splendid engraving" (figure 1.1) and three "Border Ballads." The ballads closely parodied texts in Scott's anthology *Minstrelsy of the Scottish Border*. The *Herald*'s presumably inadvertent addition of *wars* to Scott's title is telling, as two of the ballads parodied pertain to historic Scottish battles. In keeping with this theme, the *Herald*'s elaborate engraving was titled, "The Insurrection in Helderbarrack." Yet the emphasis on factional struggle is ambivalent; image and poetry simultaneously elevate local matters to international import while poking fun at the parties involved.

Two of the three Helderberg border ballads, "The Bloody Battle at Clarksville Ale House" and "Marcy's March" were based on tunes published in James Oswald's mid-eighteenth-century anthology *The Caledonian Pocket Companion*, an important source for Scots folksong. The tune intended for the third Helderbergian ballad is unknown. It is unclear whether the somber "Barthram's Dirge"—which the *Herald* transformed into "The Dutchman's Dirge over His Dead Pig"—was meant to be sung, despite its reference to a musical genre. A text called "Barthram's Dirge" appears in Scott's *Minstrelsy*, but no tune is indicated. Although it is possible that a melody was known to Scott's contemporaries, it is not necessarily recoverable now. Some traditional Scots tunes were never published.[20] Plate 2 aligns the *Herald*'s "Dutchman's Dirge" with corresponding verses from the slightly longer "Barthram's Dirge." The dead pig of the former may be a casualty of the Reidsville fracas, but its transformation into savory dishes is depicted with gusto.

"The Bloody Battle at Clarksville Ale House" picks up where "The Route of Reidsville" left off, waxing rhapsodic about New Yorkers marching into the Helderbergs. Among its several fanciful elements is the fact that the "New York lads"—though summoned, assembled, and drilled in the city—were not transported upstate. As described previously, the state's show of force was limited to regional outfits. The *Herald's* irreverent thirteen-verse ballad was clearly modelled on "The Battle of Pentland Hills" from Scott's *Minstrelsy of the Scottish Border*.[21] The poems' verses are compared in plate 3a. Scott's original chronicles the brutal seventeenth-century Battle of Rullion Green against Covenanter dissidents. The bloodshed at Clark's tavern, in contrast, was confined to the chickens and pigs consumed by the conflict's hungry participants.

Both Scott's original and the *Herald's* parody state they were "copied verbatim" from an old woman's recitation. No music is given by Scott, but Oswald published a tune called "Pentlend Hills" in *The Caledonian Pocket Companion* (plate 3b).[22] Its character is more pastoral than battlefield, as listeners familiar with Haydn's setting will recognize.[23] Plate 3b shows that Oswald's successive strains are variations on the initial eight bars, a treatment more idiomatic for flute or violin than voice. Nonetheless, the successive verses of "The Bloody Battle at Clarksville Ale House" fit the opening strain of "Pentlend Hills" reasonably well. Plate 3c sets the first verse of "The Bloody Battle" to the initial eight-bar strain to suggest how the ballad might be sung.

The third border ballad was "Marcy's March," which the *Herald* indicated was written "after the manner of Da Capo's famous Lesley March." David Lesley, First Lord Newark (ca. 1600–1682), instructed his troops to play this excellent and energetic tune as they "entered or left every town on their route." The leader's favorite tune thereby came to be used by opponents to criticize and mock him. The Scottish poet and ballad collector James Hogg, who published two settings of "Lesley's March," observed that Lesley was "a brave and resolute officer, but one who made a pretense of zeal for religion a cloak for the most brutal acts of barbarity, as well as dishonor." Hogg's excoriating text describes two different battles. The first is "Lesley's March to Scotland"; the second is "Lesley's March to Longmaston Moor." They are intended to be sung to the same tune, an air "copied from Mr. Oswald's ancient Scottish music," though only the first is notated.[24]

A poem virtually identical to Hogg's "Lesley's March to Longmaston Moor" was included in Walter Scott's *Minstrelsy of the Scottish Border* with the simpler title "Lesly's March." Scott mysteriously ended the poem with "Da Capo," which the *Herald* understood as an attribution.[25] The close resemblance of "Marcy's March" to the poem published by Scott and Hogg can be seen in the comparison of texts in plate 4a. As portrayed in the *Herald*, William Marcy's dishonorable behavior, like that of John Van Buren, consisted of flirting with the Helderberg women and seizing farm products. "Marcy's March" satirized their attempts to kiss the vrows and kill the sows, "Knock down the one and knock up the other."[26] The newspaper had already immortalized Marcy's quandary over torn breeches in "The Route of Reidsville," which was based on its report that "Governor Marcy, who tore his breeches, . . . staid all night with the Dutch girls, to get a patch put in" (December 13, 1839). Like Hogg's critique of Lord Lesley, the *New York Herald* was unrestrained in castigating the behavior of the former governor and current president's son, though with much more humor.

The tune indicated by Hogg had been published—without lyrics—in James Oswald's *Caledonian Pocket Companion* (plate 4b).[27] Called "Lasly's March," it seems more modern than "True Thomas." The 6/8 meter, D major march is sectional, with three eight-bar strains, each immediately repeated (AABBCC) and ending with the same two-bar gesture. The first and final strains (A and C) include tonal sequences a step above the initial motive, with the final strain featuring a triadic motif outlining the tonic. Interestingly, the concluding gesture lacks the leading tone (C-sharp), which would give the melody tonal closure. Instead, each strain approaches the cadence through scale degree 6 (B) and sounds scale degree 2 (E) on its last strong beat, creating the propulsive feeling characteristic of many traditional tunes toward starting again (i.e., cycling into the next verse, "da capo"). In military marches, this quality has functional application as the accompaniment to long treks. As we'll see, such cyclical forms take on other meanings when used in the context of community solidarity, a quality Ruth Crawford Seeger identified as "keep-going-ness."

Aside from the initial exhortation to "March!" the rollicking phrases of "Lasly's March" are not an easy fit with the *Herald*'s pithy lines. The same is true for Hogg's text, an awkwardness he attributes to its probable origins in a "garbled copy taken from some singer." Although Hogg and Scott refrained from publishing a musical setting of the corresponding text (i.e., "Lesley's March to Longmaston Moor"), I have provided a representative alignment of "Marcy's March" to Oswald's melody in plate 4c. It is worth noting that the tune's rapid figuration and persistent small leaps are more suitable for instruments such as flute and violin than voice. Therefore, I have assumed an accompanying instrument would complete many phrase endings. Additionally, I have added an internal repeat of the tune's initial strain to create a thirty-two-bar ABAC structure. Hogg used the same structure for "Lesley's March to Scotland."

As these remarks indicate, performers would need ample preparation to coordinate the text and tune of "Marcy's March." It is doubtful that the *Herald*'s Anti-Rent border ballads were performed professionally. Nevertheless, it is possible that they were read and sung aloud in domestic and other quotidian settings where newspapers were shared. Bennett's publication capitalized on the way people used broadsides, sheet music, and illustrated serials, preparing and sharing items of mutual interest. Amateur and semiprofessional presentations in parlors, taverns, and other gathering places were a typical feature of musical life in this period.[28]

The *Herald* ballads' close connection to works published by the extremely popular Walter Scott gave the poems both literary precedent and folkloric appeal. Linking the Scots' historic land and religious disputes to the tenant farmers' struggle would have resonated with the many Scottish immigrants like Bennett who had settled in New York State. This path already had a long history: the progenitor of one of the most prominent patroon families, Robert Livingston, had emigrated from Scotland by way of Holland in the seventeenth century. Enclaves of Scots—and Presbyterian churches—were established throughout the Hudson-Mohawk region in the eighteenth century and developed into towns such as New Scotland in Albany County.[29] The invocation of Walter Scott and James Hogg cast the Helderberg conflict in artistic and literary terms while capitalizing on the early nineteenth century elevation of folk expression for both Scots and other communities. Scottish associations would continue regionally through the multiple contrafacta based on "Bruce's Address" and other tunes that circulated in the Anti-Rent movement's later years. As Charles Hamm observed in his pioneering study of American vernacular song, stylistic features such as the Scotch snap were highly influential in the late eighteenth and early nineteenth centuries. A "small but hardy group" of Scottish songs "combined with Irish songs to form a most significant segment of popular song."[30] The contrafacta discussed here provide additional evidence of that impact on musical life in the United States.

Tin Horn Obbligato, 1840

The Anti-Rent conflict became relatively quiet as the participants awaited the consequences of Governor Seward's pledge to address their situation and land reform more broadly. The legislature, after considerable wrangling between Whigs and Democrats, formed a select committee to study the issues affecting patroons and tenants. Its recommendations led to the appointment of a Manor Commission to mediate between the sides and negotiate a settlement. Meanwhile, a stay on rent collections benefitted tenants and perpetuated their strike.[31] Summer gave way to the election season and the Whigs' successful "Log Cabin" campaign, which afforded an unprecedented role to song and spectacle, as we will see. It was during this year that the sole instrumental depiction of the Anti-Rent conflict appeared.

Several mysteries surround the programmatic "Halderbarak Quick Step" (plate 5).[32] Just two imprints are extant, held by the New York State Library and the American Antiquarian Society. The Library of Congress does not possess the work, despite the sheet music's indication that it was entered for copyright in 1840 by its New York City publisher, Hewitt & Jaques. The well-respected firm was led from 1837 to 1841 by James Lang Hewitt and Edward Jaques.[33] A further mystery is that the composer is identified only as a "member of the Troy Citizens Corps." The voluntary militia was one of three companies from Rensselaer County summoned the week of December 10, 1839. Archivists at the New York State Library have tentatively identified the quick step's creator as John C. Andrews, a multifaceted local musician and publisher. He joined the Troy Citizens Corps around 1837 and was a private in its Helderberg campaign.[34] It is easy to imagine that this ambitious composer, having been called to duty in December 1839, was inspired to capture something of the experience and its local color. We will return to Andrews's authorship shortly.

What we do know about the "Halderbarak Quick Step" is that it was "Respectfully Dedicated to the Ladies of Rensellear Ville," as the sheet music indicates. The Troy Citizens Corps was briefly quartered in Rensselaerville in mid-December. The Albany County township had been among the first new areas parceled out to prospective tenants (in 160-acre plots) as Stephen Van Rensselaer III figured out how to retain his claim to the patroonship after the Revolutionary War. It was also among the first to refuse Stephen IV's demand for back rents, sending a representative to him in spring 1839 and contributing "ringleaders" to the December resistance. The Troy Citizens Corps was stationed in the town for three days, sheltering in an empty house. The *Albany Argus* reported on their "high discipline and [the] propriety of their conduct . . . both in camp duties and their intercourse with the people of the towns."[35] It seems one of these temporary occupants composed the "Halderbarak Quick Step" as commemoration and souvenir of the episode and offered it to the women of Rensselaerville.

Without this context, the "Halderbarak Quick Step" seems a conventional and undemanding composition based on 2/4 march time. Its most notable feature, and the one distinguishing it as an expression of Anti-Rent sentiment, is its specification of tin horn solo. The composer, as a corps member, might have chosen a military bugle instead. Certainly, locals heard the daily calls of reveille. But incorporation of the tin horn acknowledges and prioritizes the tenants' cause. It sounds in the third section, designated "The Gathering." After two heralding blasts on a single tone (these were not pitched instruments), a sudden shift to the parallel minor forms a two-bar "tutti" response by the piano. This dramatic gesture was foreshadowed by the direction of "Tasto" for the piano's initial eight-bar strain (A), indicating that the opening fanfare is not to be adorned. Directions for the second eight-bar strain (B) designate the successive entrance of bugles, snares drums, and "drums etc.," as a larger ensemble might have deployed. These sixteen bars, each of which is repeated, are followed by the eight-bar strain called "The Gathering" (C). The tin horn's short rhythmic bursts are balanced and answered by the tutti response to complete each four-bar phrase. Repetition of the strains results in a common and accessible structure: AABBAACCAA. The harmony emphasizes C major's primary chords. The only chromaticism is the parallel minor and diminished seventh chords of the tutti sections' responses, the dark cloud in an otherwise bright context.

The State Library's case for John Andrews's authorship of the "Halderbarak Quick Step" is strong. He was a prolific composer and operated a music store and publishing firm in Troy. From 1841 to 1847, he taught at the Troy Female Seminary (now the Emma Willard School) alongside his daughter, Jane Andrews, an accomplished singer who performed many of his works.[36] Andrews's compositions reflect his activities in interesting ways. For example, what began as creation of a "Troy Citizens Corps Grand March" became the piano solo, "Troy Citizens Corps Quick Step," instead. Andrews seemingly changed course after the handsomely lithographed cover was printed because its reverse side has a different title and tribute. The grand march was to be dedicated to the militia's captain, Thomas Turner.[37] The quick step is dedicated to Captain Alfred Peirce, who commanded the corps—including Private Andrews—during the Helderberg campaign. By retaining the original cover, Andrews managed to honor both officers. He also saved the time and expense involved in redoing an elaborate design that advertised his business. The image depicts a half-dozen corps members in fancy uniform and headdress at attention with J. C. Andrews's music store in the Cannon Place building in the background. A Black youth in simpler uniform stands to the side, presumably one of the five named "Servants (colored)" on the campaign's roll, as listed in a history of the Troy Citizens Corps.[38]

One last bit of evidence points to Andrews's authorship of the "Halderbarak Quick Step": his "Firemans Quick March" is similarly programmatic. "Fire bells" and brass solos are among the piano solo's performance indications. Again, Andrews's connection to the work's themes appears personal. The cover lithograph (by Nathaniel Currier) portrays a fire burning wildly at his Cannon Place music saloon. Andrews showed his gratitude to the "Officers and Members of the Troy Fire Companies" by dedicating the march to them. Interestingly, the four-story commercial building, built in 1835, has survived several fires and still stands today.[39]

Like much mid-nineteenth-century piano music, it is difficult to know how widely the "Halderbarak Quick Step" was disseminated or the social settings where it was played. But this instrumental work does preserve—through aesthetic means—significant aural symbolization of topical events. The tin horn would remain a compelling icon for the movement. It would soon be joined by another set of symbols representing the conflict.

"Playing . . . Calico Indian"

Governor Seward's Manor Commission was thwarted in its attempts to negotiate a compromise between Stephen Van Rensselaer IV and tenants during the first months of 1841. The patroon's lawyers refused reasonable property valuations and sales without reservations and continued to insist on payment of back rents. With the commission at an impasse, Stephen IV renewed rent collection. In mid-March, the new Albany County sheriff, Amos Adams, was sent to the Helderberg hills to auction off the possessions of delinquent tenants at distress sales. When the tin horns sounded, Sheriff Adams witnessed something novel. "A party of men gathered round disguised as 'Indians,' in loose pantaloons and tunics of brilliant calico, decked with fur, feathers, and tin ornaments. To prevent recognition, some had painted their faces black or red, and others wore masks of calico or painted sheepskins."[40] No violence ensued, but the sheriff and auction bidders were scared away. In late April, the Anti-Renters assembled again in Berne to renew their commitment. Invoking their Declaration of Independence, they resolved to "go into a ten year contest with the patroon" of Rensselaerwyck "until a redress of grievances be obtained."[41]

The Calico Indians made spectacular appearances again in September 1841 in defiance of Sheriff Adams and his new deputy, Bill Snyder. Confrontation with the latter resulted in one of the Anti-Rent war's most well-known skirmishes and songs. Snyder had pursued the Rensselaer family's property claims over several weeks with abusive language, stockpiled weapons, and "a gang of armed bullies."[42] The decisive episode began on September 20. Anti-Renters in "Indian" disguise managed to isolate Snyder near Rensselaerville, threatening and humiliating him before he was allowed to run off. Snyder did not arrive back in Albany until the next day, leading some to assume he was dead. He returned to Albany indignant, but the encounter concluded his pursuit of the Helderberg farmers. A humorous and lively ballad, "The Horrible Murder of Bill Snyder," was written sometime after the incident and the Fourth of July 1844, when it was sung at Reidsville and sold as a broadside (figure 2.1). The song probably circulated orally before this printing. We will treat "Bill Snyder" at length after looking at the phenomenon of the Calico Indians and related works and concepts. But before we get to that discussion, it is worth noting that a musical work paying tribute to the Van Rensselaers appeared just as the Anti-Renters' confrontation with the law intensified.

In early September 1841, the New York music vendor Joseph Atwill advertised that the "Van Rensselaer Guard[s] March" was available.[43] Presumably this was "The Van Rensselaer Guards Grand March and Quickstep," originally published in 1837 in Albany by its composer, C. L. Underner.[44] The opening section, "March," consists of two eight-bar repeatable strains in C major and a trio of equal length that begins in F major and modulates back to tonic. It is in cut time with many dotted rhythms. The second section, "Quickstep," is in 2/4 and B-flat major, with constant sixteenths and some Scotch snaps. The quickstep's proportions and modulation to its subdominant in the trio mirror the march.

The resurrection of Underner's "Van Rensselaer Guards March" seems timely. A few weeks before Atwill's advertisement appeared, the New-York Military Magazine described the Van Rensselaer Guard of Albany as a "fine corps" deserving of "the support of all patriotic citizens."[45] Although little information about the guard's origin and purpose is available, we can assume the composition was a tribute to the family. They might even have commissioned it, like the nostalgic oil portraits of the Manor house and gardens they hired Thomas Cole to create about this time.

The practice of Euro-Americans assuming the identity of Indigenous peoples as a form of resistance dates at least to the Boston Tea Party, as Philip Deloria notes in Playing Indian. In December 1773, a group of white people purporting to be from the upstate New York Mohawk tribe dumped British tea into the harbor for several hours under cover of night. Deloria calls this "a catalytic moment" for American national consciousness, "the first drumbeat in the long cadence of rebellion through which Americans redefined themselves as something other than British colonists."[46] The Anti-Renters of 1840 were generations removed from being British subjects, but their feudal condition motivated them to pursue the Revolution's unrealized goals. They were keenly aware of the Tea Party's potent symbolism. "We resolved to adopt the same kind of protection that was resorted to by the people of Boston when the tea was thrown overboard into the water of its bay," recalled Anti-Rent organizer Dr. Smith Boughton. "We then raised in the various counties a large force of men completely disguised to prevent the landlord[s] from executing their threat."[47] In fact, Indian disguises had been used by rebellious tenants in upstate New York shortly after the American Revolution, albeit with tragic consequences. In 1791, resistance to a distress sale in Columbia County led to a sheriff's death.[48] The revival of disguises for oppositional purposes by the Anti-Renters fifty years later would also have severe effects.

Farmers on Livingston Manor and the Schuyler-Rensselaer holdings in Columbia County had sought relief through continued physical resistance, rent strikes, and title challenges throughout the 1790s. The last involved a second aspect of Anti-Renter identification with Native Americans: the appropriation of land from its inhabitants. The colonial period was rife with "fraud and chicanery" concerning "unextinguished Indian claims," as Ellis puts it. Property claims during the early republic were also questionable, as land grabs by speculators accelerated after the Revolution. In 1787, for example, a large company of investors led by John Livingston (of the Manor) obtained leases of 999 years for "nearly all of the lands of the Six Nations of the Indians, in New York," for a small annual rent, modest bonus, and a generous quantity of rum. A scandal erupted when the deal was made public, forcing Governor Clinton to step in. The Livingston group's contract was invalidated, but the Six Nations' land was not returned. Instead, the state negotiated treaties to acquire most of the land in seven counties in the Finger Lakes region.[49]

Native Americans would continue to lose ground in New York and throughout the new republic in the early nineteenth century. James Fenimore Cooper gave literary shape to "the vanishing Indian" in his 1826 novel *The Last of the Mohicans*. He would deploy this trope again in *The Redskins*, in which noble, genuine Indians offer moral education to the savage "Injin" Anti-Renters and then conveniently retreat from view. By 1838, when President Andrew Jackson forced the Cherokee, Seminole, and other nations to take the "Trail of Tears" to (present-day) Oklahoma, "most native people had indeed been made to disappear from the eastern landscape."[50] This did not prevent the Anti-Renters from appropriating Native American identity for oppositional, legal, and organizational purposes.

Without doubt, Anti-Renter appropriations served their self-interest rather than that of Native Americans. Rensselaerwyck tenants insisted that the patroons' illegal maneuvers invalidated their property claims. One of their supporters, Albany attorney Calvin Pepper, summarized the tenants' disputation of the Van Rensselaers' "pretended Indian title" in a series of articles. He pointed to the family's claim that they possessed "Indian deeds" for various land parcels dating from 1630 to 1727 during an 1844 hearing before the New York Assembly Judiciary Committee. "There is no pretence that they are of record, confirmed as such by the colonial government, or attested by any formality," countered Pepper. Furthermore, the colonial "foundation of property in land possessed by the Indians" dictated that no European person "had a right to purchase of them without the consent of the government." The Rensselaers had not obtained consent from either the Dutch or the English authorities. Nor had they received explicit sanction for lands contracted with the Indians from the New York legislature as required in the state constitution. "The Patroon then can have no valid Indian deed in his possession," concluded Pepper. And even if the deeds were valid, the maps upon which they were based were highly inaccurate. Finally, the originating deeds would have been made by the Dutch West India Company, not their agent, Killiaen Van Rensselaer.[51]

A third form of identification with—and appropriation of—Native American identity by the Anti-Renters was the organizational structure replicated throughout the leasehold district in the form of local associations. Without getting too far ahead of our story, a general overview helps make sense of the many Native American allusions sprinkled through expressive works such as "Bill Snyder," "The Brave Indian," and "Ye Sons of Tuscarora." The first formal Anti-Rent Association beyond Albany County's West Manor was on the 40,000-acre Schoharie County Scott Patent, which was claimed by John Livingston's descendants. Current tenants feared the imminent expiration of the leases "in lives" that their forbears had taken. Their choices were to either capitulate to the Livingstons' terms or leave. The next Anti-Renters to form associations were residents of Schoharie County's Blenheim Patent and William Rensselaer's tenants on the East Manor. The 17,000-acre Blenheim Patent had been purchased about fifteen years earlier by John A. King, future governor of the state. By early 1845, eight more counties had similar organizations, representing as many as sixty thousand supporters.[52]

The associations had two facets: a public side to plan strategy, create petitions, and host lectures, and a secret side for Calico Indian activities. The latter were neighborhood-based cohorts with about a dozen members, led by a "chief," and coordinated regionally. Their identities were known only to each other, and they were sworn to secrecy. Pseudonyms based on Native American names were adopted. The Blenheim Hill Association, for example, had three chiefs whose namesakes were the prominent Native American leaders Black Hawk, Tecumseh, and Red Jacket.[53] The Anti-Renters' bodies were camouflaged with calico gowns and masks and their personal identities with a subterfuge that—as Deloria has charted—was becoming a white American tradition.

Anti-Rent poems and songs about the Calico Indians were a way to honor efforts that could not be openly acknowledged. "The Brave Indian" is one such work (plate 6). The original manuscript was "found among the papers" of the *Albany Freeholder*'s editor, according to Henry Christman.[54] No tune is indicated, but the poem has a verse-chorus structure. The chorus exhorts the listener to accept the Indian as a friend, and not "count him as a stranger" because "he your country stays / In the day and hour of danger." The first verse mystifies the Indians' origins: "From rocky mountains we are come / To free our land from slavery." The final verse urges the reader to accept their presence and provide for their needs by giving "of your plenties' store."

The Calico Indians' role in protecting farm families runs through several of the verses. The latter's peace is predicated on the former's vigilance and endurance. Reeve Huston offers an interesting interpretation of the theme of protection based on gender conventions. In his view, "The Brave Indian" is an explicit expression of masculinity directed toward guarding the safety of the female sex. Huston's extensive demographic analysis of Anti-Renters demonstrates that a good portion of the Calico ranks was filled by young male laborers. Lacking "the usual badges of manhood" such as "dominion over wives and children," the Calico Indians could take pride in being "selfless protectors of their (implicitly female) communities."[55] Certainly, the male pronouns used in "The Brave Indian" support this interpretation. However, the song does not include a word about female dependency and subordination. Instead, the second-person address is to all people aspiring to safe, secure homes and restful nights. As we will see, the theme of peaceful, stable family life is found in several texts, including "The Farmer's Song" (plate 17) and "Dere vos a Time" (plate 23). And women's participation as active protestors and agitators is sprinkled through contemporary accounts of the movement. Their involvement also carried symbolic weight.

A curious story about the Calico Indians is recounted in Gardner's *Folklore from the Schoharie Hills*. The collector spoke with people "who claimed to have had first-hand acquaintance with the local leaders."

> They organized as bands of Indians, each band of ten under the leadership of a chief. When the official collector of rent was due in the locality, a "chief" disguised as a squaw would go to a certain thicket where he had concealed the Indian disguises of his band, and there meet and equip his ten followers. Out of this procedure grew a "broad" ballad which related the story of a squaw who gave birth to ten full-grown Indians, and thus discouraged her oppressors, who could not hope to cope with a tribe which increased at such an appalling rate.[56]

The tale's gender-fluid framework is notable. Unfortunately, the "broad ballad" described does not appear extant. It is tempting to think the story might be the basis of the American children's song "Ten Little Indians," whose origins are obscure. It is equally possible that the informants' fanciful tale of formidable increase was inspired by the folksong.

Like several recent scholars, Gardner relates Calico Indian activity to earlier subversive folk practices. She notes that Anti-Renter "tales of cleverness and daring" are suggestive of "Robin Hood and his band of outlaws." Thomas Wermuth drew a similar parallel between the Calico Indians and the youth groups or "abbeys" of early modern Europe.[57] Huston also frames them in terms of older European practices of organized disruption and charivari, or "rough music," that attracted young men. But he emphasizes that their purpose was political and their identification with Native Americans served a specific ideological function. As the purported "aboriginal inhabitants of estate lands," the braves would "liberate their ancient home from landlord rule" and then obligingly disappear. The figure of the Indian, as Deloria soberly observes, locates "native people at the very heart of American ambivalence."[58]

"The News Flew Round . . ."

"Bill Snyder" is another expressive work about "Indian" activity (plate 7a). As described previously, the lyrics were written sometime after the culminating incident of September 1841 with Deputy Snyder and before the 1844 Fourth of July "Anti-Land-Monopoly" celebration in Reidsville. The rousing number was sung at the latter by the Euterpean Band of Rensselaerville. The community brass band sold the broadsides reproduced in figures 2.1 and 2.2 for its own benefit.[59] The first broadside's title, "The Horrible Murder of Bill Snyder" is facetious, as the deputy returned to Albany the day after the confrontation. Nevertheless, the text seems to have exacerbated rumors of his demise and the Anti-Renters' violent tendencies. The more restrained title, "The End of Bill Snyder" is sometimes used instead, or simply, "Big Bill Snyder."

The tune indicated for the eight-verse contrafactum is "Old Dan Tucker." The first verse sets the scene with the sheriff's arrival "at dead of night" while "high on a hill sat an Indian true." Successive quatrains describe the Indians' fearsome appearance, the tin horn's power to summon and intimidate, and Snyder's retreat to a bottle of rum. The chorus chants the threat of tar and

Figure 2.1. "The Horrible Murder of Bill Snyder." Broadside, Stephen Foster Collection, Center for American Music, University of Pittsburgh Library System.

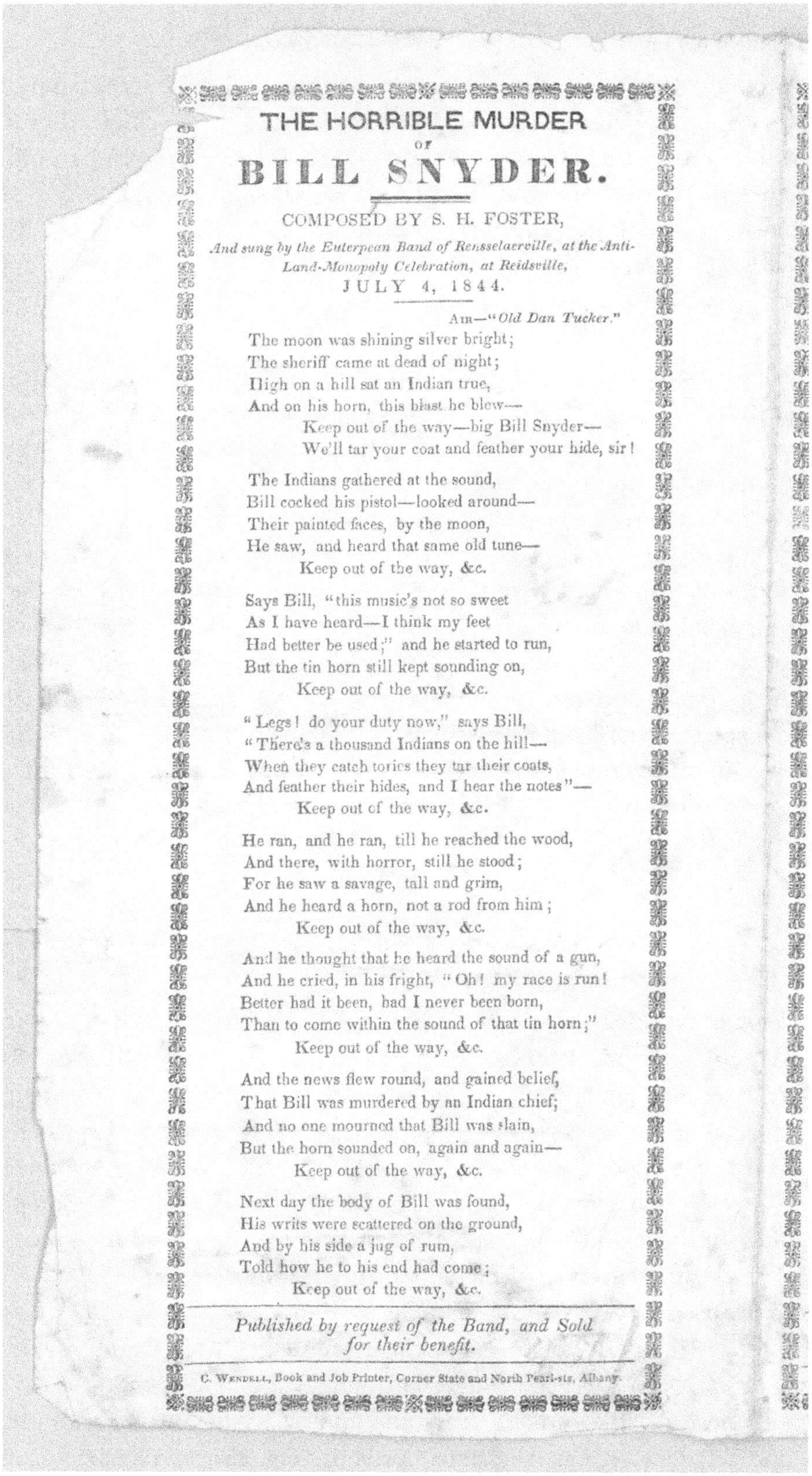

feather, which had remained only a threat in this instance. Perhaps the coincidence of Bill Snyder's and Dan Tucker's drunken dissipations inspired the lyricist, S. H. Foster (plate 7a, verse 8, and plate 7b, verse 4, respectively).

The origin of the tune that became associated with "Old Dan Tucker" has long been debated. Like much of blackface minstrelsy, it might well have been with African American musicians and traditions.[60] The first published sheet music was issued by C. H. Keith in Boston in 1843 as one selection in a set of six "Original Banjo Melodies" attributed to "Old Dan Emmit" [sic]. Dan Emmett was a member of the newly formed Virginia Minstrels, who began performing "Old Dan Tucker" that same year.[61] Evidence for its origins in African American practice includes the melodic syncopation and call-and-response structure of the "Gran' Chorus." In the 1843 publication, the chorus's first measure—which syncopates the words, "Get out de way!"—is answered by piano alone. This happens twice, making a four-bar phrase. This phrase is then repeated, but with lyrics throughout (plate 7b). My setting represents the response to the call, "Keep out of the way," with small noteheads to suggest the Anti-Renters' possible performance practice (plate 7c). The structure lends itself to use as a rally song for the Fourth of July and other gatherings.

Author S. H. Foster could have encountered the Air—"Old Dan Tucker" any number of ways, including minstrel shows in New York City. Stoked by performances and printings, the song spread rapidly across the United States. A year after its initial publication, new contrafacta appeared supporting the Whig presidential candidate and abolition. The latter was the subject of The Hutchinson Family's influential version, "Get Off the Track." "Old Dan Tucker" was soon associated with two additional Anti-Rent contrafacta, "The Working Men's League" (plate 8) and "Anti-Rent Song of Triumph" (plate 29).

Little can be ascertained about S. H. Foster except that this lyricist also authored the Anti-Rent contrafactum, "We Will Be Free" (plate 19). Its lyrics were set to another Dan Emmett–associated tune, "The Boatman's Dance." S. H. does not appear to be related to Stephen Collins Foster, despite their shared association with early minstrelsy. Perhaps the Anti-Rent sympathizer was the young Reverend Solomon H. Foster, who later became an ardent abolitionist and leader of the Wesleyan Methodist Church in northern New York.[62] Further investigation is needed to confirm this identification.

"Bill Snyder" became the movement's signature song, performed at both rallies and skirmishes. During a prolonged confrontation with the Albany County sheriff in late August 1844, for example, "women and girls enlivened the road by singing the poetical effusion," as the Illustrated London News reported.[63] "Bill Snyder" also remained in circulation longer than any other musical artifact of the Anti-Rent movement. Gardner included most of its verses in her collection of Schoharie folklore.[64] Christman, writing in the 1940s, said it was the movement's "best known song."[65] The eminent folksinger Pete Seeger released "Big Bill Snyder" on his 1976 album with Ed Renehan, Fifty Sail on Newburgh Bay: Hudson Valley Songs, Old and New. By this time, Pete Seeger (Ruth Crawford Seeger's stepson) had been performing "Old Dan Tucker" for nearly twenty years.[66] A few years later, Renehan included a setting of "Big Bill Snyder" in The Clearwater Songbook. Jerry Silverman did likewise in his 2009 anthology, New York Sings.[67]

Perhaps it is unsurprising that the penultimate and final verses describing the "end" of Bill Snyder have sometimes been interpreted literally. "And the news flew round, and gained belief, / That Bill was murdered by an Indian chief," S. H. Foster sarcastically rhymed. Seeger and Renehan perpetuated the myth of Snyder's death, and Silverman wrote that he "was killed in a skirmish with some farmers when he tried to collect rent from them."[68] As described earlier, this was far from the truth. Deputy Snyder lived to tell his version of the tale, which was reported in the newspapers as electrifying Albany. Foster's lyrics indicate that what ended was Bill Snyder's ability to serve papers. They were "scattered on the ground" rather than reaching the tenants, and the deputy refrained from ever again provoking the hilltown farmers.

A Tale of Two *Advocates*

The same month Bill Snyder was rebuffed, September 1841, marked the appearance of the first serial created to articulate and publicize the Anti-Rent cause. The *Helderberg Advocate* was a response to tenants' realization "that they needed to establish a newspaper to represent their grievances in a public forum and unite disaffected renters throughout the region." William Gallup, who already published the mainstream *Schoharie Republican*, embraced the task with vigor, writing pithy editorials. He also printed pointed columns by land reform proselytizer Thomas Ainge Devyr, who would soon play an important role in encouraging Anti-Rent poetry. In addition to serving its supporters, the *Helderberg Advocate* intended "to bring to the attention of state government in Albany the plight of the renters and the necessity of abolishing the antiquated system of land tenancy."[69] As it turned out, Gallup attracted not just politicians' notice but landlords' censure.

During the first months of 1842, West Manor and Schoharie Scott Patent tenants submitted petitions to the state legislature for redress concerning their respective leases. Their petitions were referred to the judiciary committee, which decided in April that the US Constitution's contract clause prevented the state from intervening. Nothing was to be done. Later that spring, "an armed band of 'Indians' seized the Livingston family agent" in Schoharie, threatening and subjecting him to "some personal indignity."[70] In another confrontation, a farmer intent on paying his rent to the Livingstons was abducted by Calico Indians. In a scenario that might have appeared in a minstrel show, the up-renter was brought to a tavern and forced to sit on "a chair in the center of the room for five hours until he consented to jump three times and shout, 'Down with the rent!'" Six men were arrested; two were fined and imprisoned for a month. Governor Seward issued a proclamation harshly condemning "unlawful transactions" by "tumultuous bodies of disguised and armed men."[71]

In response to the *Helderberg Advocate*'s biting commentary about the situation, Jacob Livingston made a preemptive move to prevent the spread of Anti-Rent sentiment. His lawyer and agent filed a complaint with the Schoharie County Court, which had just sentenced the tavern ruffians. In May 1842, a grand jury delivered a "presentment" declaring the *Helderberg Advocate* seditious and a public nuisance. According to legal historian Ralph Frasca, the judgment had serious implications for freedom of the press. However, formal charges were not made, and Gallup soon tempered the paper's coverage and language. He closed shop in August 1843.[72]

Despite the brevity of its existence, the *Helderberg Advocate* played an important role in Anti-Rent expressive culture through Thomas Devyr. Originally from Donegal, Ireland, Devyr moved to London as an adult, and then to Newcastle-upon-Tyne. While there, he became deeply involved with the Chartists, a radical, working-class political movement. Devyr narrowly escaped arrest for leading an armed uprising in January 1840; he and his wife immigrated to Brooklyn later that year. An experienced writer and editor, Devyr was asked to manage the newly founded Williamsburg *Democrat*. Surprised to find its mission was partisan—supporting the party rather than the political system—Devyr began reading progressive publications such as the *Helderberg Advocate* in search of like-minded activists.[73] He contributed open letters to the *Advocate* and was invited to speak at the 1842 Fourth of July Anti-Rent celebration in Rensselaerville.[74]

Devyr made the 150-mile trek from New York to join the tenant farmers and their supporters from Albany, Rensselaer, and Schoharie Counties on Independence Day. Among the participants was Dr. Smith Boughton, soon a key figure in the movement. The idealistic Boughton was born into a local tenant farm family in 1810. He received a college education, medical training, and in 1837 joined the Patriots' War in Canada. On his return, Boughton established a medical practice in Alps, Rensselaer County, and became active in the burgeoning Anti-Rent cause. He and Devyr collaborated on a "Statement of Grievances and Proposed Redress" after meeting at Rensselaerville's Fourth of July celebration. Their statement advocated for a constitutional amendment to end the leasehold system and asked the tenants to pledge they would "pay no rent until relief was secured." The widely circulated declaration reiterated the Anti-Renters' commitment "to a ten-year war if necessary."[75]

With approximately two thousand tenants in Albany County already mobilized, the movement began to expand rapidly. By the end of 1843, four thousand tenants on William Van Rensselaer's East Manor established the Anti-Rent Association of Rensselaer County. Tenants on the 17,000-acre Blenheim Patent in Schoharie County formed their own association, adopting a seven-point written platform and erecting a tall pole with a banner that said, "Down with the Rent."[76] Representatives from the three associations, including Dr. Boughton, set to work creating a new legal strategy with the assistance of sympathetic lawyers. Using New York State's 1787 "Act Concerning Tenures" as its starting point, the committee drafted an "Act Concerning Tenures by Lease" to address specifics of the manor system. If the bill succeeded, tenants would be able to challenge patroon titles and have their leases converted to outright purchases with the state's assistance. Six thousand Anti-Renters endorsed the act that summer, and Boughton presented more than 133 petitions in its support to the legislature, which began its consideration in January 1844. The opposition marshaled their resources too. "We had the whole aristocracy of the State to contend with, immense wealth and powerful political influences," recalled Boughton. "The lobbies were filled with landlord lawyers contradicting me."[77]

The Judiciary Committee's report on the "Act Concerning Tenures by Lease" savagely attacked the tenants' cause. The report's endorsement by the State Assembly in late April was a "devastating defeat" for the Anti-Renters, who had failed to counter the landlords' influence. In addition, two recent court decisions had undermined their proposal. The US Supreme Court had determined that title challenges violated the constitution's contract clause, and the New York Supreme Court disallowed the state from intervening in disputes over private property through eminent domain and related measures. Once again, the tenants' grievances were relegated to individual negotiations rather than collective redress. Predictably, the Van Rensselaer brothers Stephen and William initiated "a flurry of lawsuits" against the tenants in response to the act's defeat.[78] The Anti-Renters' next attempt at land reform would be to agitate for revisions to the state constitution.

Meanwhile, Devyr continued to support the Anti-Rent cause from his base in New York City. An important conduit arose in February 1844, when George Henry Evans asked Devyr to help found the National Reform Association (NRA). The English-born Evans was already a major leader in the American workers' movement. From 1829 to 1836, he had edited the weekly *Working Man's Advocate*, "arguably the most important labor newspaper" of the antebellum period. While the lingering effects of the Panic of 1837 exacerbated the workers' situation, Evans derived a plan to alleviate their plight through land reform. Devyr was a likely ally. His 1835 pamphlet, *Our Natural Rights*, condemned the aristocracy's monopoly of the land in the United Kingdom. In 1842, Devyr reprinted the original with a lengthy appendix reflecting his recent Anti-Rent experience.[79] Evans and the NRA's other founders agreed that individuals' natural rights included an "Equal Right to Land."[80] As historian Helene Zahler expressed this ideal, "the natural right to life implied a right to the means of living, that is, to land enough to live on."[81]

The National Reform Association's ambitious proposal involved opening public lands to actual settlers. Equitable distribution of agricultural land would reduce crowding and competition in urban areas, thus solving the problem of surplus workers and low wages. The US government, in accordance with the 1785 Land Ordinance, already required the survey of federal lands into six-mile square townships. The NRA proposed that each township be subdivided with modest farms on the outskirts and smaller lots for tradespeople at the center. To combat the tendency toward monopoly by speculators, possession (i.e., lifetime usufruct) would be limited to 160 acres and actual settlers. Zahler observes that the NRA plan linked the interests of labor and the small-scale farmer in a novel way. Its first manifesto "insisted the only remedy for social injustice was a land policy that gave the worker an alternative to wage-labor."[82] Although the particulars would differ, the NRA's basic goal was realized in the 1862 US Homestead Act.

During spring 1844, the National Reform Association held public meetings, sponsored lectures, and distributed printed materials. Female membership was cultivated, along with cultural and educational activities. The NRA's central committee was charged with providing "Vocal and Instrumental Music at the general meetings." It was also expected to "publish, and widely circulate a collection of the best Songs and Ballads having a bearing on the condition of the working classes, and encouraging them to unite for an effectual remedy."[83] Evans revived his earlier newspaper, *The Working Man's Advocate*, with a new series that launched mid-March. Now called *Young America*, the masthead identified it as the "Organ of the National Reform Association." Long columns of prose elaborated the alliance between National Reform and the Anti-Rent cause, and soon the weekly published poetry reflecting that link. Two poems published within a couple weeks of each other were contrafacta. The first to name a tune was "The Working Men's League," published May 25, 1844 (plate 8a). The second was "The Agrarian Ball" (plate 9a).

The tune indicated for "The Working Men's League" by its anonymous author was "Old Dan Tucker." The first seven of the contrafactum's eleven verses share a refrain. "Get out the way you speculators, / You shall no longer be dictators" deploys the original chorus's rhythmic drive to critique land speculation. Beginning with the eighth refrain, this idea is expanded through endorsement of "the People's Cause" over "loafing, crafty" land sellers. The verses mention "reform" twice (and again in the penultimate refrain). Speculators, who do not live on their land, are contrasted with the happy home dwellers of this "great Yankee nation." As in "The Brave Indian," the song places value in personal security. Here, the security is financial, proposing homes that are "all smiling, sunny / Without price and without money." For many years, Evans had promoted the exemption of family homes from seizure for debt. His 1829 "Working Men's Declaration of Independence" advocated abolishing "the lien law in favor of landlords against tenants" so that those "who are *not* wealthy," would have "*equal means* to enjoy '*life, liberty, and the pursuit of happiness.*'"[84] The NRA adopted home exemption as one of its primary goals while New York's legislation on distress was in flux. The Republic's founding ideals could not be realized until each person had access to adequate resources to live and flourish.

Other verses explicitly connect workers—who "used to *beg to labor*"—to farmers and "Nature's gift, *the Land*," through the "Agrarian Ball," foreshadowing the contrafactum with that title. In "The Working Men's League," the ball is depicted as rolling to "every station," tolling "the knell of Avarice," a mellifluous mixed metaphor. The associated (i.e., eighth) refrain has altered lyrics, linking the ball's movement to improvements in "The People's Cause": "Push along and keep it moving." The figure of a ball's unstoppable momentum had long been part of the Anti-Rent imaginary from within and without. "We will take up the ball of the Revolution where our fathers stopped it and roll it to the final consummation of freedom and independence of the masses," the Anti-Renters claimed in conjunction with their 1839 Declaration of Independence.[85] The image was famously harnessed during the presidential election season of 1840, when Whig parades included an enormous actual ball pushed in front of horse wagons. The spectacle was seen by crowds that reached "upwards of a hundred thousand by the end of the campaign."[86]

Nicknamed the "Log Cabin and Hard Cider" campaign, the Whig promotion of William Henry Harrison in 1840 is now regarded as having launched modern strategies of electioneering involving spectacle, material objects, and music. Both Democrats and Whigs came to understand the persuasive power of political song during the contest between Harrison and incumbent Martin Van Buren. As Horace Greeley explained to fellow newspaperman and strategist Thurlow Weed, "People like the swing of the music. . . . After a song or two they are more ready to listen to the orators."[87] The most well-known of these songs is "Tippecanoe and Tyler Too." We will discuss this tune in the context of the 1846 song, "This Great Commotion" (plate 26), in the next chapter.

The contrafactum entitled "The Agrarian Ball" appeared in the *Working Man's Advocate* on June 8, 1844. Its anonymous author set it to another Log Cabin favorite, "Rosin the Bow." Also known as "Rosin the Beau," the tune had formed the basis for at least six campaign contrafacta during the 1840 election season.[88] "The Agrarian Ball" combined its catchy melody with a vivid verbal image to express and arouse Anti-Renter sentiments (plate 9a). The contrafactum's six quatrains exhort listeners to unite across party lines—whether Democrat or Whig—"And roll on the Agrarian Ball." The Anti-Rent cause is heralded in verse five, which promises the "Agrarian army" will destroy the "Monopoly of Land." Ultimately, beauty and duty beckon the listener to "attend to humanity's call."

The ubiquity of "Rosin the Beau" went beyond political campaigns. According to folklorist Ray Browne, it was "perhaps the most popular comic song of the mid-nineteenth century" in the United States.[89] Yet, the melody's origins are murky. Prominent Scotch snaps suggest a Scots precedent, but it has Irish stylistic features as well. Piano-vocal sheet music for "Old Rosin the Beau" was published in 1838 in Philadelphia (plate 9b). The arranger is J. C. Beckell, but neither composer nor lyricist are named. The tune's catchiness and rolling 6/8 meter were amenable to numerous parodies and adaptations, such as a set of piano variations published by W. C. Peters in 1842. The lyricist of "The Agrarian Ball" could have known "Rosin the Beau" from any number of sources. It was put to serious purpose in the 1845 abolitionist song, "The Liberty Ball," later repurposed by The Hutchinson Family as "Lincoln and Liberty." The melody continued to be used in shape-note singing, minstrelsy, and songsters for several decades, persisting into the twentieth century as the Appalachian murder ballad "Down in the Willow Garden" and the folksong stalwart "Acres of Clams."[90]

The 1838 sheet music has an F major key signature, but the melody is essentially hexatonic, incorporating the leading tone (E) just once. The tune has features identified by Edward Bunting as typically Irish, including the absence of scale degree 4 (B-flat) and emphasis on scale degree 6 (D).[91] Arranger Beckell draws attention to the latter with fermati and harmonization on a diminished seventh chord (using B natural). The structure of the self-deprecating lyrics suggests a participatory drinking song. Repetition of the second couplet of each verse creates a refrain audiences could easily join. My setting of the first verse reflects this invitation to group participation. In plate 9c, "Roll on the Agrarian Ball" is stated four times. The phrase returns to close the fourth and final verses of the text, driving the lyricist's message home.

While these songs were enlivening National Reform meetings, the organization was attracting a substantial following.[92] By September 1845, "there were land-reform groups in six or eight states and in twelve New York counties."[93] "The Working Men's League" and "The Agrarian Ball" were disseminated through their reprinting in John Pickering's 1847 *Working Man's Political Economy*, which brought the message of Anti-Rent-inflected National Reform to Ohio and beyond.[94]

Fourth of July and More

Celebration of the nation's Independence Day in 1844 allowed the Anti-Renters to reaffirm their commitment to the cause in response to recent legislative defeats. Their agitation had been underway for five years at this point. The first time farmers had assembled on the Fourth of July to articulate their goals was in 1839, when Rensselaerwyck tenants created the "Anti-Renters' Declaration of Independence." From then on, the annual holiday became a time to express hope and rouse solidarity. "Every Fourth of July between 1840 and 1847, hundreds of wagons, bedecked with banners, converged at a central location in each anti-rent county," observes Huston. Parades, brass bands, and oratory were typical elements in these rituals. Poems were recited, the 1776 Declaration of Independence was read, and on at least one occasion, "27 ladies dressed in white to represent the states of the Union" joined the procession.[95] Poetry, song, and music became essential features of Anti-Rent pageantry.

The gatherings proliferated as Anti-Renters formed associations beyond the three core counties of Albany, Rensselaer, and Schoharie. Notably, a delegation from Schoharie's Blenheim Association began organizing on the Hardenbergh Patent, which covered nearly half of Delaware, Greene, Sullivan, and Ulster Counties, in June 1844. Comprising as many as two million acres in the early eighteenth century, various Hardenbergh parcels were now controlled by the Livingston, Verplanck, and other families. Competing land claims based on imprecise descriptions of the Delaware River's branches, lack of compensation to Native Americans, and other issues were long-standing. Nevertheless, many tenants had become bound by cumbersome leases to those asserting title. Anti-Rent organizers encouraged patent farmers to challenge those claims. The Blenheim Association was especially effective in Delaware County.[96] As chapter 3 describes, one of those challenges led to the movement's climactic episode at a Verplanck distress auction the next summer.

Figure 2.2. "We Are True Anti-Renters." Broadside, Stephen Foster Collection, Center for American Music, University of Pittsburgh Library System.

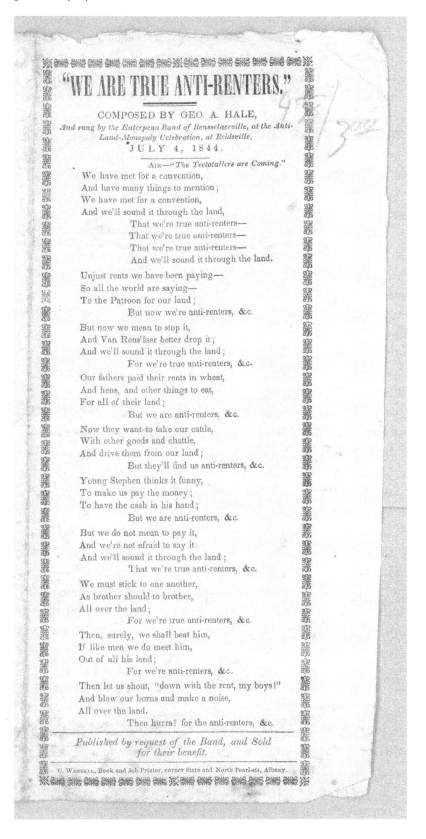

On July 4, 1844, the Euterpean Band of Rensselaerville sang two rousing numbers during the "Anti-Land-Monopoly" celebration in Reidsville. As discussed previously, one was "Bill Snyder." The other was "We Are True Anti-Renters" (figure 2.2). Both are "rally songs," defined by Roger Hecht as pieces "aimed at lifting up the spirits and forming solidarity."[97] Like "Bill Snyder," the band sold "We Are True Anti-Renters" as a broadside for its benefit. The latter's first line—"We have met for a convention"—suggests it was written after summer 1843, when association members from Albany, Rensselaer, and Schoharie Counties endorsed the "Act Concerning Tenures by Lease" (plate 10a). Lyricist George A. Hale indicated that "We Are True Anti-Renters" was set to the energetic temperance song, "The Teetotallers Are Coming."

Also known as the "Cold Water Pledge," the text of "Teetotallers" was linked to the tune, "The Old Granite State," which itself had a complicated set of associations. The latter was quickly becoming one of The Hutchinson Family's most popular songs. Jesse Hutchinson created "The Old Granite State" to tell the singing family's origin story. Their version of the tune was based on a Second Advent hymn known as "Old Church Yard."[98] The Hutchinsons made multiple appearances in the Albany area in August 1842, and "The Old Granite State" was published the following year.[99] The family's local appearance may well have inspired the Anti-Renter contrafactum. It is also possible that George Hale encountered the same tune through the temperance societies proliferating in the region, as suggested by his use of the title, "The Teetotallers Are Coming."[100] Unfortunately, nothing further is known about Hale. But following his lead, my setting of "We Are True Anti-Renters" relies on the earliest notated score of "Teetotallers" that could be located. Plate 10b is from the collection *Temperance Chimes*, published in New York in 1867.[101] After discussing its features, I will compare it to the Hutchinsons' more elaborate version of the tune.

"The Teetotallers Are Coming" must have seemed destined for Anti-Rent expression, as the four-part chorus's echoing, repeated first line is, "We're a band of freemen" (plate 10b). Interestingly, George Hale's contrafactum doesn't use this phrase but positions "That we're true anti-renters" to resonate in its place, as seen in my setting (plate 10c). The chorus's short phrases—incorporating a form of call and response that is also reminiscent of American psalmody's fuguing technique—are especially infectious and invite participation.[102] Another inventive feature is the chorus's second (and seemingly final) ending, a deceptive cadence. The unresolved submediant harmony (vi), with scale degree 6 in the melody, metaphorically allows the chorus to "sound through the land" forever.

It is worth noting that the corresponding phrase ending in the two-part setting of "Old Church Yard" has scale degree 5 in both soprano and bass, an unresolved dominant.[103] The Hutchinsons transformed this open-endedness in their "Old Granite State" by dramatically repeating and lingering (with fermati) on scale degree 6 in all four parts at the song's midpoint and conclusion (mm. 24–25 and mm. 49–50). While this gesture gives shape and flair to the arrangement's many verses, the Hutchinson song has a lengthy coda with repeated V^7–I cadences to bring the piece to a proper tonal end (mm. 50–71). "Teetotallers," in contrast, leaves its submediant harmony unresolved. I believe this feature may have influenced Hale's designation of the tune for his rally song.

The conjunction of musical and poetic meaning in "We Are True Anti-Renters" is an excellent example of what Crawford Seeger describes as the "keep-going-ness" of folksong. She identified the "unfinished" quality of folk expression as "one of the notable characteristics in traditional performance of music."[104] For the Anti-Renters gathered on the Fourth of July at Reidsville, the Euterpean Band's songs were rallying cries meant to lift participants' spirits and create solidarity in the face of unresolved conflict. As the struggle continued to grow in scope, songs of this type were crafted increasingly often. In the next chapter, we will examine the many rally songs published when the *Albany Freeholder* was established the following spring.

Across the Hudson River, a large crowd gathered to celebrate July 4, 1844. East Manor tenants from Rensselaer County assembled at Hoags Corners to hear the "magic voice" of "Big Thunder," Dr. Boughton's assumed identity. In addition to his legislative work, Boughton was a tireless organizer of Anti-Rent associations and Calico Indian bands. Many were prompted to join by "his warm confidence and sound argument." Christman gives a vivid and moving description of the acoustic environment shaping the Indians' dramatic appearance at Hoags Corners on the Fourth of July. Announced with fife and drum rolls, they emerged from the surrounding woods in "fantastic dress," with war whoops, clattering spears, and tin horns. Their leader wore a "brilliantly colored calico dress and gay pantaloons. . . . His head was decked with colored feathers, and his mask was varicolored with war paint." Big Thunder addressed the crowd "in a clear, eloquent voice that almost sang." At that moment, Boughton's wife, Mary, realized that the grand orator was her husband. Though she could not see through his disguise, she knew his voice.[105] This would not be the last time Boughton's voice gave him away. Six months later, he would be separated from Mary and their young child and struggling to survive in the Hudson jail.

Skirmishes proliferated during summer 1844 as the associations and Calico Indian bands stepped up their activities. The future railroad magnate Jay Gould witnessed his father defend their modest family home in Roxbury, Delaware County. On July 6, five "artificial Indians" confronted Gould's father for defying the Anti-Renters' restriction on sounding tin horns when he used one to call workers to meals. The defiant up-renter compelled the braves to retreat from the premises "to the tune of the 'old king's arm and shell.'" (Unfortunately, nothing further is known about this song.) A larger contingent returned the next day but were similarly rebuffed. The "frightful appearance" of the Indians was agonizing and formative for the eight-year-old Jay. At the age of twenty, he published a lengthy history of Delaware County that criticized the tenants' efforts to "repudiate solemn contracts, and defraud the landlords of their honest dues."[106]

On the East Manor, William Rensselaer renewed his pursuit of distress for rent, which was once again legal. Despite Sheriff Reynolds's sympathy for the tenants, he was pressed into serving writs. A late July standoff with one hundred Indians was quickly followed by two deputies being tarred and feathered. Not infrequently, law officers were coerced to shout, "Down with the Rent!" as part of the intimidation. Once again, a county sheriff appealed to the state's highest executive. In August, Governor William Bouck met in West Sand Lake with Anti-Renters from Rensselaer County's eight townships and agreed that Sheriff Reynolds would stop serving papers for the time being. A few months later, a new, less sympathetic governor—Silas Wright—was in charge.

"Lecturers Spread the Good News"

While Anti-Rent associations replicated across the leasehold district, the National Reform Association sponsored lectures to disseminate its platform. Crowds gathered to hear Thomas Devyr, George Henry Evans, and Alvan Earle Bovay on New York City streets during summer 1844.[107] Devyr took the message upstate that October. Such activity was the logical extension of his Chartist-inspired epiphany that the laboring class could determine its own course through education. While in Newcastle-upon-Tyne, Devyr met "workers, many of them quite poor, who read deeply [and] debated ideas intelligently." Chartists rejected paternalism in favor of "collective *self*-education, *self*-uplift, and *self*-mobilization."[108] By spreading the "good news" of land reform and equal rights, Devyr could assist tenants in this process. He would expand this effort in 1845 while editor of the *Albany Freeholder*, as we will see. Additional lecturers would circulate among the Anti-Renters that year, provoking a backlash from up-renters.

It was most likely late autumn 1844—after Devyr's upstate tour—that the broadside, "Anti-Rent Lyrics. A Correct Likeness of an Anti-Renter Lecturing," was created (figure 2.3).[109] Although the sheet is rich with poetry and image, no explicit information about its date, author(s), artist, or printer is included. The image, while striking and dynamic, is difficult to place. The crude and perhaps humorous figure seems vaguely Native American, suggesting the Calico Indians. But instead of the latter's camouflaging gown and mask, the figure has draped shoulders, an exposed midriff, knee-length skirt, and cap. These elements are reminiscent of first-encounter Native American imagery, which drew on classical mythological iconography. Similar imagery was used by various fraternal organizations such as the Society of Red Men throughout the early republic.[110] In the early 1840s, clubs devoted to combining Indian and classical elements were founded by local son and future anthropologist Lewis Henry Morgan.[111] Although the figure's boots lack wings, the travel cloak and dynamic pose subtly evoke Hermes-Mercury, the Greco-Roman messenger god. Ultimately, the image effectively conveys that the lecturer's mission is to disseminate ideas from place to place.[112]

The broadside has two sets of lyrics, neither of which is titled. The contrafactum on the left, labeled Lyric No. 1, hails "Ye sons of Tuscarora" in its first line. On the right, Lyric No. 2 begins, "With his mask upon his brow." Although each side includes a place to indicate a tune, none is specified for Lyric No. 1. The entire poem is transcribed in plate 11. Its title refers to the Tuscarora, the sixth Native American tribe to join the Ho-de-no-sau-nee-ga (Iroquois Confederacy) during the early eighteenth century. Here, the term alludes to one or more Calico Indian organizational cells. An eyewitness to Governor Bouck's August 1844 meeting at West Sand Lake reported hearing someone "designated as the 'Tuscarora chief.'" The second verse invokes the renowned Shawnee orator, Tecumseh, who campaigned against US encroachment on Native lands. The leader of the Gilboa cell in Schoharie County assumed his name.[113] In Lyric No. 1, Tecumseh is a "gallant chieftain" inspiring loyalty from the "brave Indian Boys" who are invoked in the refrain ending each of its six verses.

The tune indicated for Lyric No. 2, "With His Mask upon His Brow," is "With Helmet on His Brow." The latter, however, was not a tune name. It was a short poem by English author James Robinson Planché long associated with the French folksong "Le petit tambour."[114] Plate 12a is a transcription of Lyric No. 2, "With His Mask upon His Brow," set side-by-side to the entirety of Planché's "With Helmet on His Brow." The Anti-Renter contrafactum, which with six verses is significantly longer, follows its model's rhyme scheme and verse-chorus structure. Although it is difficult to know the broadside author's source, I have relied on an 1830 printing of Planché's poem that names the associated tune, "Le petit tambour" (also known as "Je suis le petit tambour").[115]

"Le petit tambour" enjoyed its own popularity, inspiring numerous compositions, both with and without lyrics. American settings were written by John Hill Hewitt and others.[116] Plate 12b presents the basic tune as it appeared in *The Sky-Lark: A Collection of Songs set to Music* published in London in 1825.[117] The original French lyrics include six verses and chorus. Its tonal melody (in

Figure 2.3. "Anti-Rent Lyrics. A Correct Likeness of an Anti-Renter Lecturing." Broadside, BDSDS, 1839. Courtesy of the American Antiquarian Society.

D major) is probably of recent rather than ancient vintage, as suggested by the secondary dominant (G-sharp) in the verse (measures 9 and 23).

Plate 12c sets "With His Mask upon His Brow" to "Le petit tambour." The metrical fit is good, particularly if adjustment is made for the numerous repeated pitches of the original French syllabication. Performers of the English-language "With Helmet on His Brow" would have made similar adjustments. Another accommodation involves structure. Whereas "Le petit tambour" begins with its chorus (mm. 1–8), "With His Mask" and "With Helmet" begin with their respective first verses. My setting uses the initial statement of the chorus for the first verse, which is lengthy enough to include the melody of "Le petit tambour's" first verse. In addition, I have written out the latter's return to its opening music (*da capo*) so that the contrafactum's chorus reaches the tonic, D major (mm. 25–32). Presumably, the many musicians who performed "With Helmet on His Brow" on stage did the same; no sheet music for Planché's poem appears extant.

Successive verses of Lyric No. 2, "With His Mask upon His Brow," allude to the stock Englishman Johnny Bull, the Boston Tea Party, and Rhode Island, where Thomas Dorr's recent agitation to abolish property requirements for white male voters landed him in prison. The poem's general theme is that "English Laws" are responsible for present difficulties, an allusion to the persistence of feudal relations and common law in the United States. The final verse appeals to youth who "cannot marry yet," but will seek their pretty mates when the troubles are done.

Further evidence for dating the Anti-Rent broadside comes from the contrafacta. Both poems present martial imagery encouraging the Calico Indians to fight. "To arms!" Lyric No. 1 beckons. " 'Tis time to take your guns in hand." Lyric No. 2 substitutes mask and rifle for Planché's helmet and saber. Its chorus consists of variations on "living free or dying." Yet, the role of violence is restrained, as in the ambivalent assertion of Lyric No. 1 that the band wants "no treacherous murderers" among its members and the emphasis in Lyric No. 2 on self-sacrifice. In January 1845, the Anti-Renters disavowed masks and the state legislature criminalized their use. It is doubtful that a contrafactum beginning "With his mask upon his brow" would be authored after this date.

While the poems on the broadside were already a bit dated by 1845, lecturers continued to circulate in the leasehold district with the National Reform Association's support. New England labor activist and Brook Farmer Lewis Ryckman spoke to thousands during February and March. That summer, Alvan Earle Bovay addressed five thousand in four counties. A well-educated lawyer from northern New York, Bovay would help found the anti-slavery Republican party a decade later from his new base in Ripon, Wisconsin.[118]

To up-renters, lecturers were outsiders wielding undue influence on tenant farmers. Jay Gould complained about the "followers of Fourier and Owen" who (like the politicians) saw that "this excitement" could become a "popular doctrine with the great body of those living" under leasehold tenures. Certainly, the philosophical ferment of the era included Charles Fourier's social utopianism, known in the United States as Associationism, and Robert Owen's concept of industrial organization, implemented at New Harmony, Indiana. But what alarmed Gould gave hope to others. The key was the open dissemination of ideas, which the Chartists' "Political Methodism" and the Anti-Rent lecturers attempted to provide.[119]

Unfortunately, the Anti-Renters' situation would worsen before it improved. Christman's estimation is that the landlords, "in a final attempt to destroy public sympathy for the tenants' cause, made a concerted drive to provoke violence." With "The Act Concerning Tenures by Lease" defeated, they pressed sheriffs to serve writs and hold distress sales. The result was a series of hostile confrontations with Calico Indians during autumn 1844. Only the patroon Gerrit Smith, one of the largest landowners in central New York, declared a moratorium on rent collection. Twenty other proprietors, led by John Livingston, Gulian C. Verplanck, and John A. King, formed the "Freeholders Committee of Safety" in New York City to strategize, raise funds, and promote their interests upstate. By mid-December, they recommended criminalizing the wearing of disguises.[120]

Meanwhile, Dr. Boughton led efforts to organize the eight hundred families still under feudal leases on Livingston Manor in Columbia County. Disguised as Big Thunder, he gave speeches during late autumn 1844 at rallies where "Bill Snyder" was sung and costumed braves performed intricate drills. County Sheriff Henry Miller became determined to learn the chief's identity after an obstructed distress auction where Big Thunder ordered his papers burned. Through an informant, the sheriff confirmed that Boughton was indeed the Calico leader. "The voice of Dr. Boughton was unmistakable," relates Christman.[121]

On December 18, a pretext was found to arrest Boughton and two others. Tragically, the young William Rifenburg was shot and killed during a meeting of the newly established Columbia County Anti-Rent Association. No one was ever charged with the teenager's death, which the coroner later deemed accidental. But by day's end, Boughton, Mortimer Belden, and Samuel Wheeler were behind bars in the town of Hudson, the county seat. The next day brought another tragedy that stoked the anti-Anti-Rent fire. On December 19, up-renter Elijah Smith was shot in a confrontation with Calico Indians while cutting timber for William Rensselaer. Fifty men were eventually indicted for rioting or conspiracy to riot. "The conservative press branded all antirenters as supporters of terrorism," observes Ellis.[122]

As protestors assembled at the Hudson jail where Boughton and the others were held, Sheriff Miller appealed to outgoing Governor Bouck for assistance. By New Year's Day 1845, more than three hundred armed guards, including a contingent from New York City, were assembled to protect the small town. Again, the state's show of force temporarily quieted the situation. Hudson's mayor could happily report "the public burning of many of the masks and dresses" and that Rent Day, January 1, was unusually successful. "Many of the wheat rents were yesterday paid promptly, and by several of the most noisy anti-renters."[123] Meanwhile, bail requests for Boughton, Belden, and Wheeler were repeatedly denied.

Chapter 3

_____

Climax and Denouement, 1845–1846

A duty still remains, to arm the muse
    With powers of truth-depicting song,
As from the rolling sounds and flying news,
    The rumor of the conflict floats along . . .

—H. R. Schoolcraft, *Helderbergia*[1]

1845: Unmasked

The new year brought a vigorous attempt to suppress Calico Indian activity. Governor Wright's inaugural address to the legislature recommended criminalizing camouflage. "Resistance to the law and its officers has been renewed," he pointed out on January 7, 1845. "Organized bands of men, assuming the disguise of savages, with arms in their hands, have already bid defiance to the law." Wright's lengthy exposition described "outrages" large and small; the two recent "wanton sacrifices of human life" necessitated the "prompt and effectual restoration of the reign of law and order." He urged "making the use of the disguise itself an offence."[2] By the end of January, the Senate and Assembly approved "An Act to Prevent Persons Appearing Disguised and Armed," which outlined punishable offences. Anyone "having his face painted, discolored, covered, or concealed" could be charged with vagrancy and held in the county jail for up to six months. Arrests could be made "without process," and any male citizen could be commanded by officials to assist such seizures or risk up to a year imprisonment. Three or more disguised people appearing in a public place without a permit was deemed a misdemeanor; transgressors could be jailed for as much as a year. Facial concealment while carrying a weapon was punishable by up to two years in state prison.[3]

    While the governor's recommendation worked its way through the legislature, the Anti-Renters and their allies held their first political convention. The meeting's explicit goals were to endorse political representatives sympathetic to the cause, draft petitions addressed to the legislature, and disavow violence. On January 15, 1845, nearly two hundred delegates from eleven counties convened in Berne, a great expansion of the first gathering of Albany County tenant farmers in the same town in 1839. Delegates were sent from Rensselaer, Schoharie, Delaware, Columbia, Montgomery, Schenectady, Greene, Sullivan, Ulster, and Otsego counties to meet those from Albany. The conventioneers passed resolutions disassociating the movement from masks and violence, a direct rebuttal to Governor Wright's portrayal. They also constructed a petition renewing several demands: abolishment of distress as a remedy for non-payment of rent, taxation of landlords' rental income, and passage of the "Act Concerning Tenures by Lease." More than twenty-five thousand signed the petition.[4] Nonetheless, its claims were largely rejected by the legislature that spring. Meanwhile, candidates endorsed at the Anti-Rent convention "swept the local elections" in at least four counties.[5] As a result, both Whigs and the Democrats' two factions—Hunkers and Barnburners—became increasingly determined to court the Anti-Rent vote.

Despite the convention's disavowal of violence, tension escalated after the mask law took effect. In mid-February, Delaware County Undersheriff Osman Steele raided the homes of tenant leader Daniel Squires and several others. The cousin of a patroon land agent, Steele had a reputation for bullying and harassment. His determined pursuit of distress sales and Anti-Rent resisters in early 1845 foreshadowed the climactic episode leading to his death that summer. Squires, who was suspected of various "Indian" activities, was brought to the county jail in Delhi. The facility was heavily guarded while rumors of an attempt to free him circulated. Several weeks later, the Calico Indians retaliated by entrapping Osman Steele in an Andes tavern and holding him hostage overnight. Sheriff Green More summoned a posse in Delhi, but Steele's captors ran off before the assembly completed the twelve-mile trek from there to Andes. On March 15, the undersheriff led a contingent that seized about a dozen Anti-Renters. Various charges and fines were levied, and several were sentenced to the state prison at Sing Sing for two years.[6]

An anonymous twenty-three-quatrain poem satirizing the officers and landlord agents' aggression appeared as a broadside that spring. It began:

> The Delaware invincibles,
>   The wonder of the day,
> And Sheriff Green, that valiant man
>   Whose fame can ne'er decay.

After recounting several confrontations and their legal consequences, the poem ends optimistically.

> And shall the evils here described,
>   Forever be endured?
> No! by the Ballot-Box we'll show,
>   Such evils can be cured.[7]

Squires was released in May 1845 when a grand jury failed to secure an indictment. The several men sentenced to state prison would be released and their citizenship restored by Governor Wright in September 1846, shortly before their sentences expired.[8]

Additional skirmishes took place in Schoharie and Ulster counties; Governor Wright sent munitions to Kingston to quell disorder in the latter. March 1845 also brought Dr. Boughton's trial. Along with Mortimer Belden and Samuel Wheeler, Boughton had been held in the Hudson jail without bail or explicit charges since mid-December. He was finally tried alone for robbing the Columbia County sheriff of papers and conspiracy to obstruct justice. The presiding judge was Amasa Parker, who was not particularly sympathetic to the Anti-Rent cause. John Van Buren assisted the prosecution. A lawyer in private practice in 1839 when he opposed the Anti-Renters at Reidsville, the former president's son was now New York's attorney general. Boughton's trial resulted in a deadlocked jury, and he was returned to the Hudson jail. He would remain there until mid-July 1845, when all three prisoners were quietly released on bail.[9]

Young America

The National Reform Association and its organ, *The Working Man's Advocate*, became ever more committed to the Anti-Rent cause. On March 29, 1845, the paper adopted a new name, *Young America*. The change was indicative of editor George Henry Evans's evolving view of the detrimental effect of land monopoly on social stability. It seemed inevitable that upstate farmers would eventually refuse to pay rent to landlords. One remedy was to limit the amount of land an individual could own, precluding large-scale speculation. Another was to open the public domain to the landless so that wage workers could become self-sufficient. To promote these ideas, the NRA published a circular titled "Vote Yourself a Farm." The widely disseminated pamphlet posed a series of questions, each of which was answered by the title. One question explicitly referenced the upstate farmers' plight: "Are you endowed with reason? Then you must know that your right to life hereby includes the right to a place to live in—the right to a home. Assert this right, so long denied by *feudal robbers and their attorneys*. Vote Yourself a Farm."[10]

On May 31, *Young America* printed "Downfall of Feudalism," a contrafactum that similarly disparaged the social hierarchy addressed in the pamphlet (plate 13a). The song proclaims the triumph of democracy over land monopoly.[11] Its second verse boldly asserts, "Base feudalism has foundered, / The demon grasps for breath." The third and final verse pictures a personified democracy bringing feudalism down by striking "at the monster's heart." The refrain chants "Victorious!" and extols the beacon that will "illume the social waste," a heartfelt if not entirely elegant phrase.

The tune indicated by the anonymous poet of "Downfall of Feudalism" is "Blue Eyed Mary," a very popular contemporary song. At least a dozen editions were published in various cities during the early nineteenth century.[12] Among the first were two works with similar lyrics that were brought out in Philadelphia in the mid-1810s. A Robert Tuke is named as the composer of the version published by G. E. Blake, but the more enduring musical setting was published without a composer or lyricist's name by George Willig's Musical Magazine around 1817 (plate 13b). Willig's setting was widely disseminated with only minor variants for a long time. In the 1881 anthology *Our Familiar Songs*, "Blue Eyed Mary" is identified as an "old German convivial song," but no evidence is supplied for the claim.[13] The vague description suggests that the song had gained the status of folksong by this time, its origin of less importance than its continued attraction for users.

It is often challenging to account for a work's endurance, particularly in the realm of vernacular music. A clue to the appeal and circulation of "Blue Eyed Mary" soon after its initial publication comes from a surprising source: a personal letter by the aspiring poet and future newspaper editor,

William Cullen Bryant. I propose that the anonymous author of "Downfall of Feudalism" chose this tune for the same reasons that Bryant's social circle embraced it. An explanation of those reasons, however, involves several steps, a few other aesthetic works, and some gender politics. I will return to the Anti-Rent contrafactum after tracing these connections.

Bryant provided eyewitness observations about the song's appeal in an 1821 missive to his sister, describing it as a "bran[d] new song imported from Albany" that had become "all the rage." Bryant did not approve, however. "Parties were made for the purpose of singing 'Blue-Eyed Mary,'" he complained at length. Bryant considered the lyrics "the most perfect nonsense," while acknowledging that at its performance, "the young ladies were all dissolved in ecstasy."[14] His dismissiveness—in the face of his cohort's enthusiasm—suggests that some of his peers (including his fiancée) had a different understanding of the subject's backstory. I believe the song was a gloss on Edward Rushton's 1796 melodramatic poem "Blue Eyed Mary," which circulated in American newspapers and poetry anthologies. With pathos and empathy, the radical Liverpool poet tells how the young Mary, seduced and abandoned by an aristocrat, turns to prostitution and alcohol and dies of a "dreadful disease."[15] The lyrics of the American song give none of this detail, alluding only obliquely to "Mary's truth" in the final verse.

My reading of the song's fascination puts Mary in line with the emergent literature depicting female subjectivity, such as Zerlina in *Don Giovanni* and Gretchen in *Faust*. Rushton's "Blue Eyed Mary" was the first entry in the *American Poetical Miscellany* published by Mathew Carey et al. in Philadelphia in 1809. A short preface positions Rushton's work as an answer poem to Hogarth's *A Rake's Progress*. In depicting an "affecting picture of the progress of a seduced Female . . . our whole soul is absorbed in the deep distress of poor *blue-eyed Mary*."[16] The Tuke and Willig settings were published within a decade of the *Miscellany* in the same city. Although it may seem incredible that the literary Bryant was unaware of Rushton's Mary while the young ladies understood her plight, discrepancies of this type reflect the separate spheres in which the sexes were educated and socialized. The American "Blue Eyed Mary" may not be on par with Schubert's "Gretchen am Spinnrade," but both songs put the receptive listener in the title character's place.

Plate 13b is the setting of "Blue Eyed Mary" published by G. Willig's Musical Magazine. After an eight-bar solo piano introduction, the song consists of three eight-bar phrases (ABB¹) over primary chords (I–IV–V). The second phrase (B) ends like the first (A), with the melody of the last (B¹) leaping to the higher octave. The song is entirely diatonic, its simplicity a foil for Mary's lost innocence. A virtually identical edition was published by the piano makers Geib and Walker in New York City. The firm was active during the 1830s, close to when the *Young America* contributor used its tune for an Anti-Rent contrafactum.

The lyrics of "Downfall of Feudalism" fit "Blue Eyed Mary" well enough, as shown in plate 13c. Here, the music's straightforward accessibility reinforces the refrain's optimistic cry, "Victorious!" The central—if oblique—poetic correspondence, and seemingly the author's inspiration, is between a young woman's downfall and a societal system's demise. Although it is impossible to say whether the author was directly influenced by Rushton's literary work, the texts' shared urgent expression of progressive ideals is evident.

By the time "Downfall of Feudalism" appeared in print, Bryant would have been reading *Young America* as long-time publisher of the *New York Evening Post*. Like fellow editor Horace Greeley at the *New-York Tribune*, Bryant was a perceptive commentator on the Anti-Rent struggle.

Their strong support of progressive causes formed a sharp contrast to James Gordon Bennett's increasingly conservative stance at the *New York Herald*.[17] By late spring 1845, all three New York City publishers were able to read the newly established *Albany Freeholder*, the first major serial devoted to news and analysis of the movement across the entire leasehold district. The *Freeholder* would also begin publishing contrafacta later that summer, as we will see. But while its editorial policy was taking shape, a novel excursion reached the Albany area and the young Herman Melville returned to his family home in Rensselaer County. The coincidence of these occurrences would result in a major work of American literature.

Showboat Summer

> This farm has, I hear, been in your family for sixty years: may it remain so while the country stands! To-morrow shall give you a freeholder's right to it.
>
> —Douglas Jerrold, *The Rent Day*[18]

These words, which seem to express the Anti-Rent imaginary, were penned by the English dramatist Douglas Jerrold for his 1832 play, *The Rent Day*. The melodrama was widely produced on both sides of the Atlantic, including a highly lauded production in New York City that year.[19] A brief notice in the *Albany Argus* indicates it was part of a benefit for a local actress in 1841.[20] And according to Carl Carmer, *The Rent Day* made a spectacular appearance upstate during the summer of 1845 on a floating theater barge on the Hudson River, replete with accompaniment by "Pop Robertson's orchestra of Jersey City musicians."[21] The producers had wagered that the Anti-Renters would see themselves in the central husband and wife whose existence is threatened by the landlord's hired villains. In a passage strikingly evocative of the Rensselaers' demand for back rents to clear the family debt, a character opines: "If the landlord lose at gaming, his tenants must suffer for [i]t. The Squire plays a low card,—issue a distress warrant! He throws deuce-ace,—turn a family into the fields! 'Tis only awkward to lose hundreds on a card; but very rascally to be behind-hand with one's rent!"[22] *The Rent Day* was also offered at the Albany Museum Saloon on June 10, 1845. Presumably the same river players appeared indoors that evening, when dancer Julia Turnbull and a "Cosmorama" offered additional interest. Whatever the arrangements, *The Rent Day* "contributed its share toward arousing public opinion against manor rents" that summer.[23] The play's origins and impact are worth examining a bit further.

With *The Rent Day*, playwright Jerrold was following up on the penchant for social commentary shown in his wildly successful nautical melodrama, *Black-Eyed Susan*. His 1832 play was inspired by David Wilkie's paintings, *Rent Day* and *Distraining for Rent*, which depicted the English tenantry's dire condition in the early nineteenth century.[24] By the 1830s, their situation had been exacerbated by restrictive British trade policies known as the Corn Laws. Jerrold developed a subgenre of domestic melodrama that explored "the abuses of absentee landlordism" in *The Rent Day*.[25] The play's principal device is the foreclosed mortgage; its principal villain is the calculating rent agent, who attempts to swindle his employer, rape the farmwife, and evict her family. Carmer surmises that upstate Anti-Renters identified with the victims' suffering and thrilled to "the sounding speeches of the honest farmers damning the manor lords."[26] Jerrold's play offered a mirror reflecting the tenant farmers' predicament back to them and cast a sympathetic light by which others might see their troubles.

The Rent Day may well have had an impact on Herman Melville, recently returned from worldwide travels to his mother's home in Lansingburgh, Rensselaer County (now part of Troy). Nancy Fredricks argues that the aspiring author found a vehicle for dramatizing social inequality in Jerrold's pioneering form of melodrama, with its "thematic of the foreclosed mortgage and landlord-tenant relationship." The result was Melville's novel, Pierre; Or, The Ambiguities. Like the author, the title character is from a prominent landholding family in the region. An eyewitness to the patroon system's turmoil, Melville used melodrama to "critique the injustices of America's class structure."[27] Pierre was the first major literary work that utilized the upstate manor system as a setting but did not aggrandize the landlords, a stark contrast to James Fenimore Cooper's avowedly up-rent works. In the next chapter, we will compare the two New York authors' perspectives.

Original Poetry

The establishment of the Albany Freeholder in spring 1845 marks a major new phase in the Anti-Rent movement's expressive culture. Not only was the weekly the first significant publication primarily devoted to the expanded movement but it also served as an outlet for poetry, song, and story. Headquartered in the city of Albany, the Freeholder was financed by longtime Anti-Renter Charles Bouton and newly elected state assemblyman Ira Harris. The inaugural issue appeared April 9, 1845, with Thomas Devyr as editor. Within a year, the Freeholder's circulation reached 2,700; its estimated readership was more than 10,000 as the paper passed from hand to hand.[28] Devyr's new position allowed him to promote the Chartist principle of worker empowerment through self-improvement. Chartism, in addition to its political goals, "was a cultural movement in which self-educated laborers embraced literature and philosophy and created reading and debating societies to enact an intellectual emancipation that was a necessary precondition for political liberation."[29] Devyr had contributed to such endeavors as an Anti-Rent lecturer; as an editor, he could cultivate the tenant farmers' desire to give their thoughts and feelings aesthetic form by publishing their works.

As a prelude to this initiative, the Freeholder published poetry from outside upstate New York early in its run. Selections by major British and American authors were published alongside reprints from radical Chartist newspapers like the Northern Liberator, which Devyr had formerly edited. The Freeholder's selections typically "condemned the sufferings of the poor, celebrated the labors of farmers, and encouraged solidarity for the movement." Oliver Goldsmith was a particular favorite; Devyr used his "condemnation of the Parliamentary enclosures of the English commons" for the Freeholder's motto.[30] Within a couple months, Devyr actively elicited poetry from readers and included verse by locals in a weekly section entitled "Original Poetry." He explained the decision at the column's head. "We prefer it to selected. Because we wish to give the native talent of our hills an opportunity of developing itself. Because the subjects, generally, will be of local interest. And because 'no other paper will have the news'—till we give it to them."[31]

With Devyr in the editor's chair, the Albany Freeholder included many Anti-Rent poems written expressly for the newspaper. Among them were seven contrafacta published in the first two weeks of July 1845. The "Original Poetry" column of July 2 included "The Native's Enquiry," a contrafactum set to "Bruce's Address." It was followed by two poems, "Thoughts in Prison" and "The Farming Men," by the pseudonymous contributor The Forest Minstrel. Another contrafactum to "Bruce's Address," "Hardy Tillers of the Soil," appeared in a different section of the paper. It is worth noting that "Bruce's Address" became an especially productive inspiration for new song as the Anti-Rent movement intensified. The Forest Minstrel penned the lyrics to another two published later that year, "The Contest" and "Haste to Delhi." A fifth, "Rouse, Ye Anti-Renters, Wake!" appeared in 1846. In contrast to the *New York Herald*'s brief satirical allusion to "Bruce's Address" in 1839, the Anti-Renters' contrafacta were serious outpourings. Their songs railed against oppression in concise, forceful verses. Like Robert Burns's poem, the farmers' lyrics juxtapose tyranny and domination with freedom and liberty.

Robert Burns is credited with giving the music of "Bruce's Address" its modern shape. Traditionally known as "Hey Tuttie Tatie" or "Hey Now the Day Dawis" (*sic*), the tune was said to have been played by the army of King Robert the Bruce at the Battle of Bannockburn in 1314, a decisive Scottish victory over English domination. It retained symbolic impact long after the two kingdoms joined to form Great Britain in 1707. Robert Burns's 1793 poem imagines Bruce inspiring his troops to fight for liberty over "chains and slavery." In a letter describing his creative process, the poet obliquely acknowledged the tune's relevance to his generation. "Hey Tuttie Tatie" evoked "that glorious struggle for freedom, associated with the glowing ideas of some other struggles of the same nature, not quite so ancient."[32] Burns's song was widely considered Scotland's unofficial national anthem during the nineteenth century. Berlioz's 1831 *Rob Roy* Overture, commemorating another legendary Scots hero, makes extensive use of its melody.[33] "Bruce's Address" also forms the basis of the fourth movement of Max Bruch's 1880 Scottish Fantasy.

"The old air was susceptible of stirring up or assuaging the passions, according to the different styles in which it may be played or sung," observed Burns's editor William Stenhouse.[34] This mutability helps explain its frequent reuse by the Anti-Renters, who expressed a range of sentiments with its aid. The melody can be interpreted as major ending on scale degree 5 or Mixolydian authentic as the user wishes. Either way, the tune's effectiveness lies primarily in its structure. Plate 14b provides a representative variant of the melody, which spans an octave beginning and ending on G. The initial motive develops incrementally, beginning with a repeated tone that rises to the fourth above (C). The shape is sequenced up a whole step (m. 2), leading to the responding two bars beginning at scale degree 6 (E), followed by a descent to the initial pitch (G, mm. 3–4). The tune's second half begins at E and pushes up (mm. 5–6), with the concluding gesture starting at high G and rapidly descending an octave (mm. 7–8). The pattern of beginning a melody's second half at a high point is shared by many Scots tunes.

"Bruce's Address" sounds the third and seventh steps above G only briefly as passing tones, suggesting a Mixolydian modal interpretation. On the other hand, the tonal keyboard arrangement of plate 14b harmonizes the final phrase with a plagal cadence in the key of C major. Such an ending evokes the sense of keep-going-ness noted in other Anti-Renter songs. And as with many settings of traditional tunes, the tension between modal and tonal languages is part of their fascination and effectiveness.

Plate 14b, "Bruce's Address to His Army, a Favorite Scotch Song," is a facsimile of one of at least a dozen arrangements published in the United States during the early nineteenth century.[35]

Plate 14b was brought out by G. Willig's Musical Magazine in Philadelphia around 1819, after Arthur Keene sang Burns's song at a New York concert.[36] It is worth noting that the London publisher William Blackwood brought out an edition in 1839 that included the late William Stenhouse's commentary and a Scotch snap in the melody, a figure also found in other variants.[37]

While Robert Burns was effectively invoked through the many Anti-Rent songs set to "Bruce's Address," their sentiment also resonates with works by his contemporary, the New England composer William Billings. The latter's secular hymn "Chester," for example, rallied moral indignation against British rule in anticipation of the American Revolution. "Let tyrants shake their iron rod," Billings wrote. "We fear them not."[38] Many of the Anti-Rent rally songs are jeremiads portraying the farmers as patriots of the American Revolution who personally sacrificed to make the land productive, only to be trapped in oppressive leases running from generation to generation. For them, the Revolution "was only a partial victory that would not be completed until the leasehold system, with its restrictive clauses and quarter sales, was eliminated."[39] This pattern formed a compelling narrative that was crucial to shaping the Anti-Rent imaginary.

"The Native's Enquiry" (plate 14a) engages this narrative to the tune of "Bruce's Address." The lyrics were signed "Socrates" and sent to the *Albany Freeholder* from an undisclosed location in "Helderberg" on June 20, 1845. Like The Forest Minstrel, Socrates was a regular contributor of prose and verse. The Anti-Rent philosopher, in keeping with this namesake, repeatedly challenged readers to think for themselves. "[T]he present animosity" should be considered "according to the principles of reason and an unbiased judgment," urged a letter to the editor a few weeks earlier.[40] "The Native's Enquiry" conjures the Socratic method by posing a series of questions in its first six verses. "Let strains triumphant rise around," the strophic song optimistically begins. "Shall a free people live unbound, or chained in tyranny?" The third verse invokes the American Revolution by asking whether its patriots will see their descendants' liberty. The final four verses proclaim justifiable responses, culminating with freemen pushing "the cause of equal rights." In Robert Burns's poem, the last line of every quatrain rhymes across verses (i.e., AAAB, CCCB, DDDB, etc.). Here, the final lines' correspondence is that "tyranny," or its topical synonym "patroonery," ends all but two of the ten verses.

The determined, steady gait of "Bruce's Address" effectively reinforces the narrator's resolve, as shown in my setting of "The Native's Enquiry" (plate 14c). Like Burns's poem, it takes two verses to sing through the entire tune. Socrates contrasted the expected rising inflection of questions in spoken English with the melody's shape to great effect here. Because each half of the melody ends with a descent (mm. 3–4 and 7–8), the word *tyranny*—while grammatically part of an inquiry—is repeatedly experienced as a heavy weight. The contrafacta concludes with an allusion to the ballot box: "November ides" shall put "the imps of tyranny" to flight. The poems of this period often progress from righteous complaint to resolution through peaceful means, disavowing violence. In "The Native's Enquiry" "a million" voices and hands will be raised, but weapons are not mentioned. As we will see, organizing and the ballot box are similarly prioritized in "Hardy Tillers of the Soil."

Fourth of July 1845: Albany County

In addition to "Original Poetry," the *Albany Freeholder*'s July 2nd issue anticipated the upcoming Fourth of July celebrations with two airs intended for D. G. Seger's New Salem Hotel. Neither was titled, but the initials "W. H." appear after the second. This suggests they were both authored by

William Holmes, who read the Declaration of Independence in New Salem on the Fourth. One set of lyrics, which has come to be known as "Hardy Tillers of the Soil," is discussed in conjunction with the festivities in Schoharie County. The other air published July 2 begins, "Hail to the glorious birth-day of the nation!" Its complete lyrics are transcribed in plate 15a.

The tune indicated for "Hail to the Glorious Birth-day of the Nation" is "Hail to the Chief." The latter had been used for ceremonial tribute from the presidency of Andrew Jackson to the recently inaugurated James Polk and is still associated with American leadership. "Hail to the Chief" was originally composed by English theater musician James Sanderson as a setting for "The Boat Song," a "lyrical interpolation" added to Walter Scott's *Lady of the Lake*. Scott's narrative poem had been quickly adapted for the stage and widely produced in Britain and the United States after its 1810 publication. "The Boat Song" provided a grand choral entry for the protagonist Sir Roderick Dhu, a Highland chieftain opposed to the King of Scotland. Sanderson was known for adapting traditional melodies for the stage and may have modelled his composition on the Highlander genre of the *sorrain*, a type of boat song honoring a favorite chief. As music historian Elise Kirk observes, "Hail to the Chief" may "originally have been an ancient Scottish air—or, at least, a good imitation."[41]

Curiously, the earliest known imprints of Sanderson's "Hail to the Chief" were published in the United States. Plate 15b is the edition brought out by William Dubois in New York circa 1817. Scored for three voices and piano "in the homophonic style of the English glee," the principal melody is in the middle voice.[42] Plate 15c shows "Hail to the Glorious Birth-day of the Nation" set to "Hail to the Chief." To align with Sanderson's composition, I have repeated the contrafactum's initial four lines to new music (mm. 11–18) and set the remainder of the first verse to Sanderson's second section. This section, which is rarely heard today, has a different meter from the first (i.e., 2/4 rather than common time). Its tempo marking is *allegro*; traditionally, the first section—with its opening fermati—proceeds at a stately pace.

The tune of "Hail to the Chief" was widely disseminated in the early nineteenth century. As Kirk describes, it was often copied into instrumental tutors and other pedagogical materials, supplementing its theatrical and ceremonial use. By the time W. H. gave the tune new words, its patriotic connotation was well-established through association with several presidents. Rather than paying tribute to an individual, however, the Anti-Rent contrafactum honors an abstraction: the nation. Instead of hailing the chief "who in triumph advances," every freeman is exhorted to rejoice in the country's origin story. In W. H.'s treatment, Roderick Dhu's symbolic alpine evergreen became the "time-honored lofty tree / Sacred to liberty." It is easy to imagine an Anti-Renter penning these words while preparing to deliver the Declaration of Independence at the Fourth of July in the New Scotland village of New Salem.

Devyr's vivid report of the "Anti-Land-Monopoly celebration" in New Salem appeared in the July 9 *Albany Freeholder*. Festivities included a three-gun salute, a procession from Seger's hotel "to the Grove," readings, and speeches. The editor made special note of women's involvement. There was also singing by "the Choir" and music by the Euterpean Brass Band of Rensselaerville. "In addition to their soul-stirring, patriotic and martial airs, they sung two up-rousing Anti-Rent songs, which we publish in another column," wrote Devyr. The band's singing of "In Days of Yore" "called down thunders of applause" (plate 18). In a rough-hewn iambic tetrameter, author H. B. Evans succinctly versified the tenant farmers' story in rhymed couplets across four 8-line stanzas. The manor system's major stages are interrogated, from the false premises of foreign land grants to the false promises that lured settlers and then anchored them with perpetual debt. The author concludes with a call to overcome such conditions. Should the patroon continue to demand service, quarter sales, "[t]he rent, mines, water and fowls beside,"

> Tell him to get them where they are due,
> For with such fellows you have nothing to do.

Unfortunately, Devyr does not indicate a tune for the band's singing of "In Days of Yore." Nor do we know anything further about its author, who happens to share a surname with George Henry Evans and his brother, Shaker activist Frederick William Evans.

A second set of lyrics published July 9—and the third associated with Independence Day at New Salem—was "We Will Be Free." This contrafactum's "up-rousing" lyrics are transcribed in plate 19a.[43] Devyr identified its author, S. H. Foster, as the creator of "Big Bill Snyder," performed by the Euterpean Band the previous year. As described in chapter 2, both of Foster's contrafacta were based on minstrel tunes. "We Will Be Free" is predicated on "The Boatman's Dance," which was initially published as "an original banjo melody" by Dan Emmett in 1843. It is perhaps best known today in Aaron Copland's arrangement for the 1950 set *Old American Songs*. The minstrel number enjoyed immediate widespread popularity, as suggested by the several variants published in 1843 with closely related titles, including "Boatman's Dance" and "Boatman's Song." Plate 19b is an imprint titled "De Boatmen's Dance" issued by C. H. Keith in Boston the same year.[44] "Old Dan D. Emmit" is identified as the composer and leader of the Virginia Minstrels. The work's dramatic opening vocal gesture—marked "chorus"—which announces the boatman's appearance on the river, spans a ninth. The melody that follows encompasses close intervals within a narrow range, a feature shared by many minstrel tunes. The song's catchy pentatonic melody is harmonized simply with the primary chords of F major (I–IV–V).

Plate 19c sets "We Will Be Free" to "De Boatmen's Dance." The four-bar repeat indicated for the chorus in plate 19b is written out here to the contrafactum's "Huzza! Huzza! We will be free / From feudal rents and tyranny." This is a slight reordering of the text as it appeared in the *Albany Freeholder*. (Although the sheet music [plate 19b] does not indicate a return to the chorus, that was undoubtedly an option in performance.) Several Anti-Rent verses pit the farmer's labor against the patroon's leisure, a thematic connection to the minstrel song's subject: the worker's life. "They ne'er remember that the bread . . . and the rich viands they eat / are products of the farmer's wheat." Depictions of the luxuries enjoyed by the idle rich are laced through, and the concluding verses reference controversies over titles, tributes, water rights, and quarter sales. The refrain—"shout brothers shout"—calls for collective sound-making through voices and horns, which in this context were undoubtedly tin.

Fourth of July 1845: Schoharie and Delaware Counties

The anonymous contrafactum "Hardy Tillers of the Soil," which the *Albany Freeholder* anticipated was intended for New Salem, was later reported to have been sung at Summit in Schoharie County on the Fourth of July. The day's festivities began under the watchful eye of "law and order," represented by the sheriff's posse of one hundred men. Participants assembled from all directions in colorful processions, such as the conveyance "drawn by seventeen yoke of oxen" with "good music on the carriage, and from fifty to sixty persons," described by a *Freeholder* contributor. There were banners, flags, and "singing by the choir." Three thousand gathered to watch 1,500 Calico Indians drill at Treat Durant's Grove.[45]

The celebration concluded with "Hardy Tillers of the Soil," whose lyrics are transcribed in plate 16a. Listeners are directly addressed by the opening lines:

Hearts to whom your freedom's dear . . .
Hail ye now, the epoch near,
Of your liberty.

This stanza was apparently intended as a spoken introduction, as it has a different ending from the other six. Also, the contrafactum's associated tune—"Bruce's Address"—requires an even number of stanzas. The setting in plate 16b thus begins with "Hardy tillers" and incorporates the next stanza to make a full statement of the tune. The poem's trochaic meter (strong-weak) corresponds well to the heavy downbeats of "Bruce's Address," as does the strong ending accent of each line. This also fits well with the six stanzas' final word, *patroonery*. Good use is made of the melody's structure, whose second half begins at a high point—scale degree 6 going to the octave (mm. 5–6). In the song's first full statement, this height corresponds optimistically to "Rally, organize anew." In the last, it corresponds to the Helderberg mountains and "Alps high hills." (The Rensselaer County town of Alps was home to Dr. Boughton.) As the melody makes its final descent across the octave (mm. 7–8), the lyrics conclude with all the voices of the valley shouting, "Down Patroonery."

According to the *Albany Freeholder*, the Middleburgh Brass Band performed at another Schoharie County Fourth of July celebration. A procession "composed of from 300 to 400 ladies and about 2,000 gentlemen" began at D. B. Danforth's Inn in Middleburgh. Although no specific repertory was mentioned, the procession "marched with music by the Band to the Grove selected for the occasion," where the crowd swelled to 4,000.[46]

Advertisements for the Middleburgh and Bloomville, Delaware County, celebrations emphasized inclusivity. Both acknowledged hardship and social disparities: "Old and young, rich and poor, bond and free, are invited to attend. Let there be a general rally." The *Freeholder* reported that 3,500 to 5,000 participated in the Bloomville gathering, for which a "band of music" was engaged.[47] In addition to speeches, a procession, and toasts, The Forest Minstrel's narrative poem, "The Afflicted Tenant's Appeal" was read "with great effect." The *Freeholder* published the twenty-six-stanza poem on July 23.

Roger Hecht describes "The Afflicted Tenant's Appeal" as an Anti-Rent lament. It recounts "the labors and sufferings of hardscrabble farming made worse by unfeeling landlords who demand rent regardless of the season's yield (and thus the tenant's ability to pay). The poem is a 'tale of sorrow' that could easily be any tenant farmer's story."[48] Its universality was similarly noted by Huston. "The Afflicted Tenant's Appeal" was representative of the theme "of poverty and rootlessness [that] echoed sadly throughout the speeches, letters, and songs of the tenants' movement."[49]

That for which we'd long been striving,
     All our hopes for years to come. . . .
Often forced to change our dwellings;
     Thus, we thread our cheerless way.

The Forest Minstrel's moving description closes with a series of imploring questions, the "appeal" indicated in the poem's title.

O, ye men who rule our nation,
     Men of Legislative powers,
Is there no compassion for us;
     No redress for wrongs like ours?

The positive reception of the poem's "spirited stanzas" appears almost a foreshadowing of Delaware County becoming the focal point of Anti-Rent agitation. The same poet would write one of the movement's most poignant songs, "Haste to Delhi," in response to that development.

The Forest Minstrel, who hailed from Middletown, Delaware County, was a prolific contributor to the Anti-Rent press. Writers often masked their identities, just as the Calico Indians disguised their persons. The pseudonym is interesting because it alludes to the title of James Hogg's first song collection. *The Forest Minstrel* was published in London in 1810 with more than fifty original poems by Hogg and two dozen by other authors. An American edition was released by the progressive Philadelphia publisher Mathew Carey in 1816.[50] In chapter 2, I noted that Hogg had much to say about "Lesley's March" in his *Jacobite Relics of Scotland*. His memoir of Walter Scott was published in New York in 1834, accompanied by a 115-page biography of Hogg authored by S. D. Bloodgood. According to the latter, Hogg's knowledge of Scottish poetry and song made a deep impression on Walter Scott when the younger man helped him "to gather relics of the forest minstrelsy."[51] Although nothing further is known about New York's Forest Minstrel, it seems fitting that the writer set the lyrics of "The Contest" and "Haste to Delhi" to the meter of the Scots' enduring tune, "Bruce's Address."

The Forest Minstrel wrote "The Contest" a week after the Bloomville celebrations, and it appeared in the *Albany Freeholder* on August 6 (plate 22a).[52] Its eight verses distill the themes treated at length in "The Afflicted Tenant's Appeal." As the setting in plate 22b indicates, each full statement of "Bruce's Address" takes up two verses. The resulting four statements progress from tenantry's origins in European practices to the New York farmers' oppressive leases, quest for autonomy, and anticipation of victory.

More Original Poetry and Homespun Song

A significant portion of the poems solicited, disseminated, and preserved through Devyr's initiative used musical terms or were structured as musical forms without a particular tune being designated. "In Days of Yore" was one such work, reported to have been sung but lacking indication of specific music. Another was "The Prisoners in Jail," the first item in the *Albany Freeholder's* July 9 "Original

Poetry" column. Its author was Mortimer Belden, whose Calico name was "Little Thunder."[53] Belden, Boughton, and Wheeler had been held in the Columbia County jail at Hudson for more than six months at this point. That Belden conceived the poem in musical terms is suggested through its use of the refrain, "In these hard times."[54] And in the fourteenth and final verse, the narrator says, "I think now it's time to finish my song." The complete lyrics of "The Prisoners in Jail" are transcribed in plate 20.

Belden was allowed to have his violin with him in jail, but this brought small comfort. His health declined precipitously due to consumption. Devyr expressed incredulity about Belden's description of the jail's condition, hoping that some matters were "poetical licenses." "It is not possible that they would chain the prisoners to the floor," he worried. The poem's most bitter verses are directed at the sheriff, who "will do anything that will profit himself." Belden decries various abuses of power and suggests that distress actions, in addition to impoverishing families, led to corrupt practices by the administering officials. The poem's pointed conclusion, which reiterates that the prisoners were held "in jail without any bail," was made obsolete in mid-July when all three were released pending trial.

The second item in the *Albany Freeholder*'s "Original Poetry" column on July 9 was generically titled "An Anti-Rent Song." It was contributed anonymously from Ancram, another Anti-Rent stronghold in Columbia County.[55] The contrafactum's complete lyrics—all sixteen verses—are transcribed in plate 21a. The tune indicated is "Bold Caroline." Most likely this is the ballad "Caroline and Her Young Sailor Bold," classified today as Roud 553. The ballad's lyrics were frequently printed as a broadside during the nineteenth century. The earliest example, from about 1836, indicates its text was an answer to "The Gallant Hussar" (Roud 1146). Steve Roud surmises that "Caroline" probably used the tune of "The Gallant Hussar" initially, as was typical of answer songs. Gradually, "Caroline" assumed its own distinct identity among traditional singers and eventually eclipsed the popular dissemination of its source.[56]

Many variants of "Caroline" were transcribed by folksong collectors in the early twentieth century, with print editions appearing only later. The earliest melodies I could locate are transcriptions preserved in the Vaughan Williams Memorial Library in London. The variant reproduced in plate 20b, "Caroline and Her Brisk Young Sailor Boy," was collected in 1906 from the eighty-year-old Moses Blake in Lyndhurst, about ninety miles southwest of London.[57] While the Anti-Renters would not have had access to this transcription, it represents what they—like Mr. Blake—might have heard around 1845. Perhaps future research will reveal how the ballad, like Caroline and her sailor, crossed the ocean.

Plate 20b shows a sixteen-bar tonal melody in the key of D major with an octave range and AABA form. Although the tune is memorable, its fit with the lyrics of "An Anti-Rent Song" is not particularly smooth. Nonetheless, the author's inspiration to connect poem and tune may have come from two of the ballad's thematic elements. One is the class difference between the well-to-do Caroline and the sailor she pursues, an obvious parallel to the patroons and tenants. Another is the ballad's twist: we are told the young sailor is bold, but it takes even greater boldness for Caroline to don male clothing, spend years "on the salt seas," survive three shipwrecks, and ask her father for permission to wed the beloved with whom she had run off. While the contrafactum is structured quite differently from the original ballad, it uses that difference to good effect. Instead of the continuously unfolding narrative conveyed in strophic form represented by plate 21b, "An

Anti-Rent Song" has a verse-chorus structure. In my setting (plate 21c), the chorus takes up the second half of each full tune statement. In other words, the chorus's response to each verse is the encouragement to "be cheerful my boys / Let your hearts never fail." The song challenges Anti-Renters to be as bold as the legendary Caroline, who crossed gender boundaries and the sea to reach her goal.

By mid-summer 1845, Devyr had been dismissed from the *Albany Freeholder*. In his view, Whig and Hunker Democrats "wormed themselves" into the Anti-Rent movement to procure votes, pushing him aside for his failure to cooperate.[58] In contrast to the politicians' pragmatic goals, Devyr was driven by ideals. He began a new weekly, the *Anti-Renter*, whose circulation reached two thousand but which lasted only about a year.[59] Unfortunately, no songs by locals appeared among the many poems he published there.

Amid the *Albany Freeholder*'s early July outpouring of original poetry, *Young America* published "The Farmer's Song" (plate 17a). As we saw in chapter 2, the farmer's happy home is a recurring theme in Anti-Rent expressive works. This anonymous song conveys—presumably from a heteronormative perspective—the farmer's joy in having a "snug little farm, / with a kind and notable wife." Taking its inspiration from Henry Russell's composition "A Life on the Ocean Wave," the lyrics extol life on one's native soil, with "blossoming fields" and "whole valleys of waving grain." "The Farmer's Song" combines an appreciation of the surrounding countryside with ideas about people's right to a safe, secure home. Its pastoral lyrics float on philosophical currents.

Russell's 1838 composition was a setting of Epes Sargent's recent poem of the same name describing the ships of New York City's harbor. The English-born Russell was at the height of his popularity as a performer in the United States at this time.[60] A versatile songwriter, he became known for multi-sectional works akin to the scena of bel canto operas as well as simpler pieces "suggestive of traditional English songs."[61] Many of his later songs reflect contemporary social issues; all the more appropriate that an early one was adapted by an advocate of natural rights and land reform.

Plate 17b reproduces an excerpt from Russell's piano-vocal score for "A Life on the Ocean Wave," published by Hewitt & Jaques.[62] The composer freely repeated portions of Sargent's text to give musical form to the poem's three verses, each of which is set to the same music. Plate 17b includes a fifteen-bar piano introduction establishing G major as the tonic. Russell sets the first verse as an AABA form (mm. 16–47), with the B section suggesting the relative minor (E) before returning to the final tonic statement (A). This is followed by a coda (mm. 48–63), which features a dominant pedal (on D) and rolling piano accompaniment that nicely evokes the winds that take ships to the open sea. The second half of the sheet music is a setting of Sargent's second verse to an exact musical repetition of the first. Realization of the third verse, whose text appears on the final page, is left to the performers.

Plate 17c sets "The Farmer's Song" to the sung portion of Russell's music (mm. 16–47), incorporating a bit of the piano part and repeating portions of the contrafactum's text as needed. The contrafactum is longer than Sargent's text and Russell's setting. This results in something more like a verse-chorus structure, with the verse using musical phrases AAB and the chorus using A and the coda. For each of its three stanzas, the less sophisticated "Farmer's Song" employs the coda to prod livestock along: "Gee up!"

A second ode to the farm family's desire for stability appeared in the *Albany Freeholder* that autumn. The fifteen-stanza ballad "Dere vos a Time" was prefaced by the paper's editor with a rationale for printing a contributor's account of a typical evening in a Hudson River town tavern. "We publish the following communication because it conveys much truth in homely phrase. The song is a true relation of the manner in which perpetual leases were palmed off upon ignorant men. We have been told by old men of numerous instances of like fraud, and gross deception."[63]

The contributing writer, who was identified only as "EGO" from Clermont, Columbia County, describes the scene of the ballad's performance on a cold evening the previous winter in great detail. Most of the tavern's denizens were of "German descent," presumably reflecting eighteenth-century Palatinate immigration.[64] They smoke, chat about the weather and news, "and occasionally hear a song from some one gifted with a musical talent." The tavern-mates speculate—in dialect—about Anti-Rent meetings, "Indians," landlord titles, unscrupulous lawyers, and other timely topics until "some one proposed that 'long John' should sing a song. 'Yes, give us a song,'" chimed a dozen voices. John initially demurs but then offers his story, which he had sung "so often that it had become stereotyped upon his mind." After demanding the room's attention, and a hearty swig from a "favorite decanter," he begins.

> Dere vos a time, I knows it vell, it vos ven I vos young,
> Just thirty years ago it vos, and den I vos among
> A merry company, ven first my Katy, I did see;
> I fell in love mit her, and den, she fell in love mit me.

A transliteration of John's complete song is found in plate 23. Successive verses tell of his and Katy's desperation when the landlord demands back rent, which leads to their ejectment. "Ve had'nt anywhere to stay, nor anywhere to go," he concludes.

> Nor ve had'nt any money den, nor any thing to sell,
> And how to get another home, just then, ve could'nt tell.
> As so ve did'nt go away, 'til driven from de door,
> And den ve did; and ever since, ve have been werry poor.

Unfortunately, the *Freeholder* did not indicate a tune for "Dere vos a Time." Nonetheless, John and Katy's moving saga demonstrates literature's potential to subvert power relations in the reader or listener's mind. "Fictions humanize what the tyrants dehumanize," as author Azar Nafisi recently observed.[65] Like "Downfall of Feudalism," "Dere vos a Time" conjures sympathetic images of ordinary people's struggle. The difference is that the former is a rallying cry for collective action, while the latter restricts itself to a heart-wrenching portrait of individuals. Both are powerfully expressive, but the difference is indicative of the *Freeholder's* more restrained stance after Devyr's dismissal.

Haste to Delhi

While the *Albany Freeholder* straddled supporting the movement and shaping political coalitions, *Young America* published a set of solemn lyrics reflecting the dire situation of autumn 1845.

Christman calls "Haste to Delhi" "one of the grimmest songs of the entire Anti-Rent movement." Its complete lyrics appear in plate 24a. The Forest Minstrel's verses "grew out of the terrorism" in the Delaware County seat, where hundreds had been rounded up and jailed.[66] The episode began on August 7 when Calico Indians disrupted a distress sale at Moses and Sara Earle's farm on Dingle Hill in Andes. The family's 160-acre plot was part of the sprawling Hardenbergh Patent. The precise boundaries of the patent had been disputed for many years by tenants as well as between patroon claimants. Charlotte Verplanck, who lived in New York City, controlled about twenty thousand acres. She was the aunt of Gulian C. Verplanck, cofounder of the Freeholders Committee of Safety established by landowners in late 1844. Moses and Sara Earle were not outspoken Anti-Renters, but their "adopted" daughter Parthenia Davis had convinced Moses not to pay the two years of rent in arrears until the patroon's title was proved. In response, Verplanck's land agent arranged with local law officers to auction off the Earle horses and livestock for the $64 owed. One of the officers was Osman Steele. More than a hundred Calico Indians gathered to prevent the sale. Shots were fired, and Steele was mortally wounded. The Earles took him into their house. Despite a doctor's efforts, he died that evening. Who shot first, and for what reason, has never been ascertained. McCurdy calls the entire episode "a tragedy of errors."[67]

Local authorities responded swiftly and harshly to Steele's death. Moses Earle, who was in his sixties, was taken into custody. Multiple posses were assembled to search for others present at the distress sale and scores of arrests were made. Suspecting that some Anti-Renters had taken refuge outside Delaware County, officials requested the governor's aid. On August 27, Governor Wright declared a "state of insurrection" in Delaware, Columbia, and Schoharie Counties and sent more than three hundred troops to the region at significant taxpayer cost. Recent legislation justified sweeping arrests during the four months the governor's decree remained in effect. The mask law provided "that every fatality arising from the commission of a felony (assembling armed and disguised) constituted murder in the first degree." Nearly 350 individuals were indicted, about half of them charged with the undersheriff's killing. The great number held at the Delhi jail so exceeded its capacity that the suspects were housed in hastily erected rough log cabins, colorfully dubbed "the Delhi Bastille" by one inmate.[68] A drawing of the structures appeared on the front page of the *New York Herald* (figure 3.1).

"Haste to Delhi" was published in *Young America* on November 22, 1845. By this time, Judge Amasa Parker had sentenced Calico "chiefs" Edward O'Conner and John Van Steenburgh to hang, despite the fact that neither was proved directly responsible for Steele's death. Their execution was scheduled for the following week.[69] Moses Earle and about ten others had pled guilty to manslaughter and received life sentences, as did Daniel Squires. More than eighty were convicted of lesser crimes. At least a dozen had been taken to Clinton Prison at Dannemora, 225 miles north of Delhi, in mid-October. The editor of *Young America* commented, "There is nothing to equal it in this country since the hanging of witches in New England."[70]

The third verse of "Haste to Delhi" expressed similar bewilderment:

Justice with her blinded sight
Might have stumbled on the right,
But she's fairly to her flight
    From old Delhi.

Figure 3.1. "The Prisons of the Anti-Renters at Delhi." *New York Herald*, September 29, 1845. From the digital collection, *Chronicling America: Historic American Newspapers*. Courtesy of the Library of Congress.

The lyrics pose a stark denunciation of "law and order" proponents across seventeen stanzas. More than half begin with a second-person address to *ye*, characterizing those who stand against freedom, fairness, and equality while enriching themselves.

> Ye who wish to seize the store,
> Of the injur'd lab'ring poor,
> Crush them that they rise no more,
>   Haste to Delhi.

Plate 24b sets the initial two stanzas of "Haste to Delhi" to "Bruce's Address." The dragging dotted rhythms of the eight-bar air seem a perfect vehicle for the pseudonymous author's sentiments. The combined effect of the tune's slow climb and sustained high point is that of steady marching toward a goal. "Nothing fear, your cause is just," urges the final stanza. "Better days will come, we trust, / Tyrants yet will bite the dust." It is fitting that a full statement of the tune necessitates repetition of these lines.

A significant counternarrative arose in Delaware County around Osman Steele's death. The extended family had a long history in the area, and his funeral was very well-attended. Many saw his demise as personal sacrifice in the line of duty. Several up-rent expressions were inspired by the tragedy, including two color lithographs. *The Inhuman Anti Rent Murder* is the title of one 1845 print depicting the conflict; another is *The Death of Osman N. Steele.*[71] A dirge commemorated his passing.

> Lamented Steele! Well may we weep
> O'er thy untimely grave;
> And angels round shall vigil keep,
> Thou fearless one and brave![72]

A decade later, Jay Gould's detailed account concluded that Steele's death had "summerset" Anti-Rentism, as county residents banded together to condemn the Calico Indians and promote law and order.[73]

Descendants on both sides reside in the region to this day, and reminders of the antagonism are everywhere.[74] An historical marker near Dingle Hill reads, "One mile to scene of tragedy where Undersheriff Osman N. Steele was slain by Anti-Renters August 7, 1845."[75] The Delhi Post Office has a WPA-era mural depicting the conflict. The Andes Society for History and Culture runs the Parthenia Davis Gift Shop in the historic Hunting Tavern where the undersheriff allegedly boasted, "Lead can't penetrate Steele."[76] More of this legacy is discussed in chapter 4.

The Delaware County Anti-Renters were not the only ones remanded to state prison. While their fates were being determined, Dr. Boughton's second trial took place in Hudson. Fighting between his lawyer, Ambrose Jordan, and Attorney General John Van Buren was so fierce that the judge charged both with contempt and had them jailed overnight. In late September, Boughton was convicted of highway robbery and received the maximum punishment—a life sentence—while cellmates Belden and Wheeler were released with time served. Boughton met up with about fifteen Anti-Renters already in Clinton Prison. The newly established facility provided convict labor for the Adirondack Mountains' iron mines and foundries, and the doctor's expertise proved useful there.[77]

The harsh sentences meted out to the Anti-Renters loomed over the November 1845 elections. Numerous public and private appeals were made to Governor Wright to spare O'Conner and Van Steenburgh, the two on death row. Horace Greeley argued that their execution would exacerbate the societal problems exposed by the Anti-Rent movement in the *New-York Tribune*. G. H. Evans added a banner for the "Liberation of Boughton" to *Young America*'s masthead beginning October 4. The governor, whose term ran another year, nevertheless waited until after the election to decide the men's fate. On the day "Haste to Delhi" appeared—and just one week before their scheduled executions—O'Conner and Van Steenburgh's sentences were commuted to life in prison. They were soon transferred to Sing Sing. Exhortations to pardon them and the other imprisoned Anti-Renters would not be answered, however, until a new governor was in office.[78]

1846: The Year in Six Songs

The repression of late 1845 had a chilling effect on the movement's visible tactical resistance. The associations again disavowed "Indian" activity, and "crowd actions ceased to be part of the anti-renters' political arsenal."[79] With several leaders behind bars, Anti-Rent efforts focused on the prisoners' fate, pressing for favorable legislation, and revising the state constitution. Their surprising success at the polls that November soon had tangible results. Voters approved the constitutional convention that *Young America*, the Whigs, and progressive Democrats had advocated for several months. The Anti-Renters resumed the push for title-tests, an equitable tax code, and relief from distress actions. Their increased influence in the legislature helped them attain two goals. The "Act to Equalize Taxation" and "Act to Abolish Distress for Rent" were approved and signed by Governor Wright in May 1846.[80] The latter left the landlords' right of repossession for non-payment of rent intact, but sheriffs were not obligated to auction tenants' household goods on their behalf. Had distress been abolished the previous year, the tragedy in Delaware County might have been avoided.

In keeping with the *Freeholder's* turn toward partisanship, far fewer Anti-Rent poems and songs appeared prior to the next election season. One exception is "Come Join the Anti-Renters," published May 20, 1846. No tune is indicated, but its verse-chorus structure can be seen in plate 25. Nothing is known about the author, Henry J. Crowell, except that he composed the work "for the Freeholder." The poem offers an upbeat, optimistic invitation to join the cause and witness the demise of "Patroonery." What is striking is that the invitation is in gendered terms: young and older men are addressed first, then "dames and maidens fair." Male desire to protect wives and children is invoked, along with the joy felt when "women cheer us on." These elements suggest a male persona.

Reeve Huston sees the poem's heteronormativity as generally representative of Anti-Renter attitudes. It certainly tells us a great deal about attitudes at the *Freeholder*. In contrast, *Young America* was far more likely to emphasize women's active participation, reflecting the NRA's embrace of equal rights. Despite Huston's interpretation of the poem, he acknowledges that "a significant number of leasehold women" behaved "like independent actors in a collective effort."[81] Women sounded the tin horns, hid fugitives, disrupted distress actions, attended court proceedings, held association memberships, and wrote to the Anti-Rent newspapers. The household's welfare was a shared concern. Not surprisingly, Anti-Rent sentiment played an important role in advancing this theme at the state constitutional convention.

Celebrations for the Fourth of July in 1846 were considerably more subdued in Albany County than the previous year. Thomas Devyr spoke in New Scotland, despite Ira Harris's attempts to exclude him.[82] Delaware County's celebrations, however, drew a sizable crowd. The "Equal Rights Celebration" in Bloomville included "an impressive procession," speeches, and songs for an estimated crowd of five to eight thousand. Another gathering was held in Middletown, where Revolutionary War veteran General Erastus Root gave one of his last public speeches. He expressed appreciation for the "large and respectable" convocation of "fellow citizens, who not only profess, but aim to put in practice, the principles I have cherished from my youth."[83]

New York State's endorsement of Anti-Rent legislation during the spring seemed to bode well for the convention, which met from June 1 to October 9 to debate revisions to the constitution. Most delegates from the leasehold counties were Anti-Rent sympathizers of various degrees, such as Ira Harris and Dr. Boughton's lawyer, Ambrose Jordan. Although they made up just 10 percent of the total delegates to the state convention, the *Albany Evening Journal* was optimistic that "whatever of feudalism remains" would be purged from the constitution.[84] Among those vestigial privileges was that the property of wealthy married women could be protected from seizure for their husbands' debt through prenuptial and other legal agreements. New York's landholders had been especially eager to conserve family assets through the designation of "separate property" owned and controlled by wives as if they were *femes sole* (single women). Less affluent married women who lacked the means to secure such legal arrangements often had their assets confiscated for their husbands' debt under the prevailing common law. Norma Basch notes that Ira Harris and other Anti-Rent advocates were in the forefront of proposing constitutional revisions that would extend asset protection to all married women. Allowing wives to keep their own property could help insulate households from impoverishment. Distress legislation had addressed related concerns, as we have seen. Although the various proposals to protect married women's property were defeated at the convention, the debate "crystallized the issues, placed them in the political arena, and engendered some expectation that passage of a married women's act was merely a question of time."[85] In fact, New York's Married Women's Property Act of 1848 became a model for other states and was an important step toward women's suffrage and other forms of equity.

While the constitutional delegates concluded their mandate, the Anti-Renters held their second political convention. A great deal depended on the November election, including voter approval of the revised constitution. Nonetheless, the Anti-Renters' October 6 meeting was significantly smaller than that of the previous year. Thirty-four representatives from the leasehold district endorsed a predominantly Whig slate. The complete ticket, naming candidates for office in five counties, was published in the *Albany Freeholder* on October 28. The same issue included two new Anti-Rent contrafactum, as we will see.

The Anti-Rent ticket for Albany County also circulated through a campaign broadside. Figure 3.2 shows a contrafactum written to endorse candidates for statewide and county offices. Generically titled "Anti-Rent Song," its first line asks, "What has caused this great Commotion?" (hereafter, "This Great Commotion"). The Albany slate is laid out in the lyrics' transcription (plate 26a). Successive verses name John Young for governor, Addison Gardiner for lieutenant governor, and "other pro anti-renters" for the US House of Representatives (Johnny I. Slingerlands), state senate (Ira Harris), assembly, sheriff, and county clerk.[86] The contrafactum is both a mnemonic device for voters at the poll and a rally song. The movement's greatest aspiration is repeated in the chorus, which is written out for each of the ten verses: "For the right of soil and a title true . . . for them we'll vote to a man."

The answer to the opening question "What has caused this great Commotion?" is "the ball that's rolling on." With this proposition, contemporaries would have readily recognized the contrafactum as a parody of the wildly successful 1840 Whig song, "Tippecanoe and Tyler Too!" "This Great Commotion" also recalls the latter's chorus, which referred to the opposition—Democrat Martin Van Buren—with "Van is a used up man." The contrafactum transforms this to "in spite of Manor Van," conjuring associations with both Dutch patroon landownership and recent events. Although neither Martin nor John Van Buren were currently running for office, the lyric was a reminder of the imprisoned Anti-Renters. The seeming lightheartedness of "This Great Commotion" belies the serious ramifications many farm families associated with the election.

Figure 3.2. Anti-Rent Song, "This Great Commotion." Broadside (SCO BRO1398), New York State Library, Manuscripts and Special Collections, Albany, New York.

ANTI-RENT SONG.

TUNE.—"*The Little Pig's Tail.*"

What has caused this great Commotion,
motion, motion,
Our whole State through?
It is the ball that's rolling on,
For the right of soil and a title true,
For the right of soil and a title true,
And for them we'll go to a man, man, in
spite of MANOR VAN,
And for them we'll go to a man.

Have you heard from neighb'ring towns,
towns, towns,
This district through?
The people all are wide awake,
For the right of soil and a title true,
For the right of soil and a title true,
And for them we'll go to a man, man, in
spite of MANOR VAN,
And for them we'll go to a man.

Who shall we have for Governors, Gover-
nors, Governors,
Our will to do?
Oh, Young and Gardiner are the men,
For the right of soil and a title true,
For the right of soil and a title true,
And for them we'll vote to a man, man, in
spite of MANOR VAN,
And for them we'll vote to a man.

Who will we have for Senator, Senator,
Senator,
Who's strong and true?
Oh, Harris is the man of men,
For the right of soil and a title true,
For the right of soil and a title true,
And for him we'll vote to a man, man, in
spite of MANOR VAN,
And for him we'll vote to a man.

Hark! I hear the voice of Harris, Harris,
Harris,
I see him too;
He stands erect, he's clinching the nail,
For the right of soil and a title true,
For the right of soil and a title true,
And for him we'll vote to a man, man, in
spite of MANOR VAN,
And for him we'll vote to a man.

Who shall we send to Congress, Congress,
Congress,
Who tell us who?
Why JOHNNY I. would fight or die
For the right of soil and a title true,
For the right of soil and a title true,
And for him we'll vote to a man, man, in
spite of MANOR VAN,
And for him we'll vote to a man.

Who must we have for Sheriff, Sheriff,
Sheriff,
Who'll justice do?
Oh, Oscar Tyler would "burst his biler"
For the right of soil and a title true,
For the right of soil and a title true,
And for him we'll vote to a man, man, in
spite of MANOR VAN,
And for him we'll vote to a man.

Who shall we have for County Clerk,
Clerk, Clerk,
Who'll recording do?
Why, Lawrence Van Deusen is the man
For the right of soil and a title true,
For the right of soil and a title true,
And for him we'll vote to a man, man, in
spite of MANOR VAN,
And for him we'll vote to a man.

Have you heard of Watson, Treadwell,
Fuller & Co.,
Our friends " true blue"?
They're just the ones to wield our guns,
For the right of soil and a title true,
For the right of soil and a title true,
And for them we'll vote to a man, man, in
spite of MANOR VAN,
And for them we'll vote to a man.

Awake, Awake, ye Anti-Renters, Renters,
Renters,
Your aim pursue;
Let every soul go up to the poll,
For the right of soil and a title true,
For the right of soil and a title true,
And for them we'll vote to a man, man, in
spite of MANOR VAN,
And for them we'll vote to a man.

As described in chapter 2, the Log Cabin presidential campaign is credited with creating modern strategies of political advertising. Songsters such as Horace Greeley's *The Log Cabin Songbook* and sheet music arrangements of "Tippecanoe and Tyler Too!" proliferated. Plate 26b is excerpted from an exemplary piano-vocal score published in Philadelphia in 1840.[87] The tune was used by numerous later campaigns, and by 1846 the anonymous lyricist of "This Great Commotion" had multiple sources from which to draw. Yet, rather than indicating any of these, the broadside named "Little Pig's Tail" as its tune. The title is enigmatic. Presumably, the author's desired melody was the comic glee "The Little Pigs," the original basis for "Tippecanoe and Tyler Too!" Songwriter and entertainer Alexander Lee published "Little Pigs" in Dublin in 1820, with American editions appearing from the mid-1830s (plate 26c).[88] The melodious three-part nonsense song has singers imitate barnyard animals with snorts and grunts. The campaign song's wide dissemination, however, has almost completely relegated Lee's humorous and relatively successful original song to obscurity.[89]

Despite the great difference in their subject matter, the close musical relationship between the vocal parts of "Tippecanoe and Tyler Too!" and "Little Pigs" can easily be seen in plates 26b and 26c, respectively. Both glees are in 6/8 time and A major; their three-part harmony is virtually identical. Although Lee's song designates the middle voice "tenor," its primary melody is in the uppermost part, which is also true for "Tip and Ty." The two songs are roughly equal in length with inclusion of the latter's twelve-bar instrumental introduction.

How the creator of "Tippecanoe and Tyler Too!"—Alexander Coffman Ross—first encountered "Little Pigs" is not known.[90] A native of Zanesville, Ohio, the musically active Ross recognized the public's appetite for political song as the 1840 campaign heated up. Debuting his new lyrics with his glee club at an Ohio rally, Ross soon had an opportunity to demonstrate the new song in New York. As a later contemporary said, "What the Marseilles Hymn was to Frenchmen, 'Tippecanoe and Tyler, too' was to the Whigs of 1840."[91] The song's success can mainly be credited to its catchy and accessible melody. But Ross's arrangement is also memorable, producing a powerful link between words and music. This can be seen through further comparison with Lee's glee, which prioritizes vocables and onomatopoeic syllables to a sparse and static accompaniment. In contrast, Ross used rippling rhythmic figuration for "Tip and Ty" that reinforces the opening verse's image of motion and commotion. This is reinforced further by the melody: having become stuck on a repeated note for "motion," pent-up energy is released by a short rising figure depicting "the ball a'rolling on" over rapid, emphatic cadential harmony.

Like "The Working Men's League" and "The Agrarian Ball" (plates 8 and 9, respectively), "This Great Commotion" recalls the gigantic ball rolled through the street during Whig parades. The 1846 song clearly attempts to reproduce the Log Cabin campaign's momentum, as can be seen in my setting (plate 26d) and heard in Justin Friello's stirring period arrangement. The candidates named on the broadside were, in fact, elected to office.[92]

The *Freeholder*'s October 28 endorsement of candidates for Albany County and four additional counties—Schoharie, Delaware, Rensselaer, and Columbia—was followed by a reminder to vote "YES" on the amended constitution. The same issue included two contrafacta generically titled "Anti-Rent Song." Their respective first lines are "Keep Thy Spirit, Swell Thy Faith" and "Rouse, Ye Anti-Renters, Wake!" The lyrics of "Keep Thy Spirit" are transcribed in plate 27a. Like several earlier songs, this one directs the Anti-Renters "away from militant activities and toward the safer route of the ballot box."[93] Its penultimate verse endorses four candidates for the New York State Assembly, three of whom were named in "This Great Commotion." The *Freeholder* lauded the fourth, Willett, in a column printed next to the song, despite his having lost the nomination.

The tune indicated for "Keep Thy Spirit" is "Cheer Up, My Lively Lads" (plate 27b). The latter's title comes from the initial words of its refrain. Its origin, however, is difficult to ascertain. "Cheer Up, My Lively Lads" was already treated as a traditional song by 1840, when political and temperance contrafacta begin to proliferate. Its refrain even played a role in "The Devil-Tavern," an anonymous 1843 *Knickerbocker* short story with maritime associations.[94] One widespread temperance version was:

Then cheer up, my lively lads / In spite of all rum's powers
Cheer up, my lively lads / The victory'll soon be ours.[95]

The earliest known musical notation for the tune appeared two years after the Anti-Rent "Keep Thy Spirit" in the song collection *The Free Soil Minstrel*. Plate 27b reproduces this version of "Cheer Up, My Lively Lads," an antislavery contrafactum titled "Salt River Chorus." The two-part arrangement was made by abolitionist George Washington Clark, known as the "Liberty Minstrel" for his earlier collection of that name and his performances as a singer.[96] The simple harmonies suggested by the treble-bass score are tonic, dominant, and submediant (i.e., predominant). With its many repeated notes and the melodic span limited to a fifth, the diatonic tune is a perfect vehicle for rousing collective participation. Plate 27c sets "Keep Thy Spirit" to this melody. Although one verse endorses specific candidates, most are a general rally for the cause. As the chorus proclaims,

Cheer up my lively lads / In spite of wind and weather,—
Cheer up my lively lads / We'll triumph altogether!

The second "Anti-Rent Song" appearing in the *Freeholder* on October 28 begins "Rouse, Ye Anti-Renters, Wake!" Calls to awaken and arouse appear frequently in the movement's communications and writings.[97] The contrafactum's six stanzas are transcribed in plate 28a. Its anonymous author reaches for allegory, warning listeners about "the wight . . . with bloody hands" and the monster who is "stained with guilt and shame" for keeping the farmers enthralled. Happiness will come when "justice has its sway" and "quarter sales no more will be." In plate 28b, "Rouse, Ye Anti-Renters, Wake!" is set to its intended tune, "Bruce's Address."

The 1846 constitution, which was approved by voters on November 3, achieved certain advances in the democratization of the law. The judicial system was drastically reorganized into its modern form, with the court of appeals as the state's highest court. Judgeships and many state offices were converted from appointed to elected posts, a victory for the Anti-Renters. Certain progressive measures failed, however. The constitution of 1821 had instated property requirements for Black voters to restrict the increased enfranchisement resulting from the state's gradual abolition of slavery. Challenges to these requirements failed at the 1846 constitutional convention. In response, Liberty party leader Gerrit Smith offered free, forty-acre parcels of Adirondacks land to about three thousand Black men that would make them eligible to vote. As noted in the previous chapter, Smith was the only patroon to forego rent collection when other landholders resumed pursuit in autumn 1844. His somewhat contradictory positions on land ownership were discussed in the Anti-Rent press.[98] Smith's role in founding the Black farming community of Timbuctoo and friendship with abolitionist John Brown has recently received renewed attention.[99]

Most significantly for the Anti-Renters, the revised New York State Constitution paradoxically relegated manorial leases to the past while allowing part of that past to persist into the present. "All feudal tenures of every description, with all their incidents, are declared to be abolished," stated article 1. Quarter-sales and other reservations on alienation were thereby prohibited. "[T]he entire and absolute property" would be "vested in the owners," giving them clear title and the mineral, lumber, and water rights previously reserved to landlords.[100] Nor could leases be perpetual; new contracts for agricultural lands were limited to twelve years. However, the new stipulations applied only to future agreements. While leases for one or multiple lives would be renegotiated on the new terms when they expired, no remedy was available to families holding perpetual leases. The tenant farmers of Rensselaerwyck remained in conflict with the patroons. "As statements of the body politic's revulsion with 'voluntary slavery,' these provisions spoke volumes. As instruments of land reform, however, they had negligible utility," observes McCurdy.[101] The Anti-Rent movement had achieved a major victory in principle, but not entirely in practice. The state's third constitution went into effect January 1, 1847.

The election results brought heavy losses to the ruling Democrats. Incumbent Governor Silas Wright was displaced by John Young and others on the Anti-Rent slate. Although the struggle was not completely over, the constitutional convention and election of 1846 brought its most turbulent chapter to an end. Two songs appeared that December in the *Albany Freeholder* reflecting recent developments, the "Anti-Rent Song of Triumph" and "The Land Lord's Lament." Their authors had very similar identifications; the first contrafactum is attributed to "E. I." of Berne and the other to "E. P." of "Bern Ville."

The "Anti-Rent Song of Triumph," which was published December 9, was dated November 7 by its author. E. I. seemed to watch election results as they were announced county by county. "Tis easy told and thus 'tis done / They all did go for Johnny Young," states the initial verse. Albany's response is described in the next verse, followed by Rensselaer, Columbia, Schoharie, and Delaware Counties. The "Anti-Rent Song of Triumph" was the third Anti-Rent contrafactum written to the tune "Old Dan Tucker." Its spirited refrain declares that Silas Wright should "Get out the way" and "Make room now for honest men." The complete lyrics are transcribed in plate 29a, and the contrafactum is set to "Old Dan Tucker" in plate 29b.

The *Freeholder*'s final song of 1846, published December 30, is a remarkable satire called "The Land Lord's Lament." Written from the patroon's perspective, it mocks the landholders' dilemma to the tune of "Oh Dear, What Can the Matter Be." Longstanding themes of greed and abuse are rehearsed in highly comedic verses. The song was brilliantly performed at Old Songs' 2014 show, as will be discussed in the next chapter. The first three lines of each quatrain rhyme, and the last line of all four quatrains, are punctuated with a complaint about obtaining the rent (i.e., AAAB, CCCB, etc.) In the chorus, the persona frets, "What shall I do with my tenants / How shall I get all my *rents*?" At the end, "the friends of *equal rights*" are identified as the source of these troubles. The complete lyrics, attributed to E. P., are transcribed in plate 30a.[102]

The earliest modern references to "Oh Dear, What Can the Matter Be" appeared in the late eighteenth century, when it had great success as a duet on the British stage.[103] British and American piano-vocal scores soon proliferated, including a 1793 imprint by Philadelphia's Benjamin Carr. The sheet music in plate 30b, published by E. Riley of New York in 1823, is indicative of its continuing popularity.[104] Like Carr's edition, neither composer nor lyricist are named. The indication of vocal harmony in smaller noteheads below the main soprano melody is characteristic of the era.

Plate 30c sets the "The Land Lord's Lament" to "Oh Dear, What Can the Matter Be." As the contrafactum's biting satire reflects, regional landlords had good reason to worry about the revised state constitution's prohibition against new feudal contracts. When leases made for lives expired, new ones would have very different terms and conditions. And the Rensselaerwyck perpetual leases were far less valuable without the remedy of distress. We now turn to the ramifications of these changes and the recent election for the Anti-Renters.

Coda

To ensure he did not forget his campaign promise, the Anti-Renters sent a petition to Governor John Young with eleven thousand signatures demanding that the prisoners be pardoned.[105] By February 1847, Dr. Boughton, Edward O'Conner, John Van Steenburgh, and Moses Earle were allowed to return home. Their rights as citizens, which their life sentences precluded, were restored that September. The remaining Anti-Renters in Clinton Prison were pardoned and released. Homecoming that February included a stop in Clarksville, where they were greeted with a public dinner and "soul-stirring music from the Berne brass band."[106]

Some of the Anti-Rent leaders eventually moved west, part of a general trend among upstate farmers. Boughton resumed his medical practice and social activism. His accomplishment as "Philanthropist and Liberator" is detailed in a history of his extended family, which spanned both sides of the Hudson.[107] Boughton also had the dubious honor, eight years after his death in 1888, of being vilified by the *New York Times* in a series recollecting notable court trials.[108] Apparently, the article did not compromise his status as a local hero in the twentieth century. Three historical markers dedicated to Big Thunder were erected commemorating his home, Fourth of July oratory, and grave in Rensselaer County.[109] In the next chapter, we will discuss additional tributes to his advocacy.

With the Anti-Rent prisoners' release, the abolishment of distress, the revised terms of landownership, and a new tax code, the era of collective action came to a close. Private settlement and contractual obligation remained the foundation of property relations in New York, though feudal reservations were now prohibited. Some landlords sold outright or converted the old quarter leases to mortgages. John A. King sold about fifteen thousand acres of the Blenheim Patent in Schoharie County to tenants, clearing his path to Congress and the governorship.[110] "Half the remaining tenants on Livingston Manor bought out their landlords between 1846 and 1848," and voluntary sales on the Hardenbergh Patent were similar.[111] Nevertheless, legal battles, financial disputes, and even a few direct confrontations persisted upstate for decades.

The heirs to Rensselaerwyck remained tenacious at first through dizzying circumstances. On the East Manor, William Van Rensselaer challenged Rensselaer County's right to collect tax on rental income until the New York Supreme Court upheld the assessment in 1850. In 1848, the legislature passed a resolution allowing title-tests. Four years later, Judge Ira Harris declared the patroon claim to certain wild lands invalid in *People v. Rensselaer*. Also in 1852, none other than

Judge Amasa Parker ruled that quarter reservations in leases made after 1787 violated the first state constitution, invalidating a major source of patroon revenue and adding a new challenge to the validity of manorial titles. Harris's decision was reversed by the court of appeals in 1853, but Parker's decision was confirmed, "and so the rent strike continued with a new justification."[112] Meanwhile, Stephen IV and William had already begun selling parcels of their manors to a distant relative, the land speculator Walter Church, for a fraction of what the tenant farmers had been willing to pay in 1839.

By 1858, Church and his associates possessed what remained of Rensselaerwyck.[113] His engagement of law enforcement and private militias led to multiple bitter confrontations, occasionally arousing the Calico Indians. According to Simon Rosendale, who served as New York's attorney general in the 1890s, Church testified that he had pursued approximately two thousand lawsuits. "The court calendars of both Albany and Rensselaer counties during his most active years show how greatly he monopolized the attention of the courts and juries in the attempted enforcement of his rights."[114] Church made a good living for a time but died in poverty in 1890. The tenth patroon and seventh lord of the manor, Stephen IV, had died in 1868, as did his brother William four years later.

Rosendale was born in Albany in 1842. His recollection of tenants lining up to pay their rent to the Van Rensselaers' assignees in the 1860s was reminiscent of the Good Patroon's era. "I well remember the scene on the steps of the old manor house on North Broadway [Albany], where on New Year's Day, for a number of successive years, demands by the attorneys were publicly made of a long list of tenants, repeating in a loud tone, a demand for the skipples or bushels of wheat, the fat fowl, or the day's service provided in the respective leases."[115] Chapter 4 brings us back to the 1840s, when several monuments to the patroons' way of life were created. Some treat the Anti-Rent conflict explicitly; in others, it forms an implicit backdrop. Either way, the artistic legacy of Anti-Rentism was launched with attempts to preserve the landlords' world in living memory.

Chapter 4

Living Memory and Legacy

But take this quill—time was, some sapient goose
Once sported, high and proud, the brilliant gem;
. . . Admit—it is the right hand's diadem,
Yclept, the quill. The muses all obey the potent wand,
It is the sceptre of opinion's rights, o'er sea and land.

—H. R. Schoolcraft, *Helderbergia*[1]

Two large oil portraits of the Van Rensselaers' nineteenth-century Albany residence can be viewed today at the Albany Institute of History and Art. *The Gardens of the Van Rensselaer Manor House* (1840) and *The Van Rensselaer Manor House* (1841) were painted by Thomas Cole at the request of William Van Rensselaer. The works were nostalgic, intended to preserve memory at a time of transition. Following the death of Stephen Van Rensselaer III in January 1839, Stephen IV assumed possession of the Albany manor house and his half-brother William built a new home, Beverwyck, on the East Manor.[2] In anticipation of the relocation that autumn, William commissioned Cole to create mementos of the Albany house and gardens for his mother, Cornelia Paterson, and sisters. As he wrote to Cole, the women "naturally would like to take with them some representation of the home scenes with which they have become so familiar and which are so endeared to them."[3] William already possessed two large works on medieval subjects by the Hudson River artist, whose reputation for fine representations of aristocratic country life was well-established.

Art historian William Coleman argues that the nostalgia captured in Cole's works for the Van Rensselaers went beyond personal associations. The artist's house portraits for a variety of patrons are "visual arguments about the role of private wealth and privilege in a republic." Stately mansions were the place where civilization met the wilderness, transforming the unruly American landscape into cultivated space. Such a transformation was of necessity entrusted to a certain class of people; the natural leaders of society operated their estates for the nation's benefit. While *The Van Rensselaer Manor House* and its companion *Gardens* preserve individual memories for the family, they also legitimate the patroon's way of life. Cole's two scenes are "stripped of the industry and unrest that surrounded them in reality." Quiet and peopleless, the paintings indulge a melancholy wistfulness that Coleman identifies as "feudal nostalgia": expressions of longing for a waning American aristocracy.[4] The paintings certainly appear that way today, hanging in the museum Stephen III helped shape.[5]

With this concept in mind, I look at two up-rent works: a waltz dedicated to Stephen Van Rensselaer IV and Cooper's novel *The Redskins*. This is followed by discussion of Melville's rejection of feudal privilege in his novel *Pierre* and Schoolcraft's 1855 idiosyncratic poem *Helderbergia*. No major expressive responses to Anti-Rentism seem to have appeared in the later nineteenth century. Understandably and importantly, the Civil War and its aftermath eclipsed the regional conflict. The hiatus in Anti-Rent works is reflected in this chapter by a leap forward to the movement's centennial, which inspired new creative treatments and tributes characteristic of 1930s-style populism and mid-century progressivism. Upstate proponents of folksong found the Anti-Renters' story compelling, as did educators during the final quarter of the twentieth century. Their theatrical works take us back to where we began: Old Songs' 2014 folk theater pageant, *Down with the Rent!*

Sometime after Cole completed *The Manor House*, a similar image appeared on the cover of Oliver J. Shaw's "The Rensselaer Grand Waltz."[6] Perhaps William also commissioned this piano solo, or perhaps it was made to order for his brother, General Van Rensselaer, the subject of its dedication.[7] Like their father, Stephen IV attained the military rank of major general. The cover lithograph was created by the Boston-based artist E. W. Bouve, and its caption identifies the Albany Manor House. In contrast to Cole's isolated and lonely view, the lithograph includes several outbuildings, the Hudson river, distant mountains, and human activity. A carriage with horses and a driver waits at the Manor House's front door, a figure attends several cows in the foreground, and a steamboat passes by on the river. The pastoral scene is idyllic but active, corresponding to the music's lively indulgence of nostalgia for an untroubled time. The New York State Library dates the sheet music's publication between 1845 and 1848.

As was typical of the genre, the form of "The Rensselaer Grand Waltz" is sectional, with strains of sixteen and twenty-four bars. The E-flat major composition begins *fortissimo* with a thirty-two-bar introduction, followed by two ABA sections and a coda. The second ABA is in the key of the dominant (B-flat) and includes a passage marked "trio." Chromatic passages, octave doublings, and ornaments are used for dramatic effect. The waltz could be purchased from the publisher, W. H. Oakes, in Boston or from the composer in Albany. Oliver J. Shaw was the son of the highly accomplished, blind Providence musician and composer Oliver Shaw.[8] The younger musician wrote tribute pieces to highly placed men soon after he arrived in Albany, such as the 1842 "Governor Bouck's Grand Quick Step" and 1844 "Governor Wright's Grand March." He taught at the Albany Female Academy and a boys' school, Mansion Hall. The lithographed cover of his piano solo, "Mansion Hall, Waltz Brilliante" depicts the "venerable edifice" that housed the school, and a lengthy caption explains that the building was erected by the Van Rensselaers.[9] While Shaw does not appear to have participated in the conflict between landlords and tenants directly, his works—whether inspired or for hire—reflect the situational allegiances typically navigated by rank-and-file musicians. The loyalties of James Fenimore Cooper were entirely another matter.

Aristocracy in the Republic

In the literary sphere, Cooper was the single most significant spokesperson for the landed gentry. The prolific author was an insider to the patroon system, well-acquainted with the Van Rensselaers and other powerful families. His father, William Cooper, despite humble origins became one of the most successful land speculators of the Revolutionary Era and a political ally of Stephen III. The magnificent family home William built in Cooperstown, Otsego Hall, was modeled on the Van Rensselaers' Albany Manor. When his father died in 1809, Fenimore Cooper inherited a considerable fortune. He married Susan DeLancey, who descended from French nobility and New York patroons.[10] The unexpected loss of his inheritance was followed by lifelong financial struggle. Nonetheless, Cooper was deeply committed to the family legacy, symbolized by his restoration of Otsego Hall in the 1830s. Although Cooperstown was outside the Anti-Rent district, statewide legislation on distress, taxes, and titles concerned him deeply. He systematically addressed each of these topics in the final volume of "The Littlepage Manuscripts." By then, various setbacks had dampened Cooper's ardor for democracy and "cast a nostalgic glow over the serene days of his youth when his father was establishing a lordly estate on the shores of Glimmerglass."[11]

Cooper's professed goal in the trilogy, which appeared in 1845–1846, was to treat "anti-rentism with the utmost frankness."[12] The first volumes, *Satanstoe* and *The Chainbearer*, chronicle the Littlepage family's acquisition of a large tract of wilderness from Native Americans during the 1750s, their hard-won development of the property, and the generous terms given to their tenants after the Revolution. In *The Redskins*, nefarious forces conspire to deny the Littlepages their just return for nearly a century of diligent labor, expensive investment, and risk-taking. As Granville Hicks observed, "the anti-rent trilogy is starkly and one might almost say uniquely class-conscious, for it is both a theoretical defense of a class and an emotional expression of class-feeling at a high pitch."[13]

Much of *The Redskins* is devoted to defending New York's great landlords, as represented by the young heir, Hugh Littlepage, and his wealthy uncle. The two return to the family estate after five years in Europe to investigate reports of Anti-Rent disturbances. They sneak into the region disguised, risking violation of the recently passed anti-mask laws. Although their camouflage is necessitated by fear of Anti-Renter violence, Hugh is armed only with the flute with which he charms his bride-to-be. Coincidentally, a large contingent of Native Americans from the prairies arrive at the very same moment to visit an esteemed elder. The plot device allows juxtaposition of genuine Indigenous peoples with the ersatz Calico Indians. At the climax, the Native Americans' noble dignity bolsters the landlords' superior moral position over the Anti-Renters. In the denouement, the Native Americans quietly depart for the west, and the local troublemakers recede. With the region cleared of both Indian and Injin, Hugh and his fiancée can focus on their impending marriage. The Littlepage family is thus elevated "from mere landholding to control of the future itself," as Philip Deloria notes.[14] The novel paints an optimistic picture of racial privilege and class triumph, clouded only by potential "republican tyranny," the novel's closing words.[15]

To avoid such levelling and attain the highest order of civilization, the United States needed a landed gentry. Cooper spells this out in his preface for *The Chainbearer*: "The column of Society must have its capital as well as its base. It is only perfect while each part is entire, and discharges its proper duty. In New York, the great landlords long have and do still, in a social sense, occupy the place of the capital." To the charge of endorsing feudalism in a republic, Cooper countered that the present system was foundational to the United States Constitution. Lamenting a particular Anti-Rent victory, he opined: "High authority . . . has pronounced the tenure of a durable lease to be opposed to the spirit of the institutions! Yet these tenures existed when the institutions were formed, and one of the provisions of the institutions themselves guarantees the observance of the covenants under which the tenures exist."[16] For Cooper, "original intent" justified the status quo.

Despite its monumental originality in American letters, Cooper's monetary return on "The Littlepage Manuscripts" was disappointingly poor, and critical reception was mixed. Many regarded *The Redskins*, with its lengthy discourses on property relations and Anti-Rentism, more polemic than literature.[17] Biographer Wayne Franklin observes that the "trio of novels had little effect on the course of the public Anti-Rent debate, or the resolution—rather, irresolution—that accompanied that debate."[18] Perhaps the novel's most important impact was on the younger writer, Herman Melville.[19] Like Cooper, Melville had deep ties to the patroon system that failed to secure his socioeconomic position. But he presented readers a far less sanguine view of that system in *Pierre: Or, the Ambiguities*, published a half-dozen years after Cooper's trilogy.

The patroon heritage of Melville's title character, Pierre Glendinning, was personal for the author: his mother was a Gansevoort, an original seventeenth-century patroon family related by marriage to the Rensselaers. These connections made Melville a keen observer of class disparities. Like many patroon daughters, Marie Gansevoort's personal wealth was relatively modest. Her inheritance was squandered by Melville's father, and the family moved from New York City to the Albany area during Herman's adolescence. His father's death a short time later forced Melville to leave school and seek employment, leading to a stint on whaling ships and other travels from 1841 though 1844. He arrived back upstate as the Anti-Rent conflict was intensifying in Rensselaer County and Jerrold's melodrama *The Rent Day* was being performed along the Hudson. Melville soon began to write about his varied experiences. He published *Moby Dick* in 1851, and *Pierre* appeared a year later.

In describing Pierre Glendinning's origins, Melville invokes "those most ancient and magnificent Dutch Manors . . . whose haughty rent-deeds are held by their thousand farmer tenants" in a perpetuity that makes "lawyer's ink as unobliterable as the sea."[20] Pierre, like the author, is destined to lose the security seemingly guaranteed by his lineage. Early in the novel, he learns a secret whose revelation would materially and morally compromise the family name. In a desperate attempt to right the past and protect two women stigmatized and potentially impoverished by illegitimate births, Pierre ultimately destroys the validity of the Glendinnings' position. "Melville makes the illegitimacy of the Glendinning family titles analogous to the illegitimacy of the Glendinnings' property titles," observes Hecht.[21] In creating such a tale, Melville engaged one of the Anti-Renters' lingering goals—challenging the validity of landlord titles.

If property titles are not legitimate, then the social system built on them cannot be legitimate either. Pierre emerges as a spokesperson for the marginalized, giving voice to the voiceless. He becomes painfully aware of desperate Glendenning tenants who "abandoned an ample farm on account of absolute inability to meet the manorial rent" and now survived precariously with their four children in a "small and half-ruinous house."[22] Melville's novel, like Jerrold's melodrama, "focuses on society's injustices as seen from the perspective of the socially oppressed."[23] Furthermore, Pierre's democratic values and "sterling charity" contrast sharply with those who blithely deny there is misery in the world: "If the grown man of taste, possess not only some eye to detect the picturesque in the natural landscape, so also, has he as keen a perception of what may not unfitly be here styled, the *povertiresque* in the social landscape."[24] The neologism is symptomatic of Melville's intervention as critic of the ideological structures that maintain upper-class power. Whereas Cooper offered the picturesque landscape as nature's confirmation of the patroons' elevated position, Melville "constructs his landscapes to subvert and denaturalize not only the great proprietors' claims to their deeds and titles, but any claim to authority based on Nature."[25] *Pierre* prompted readers to question "the existence of such mighty lordships in the heart of a republic."[26]

~

Helderbergia: Or the Apotheosis of the Heroes of the Antirent War, is one of the most curious literary manifestations of Anti-Rent sentiment. For reasons unknown, its author, Henry Rowe Schoolcraft, published the work anonymously. The epic poem, which consists of 94 ten-line stanzas grouped into four cantos, was printed in Albany in 1855. *Helderbergia* received little notice from contemporaries and remains obscure today, read mainly as another example of cultural appropriation by one of the United States' first ethnologists. Schoolcraft cast the Anti-Rent conflict in mythological terms, a perspective honed from his Rensselaerwyck origins and several decades of engagement with Native American communities, including his first wife's family.

Schoolcraft was born in Guilderland, the sixth Albany County town to join the initial Anti-Rent protest.[27] He worked in his family's glass-making business as a youth, then traveled with several expeditions investigating the natural resources and Native American populations of the Midwest. Schoolcraft's sojourn in Michigan's upper peninsula led to his marriage to Jane Bamewawagezhikaquay Johnston in 1823. Jane's parents, the Scots-Irish John Johnston and the Ojibwe Ozhaguscodaywayquay, were fur-traders and community leaders in Sault Ste. Marie. The region's culturally rich métis environment enabled Schoolcraft's first significant Native American ethnographic works.[28] It also facilitated his advancement in several administrative appointments in the Michigan Territory, positions that often involved decisions detrimental to Indigenous peoples. For example, Schoolcraft negotiated the 1836 treaty ceding nearly sixteen million acres of Anishinaabe Ojibwe and Odawa land to the US Government in anticipation of Michigan's statehood. In 1839, Schoolcraft published *Algic Researches*, a collection of Native American allegories and legends that Henry Wadsworth Longfellow later acknowledged was an important source for *The Song of Hiawatha*.[29] In 1841, the Schoolcrafts and their two children moved to New York City, where Jane died the following year.

Henry visited Albany in 1845 and 1846 to prepare a census and demographic study of Native Americans in New York.[30] He probably conceived the idea for *Helderbergia* at this time, while the Anti-Rent movement was reaching its climax. Internal evidence suggests Schoolcraft followed news of the conflict, from the state's ban on masks to reports of the Anti-Renters' gatherings and subterfuges. His narrative focuses on attempts by a military corps supporting patroon interests to subdue the tenant farmers' rag-tag resistance. Ultimately, each side is shown to have its heroes. The lighthearted conclusion bestows awards for valor on an Anti-Rent wife and her broom (with which she had ejected her husband's pursuers from their home). In the final stanza, the writing quill is recognized for its power to make a "God or Goose" of its user.

While Schoolcraft seems sympathetic to the Anti-Renters, each side is also shown to have its faults, and the longest cantos lavish attention on the military corps. The first canto describes an Anti-Rent congress with Big Thunder, which leads to the tar-and-feathering of an intruding sheriff (stanzas 1–22). The second canto elaborates the responding military force's twelve-mile march west from Orania (i.e., Albany) to the Helderbergs (stanzas 23–51). Local color is dressed with ancient allusion, as when the army's march through Guilderland's sandy soil is described as a "Nilotic tramp" (II:36).[31] The next canto (III:52–82) continues the soldiers' exploits, now in "Bangall"—seemingly an allusion to Delhi—where they battle an army of goats (à la *Don Quixote*) and are spooked by ghosts and demon spirits (III:60 and 78, respectively). Humorous verses about the military's foodstuffs suggest Schoolcraft consulted earlier accounts, such as the *New York Herald*'s satires. Unsuspecting farm animals succumb to slant rhyme and the "human art" that "Alone reveals how stomachs, maws and tripes / Can be transformed to dishes of desire" (III:67). A short while later, the army discovers its supplies are low and returns directly to town, which the narrator deems an honorable decision.

> And if the Oranian army did not fight, but run it,
> 'Tis a plain proposition that they might have done it. (III:82)

In the short final canto, the Anti-Rent congress reconvenes, shares an Indian-inspired pipe, and honors its heroes (IV:83–94).

Helderbergia includes a glossary with thirty-five Dutch and Indian terms, numerous allusions to Native American legends, and gratuitous remarks on Indigenous peoples' capabilities. The Anti-Renters' appropriation of Native American cultural markers and practices must have hailed Schoolcraft (as it did Cooper).[32] Schoolcraft's career as an Indian agent depended on appropriations both political and personal. While space does not permit a thorough discussion of his "egotistical and opportunistic careerism," it is worth noting that a more precise understanding of Schoolcraft's "cultural theft" has emerged from Robert Dale Parker's research on his first wife.[33] Parker's discovery of Jane Johnston Schoolcraft's many unpublished and limited edition works among Henry's papers led to her recent recognition as the first Native American literary writer and poet. Her Ojibwe name, Bamewawagezhikaquay, means "the sound the stars make rushing through the sky." Parker used its English translation for the title of the first modern edition of her collected poetry. His introduction offers a few clues to the mystery of *Helderbergia*'s 1855 publication date.

By the mid-1850s, Schoolcraft had settled in Washington, DC, remarried, and become a virtual invalid. His second wife—a notorious racist—helped him continue to publish despite his infirmity.[34] It is not impossible that the timing of *Helderbergia* was influenced by anticipation of Longfellow's epic poem *Hiawatha*, with its prominent acknowledgment of *Algic Researches*. Schoolcraft quickly reprinted the latter with the title *The Myth of Hiawatha, and Other Oral Legends* to coincide with the poem's debut. Predictably, he again failed to acknowledge Jane's contribution. It is therefore likely that Longfellow based both *Hiawatha* and *Evangeline* on her stories "without knowing that she was the source."[35] Perhaps Schoolcraft felt a little guilty for Jane's erasure and a little nostalgic for the literary camaraderie they had once shared exchanging and printing poetry.[36] We may never know whether creating *Helderbergia* reminded him of those times, but it offers today's reader a curious, amusing, and idiosyncratic view of the Anti-Rent movement by a native son (with all that implies). It would be many decades before the next phase of Anti-Rent-inspired expressive works appeared.

Cultural Front Centennial: Regional Resonances

As the hundredth anniversary of the Anti-Rent conflict approached, several communities prepared to mark its significance. The movement appeared in a new light with the United States reeling from the Great Depression and Europe engaged in a struggle against fascism. Bitterness and unease about the tenant farmers' alleged violence gave way to empathy for their collective action and class struggle. The shift in emphasis resonated with the era's left-leaning populism, which put the common man (i.e., person) at the forefront. Aesthetic manifestations of this sentiment—the cultural front—incorporated the representation of labor and laborers into artistic works.[37] In both factual and fictional accounts of the 1930s and 1940s, the Anti-Rent movement was viewed as championing the experiences and rights of ordinary people. The next section traces this development from local histories to visual works, public commemorations, a mainstream novel and film, and Christman's sweeping narrative, *Tin Horns and Calico*.

At the vanguard of this new perspective was a rich network of regional historians and journalists who preserved and curated the Anti-Renters' story. One such figure was Arthur Gregg, author of *Old Hellerbergh: Historical Sketches of the West Manor of Rensselaerwyck, Including an Account of the Anti-Rent Wars, the Glass House, and Henry R. Schoolcraft*. As its full title suggests, Gregg's volume covers a wide range of topics and includes important documents. But its "most valuable part," observed New York State historian Alexander Flick, are "those chapters giving in greater fullness than ever before published an account of the Helderberg Wars over anti-rent issues."[38] Gregg's book was brought out in 1936 by the *Altamont Enterprise*. The regional New York newspaper had printed his work in progress during the preceding years.

An example of the period's populist orientation can be seen in a passage attributed to one of Gregg's informants, a local son "born and brought up in the heart of anti-rent country." He conveys the indignities experienced by tenant farmers on rent day and sheds light on an important motivation for their collective resistance.

> Such men . . . were well-to-do farmers, respected and influential in their community, but when they went with their annual loads of wheat or wood or poultry to the Manor House on New Year's Day, they were nothing but country tenants, serfs bearing tribute. After a long tiresome drive with their teams over treacherous country roads they found themselves invariably in a blockage of wagons. They were compelled to wait until their names were called in haughty tones by the agents of the patroon. Perhaps all day they would wait and at nightfall still be unable to unload and get a receipt. Then they must go to hostelry, put out their teams and spend the night, returning to the "Storehouses of Pharoah" in the morning. When at length they had reached their homes on the Helderberg, they had lost considerable time and money. Downright angry and disgusted they vowed never to return again.[39]

Documenting and preserving such recollections also motivated John Duncan Monroe, who brought out a limited edition of *The Anti-Rent War in Delaware County: The Revolt against the Rent System* in 1940. The local historian wanted to address a lacuna in the record; as he explained, nothing was currently available in print on the Delaware County revolt "from the anti-renters' point of view." To that end, Monroe compiled profiles of several original participants, including Moses Earle, whose farm on Dingle Hill was the site of the movement's final showdown in August 1845. Interestingly, just one hundred copies of this 128-page book were printed. Perhaps Monroe felt local factions would be antagonized or that his personal view was too radically anti-capitalist. In the preface, Monroe confesses to being motivated by his "realization that the rent system was but one form of the ever recurring problem created by the efforts of men of parasitic habits to divert the labor and earnings of other men to their own profit."[40] Monroe was invited to address the local centennial commemoration in 1945 and was named honorary president of the Delaware County Historical Association.[41] Although we may never know the reason he limited the book's reach, some of its contents found a wider audience through *Tin Horns and Calico*.

There were visible signs of Anti-Rent's resurgence, too. Historical markers commemorating the conflict began dotting the region in 1932, courtesy of the New York State Education Department.[42] In 1935, the State Normal College in Albany installed the evocative wall mural reproduced on the book cover. Entitled *An Incident of Anti-Rentism*, the caption adds, "Tenants showing discontent. Cart to the Front Door of the Manor. Their Annual Rent. 1838." In rich, warm tones and dappled sunlight, local artist David Lithgow depicted a farm couple with a wood-filled cart and oxen approach several fashionably dressed figures standing on the Manor House porch. A leafy border twined with red apples surrounds three sides of the scene, with a dozen or so fowl filling the lower border. The only obvious sign of discontent is that the farmers have dared to appear at the patroons' front door rather than the agent's office. The year 1838 was the (relative) calm before the storm.[43]

A more explicit illustration of resistance was installed in Delhi's new post office in 1940. Like the building that houses it, Mary Earley's dramatic mural, *Down-Rent War, around 1845*, was a New Deal product. Her work was sponsored by the US Department of Treasury, Section of Fine Arts, which commissioned many public works contemporaneous with the Work Projects Administration (WPA). Earley's composition incorporates the Anti-Rent movement's most prominent symbols. To the right, a youth in the distance blows a tin horn. Eight large, masked figures are clustered in the mural's center, their clenched fists brandishing knives and a sign reading, "Down with Rent." Their faces are completely hidden by hoods topped with antlers and red feathers. The middle figure, garbed in bright red, holds a roll of paper in one hand and a torch aloft in the other, poised to burn the despised writs. On the left, a startled horse and rider—presumably the sheriff—gallop away. Earley originally intended to show the central masked figure in a full-length calico gown, but the mural's installation above the door to the postmaster's office necessitated a view from waist-up. Her earlier conception can be seen in a preliminary study for the work. The mural itself can be viewed today at the Delhi post office, located not far from where a record number of Anti-Renters were jailed.[44]

In addition to the visual commemorations in Albany and Delhi, at least one musical work was inspired by the Anti-Rent legacy. Vivian Fine, a pioneer of music for modern dance, composed *Tin-Horn Rebellion* for solo piano. It was presented by George Bockman and the Adelphi Dance Theatre in New York City in December 1941 as a dramatic folk-tale of the Hudson Valley. The choreography called for a cast of eight, with a total of sixteen dancers onstage. Unfortunately, the work was not published and no further information is available.[45]

The first documented public commemoration of the Anti-Rent centennial took place in Andes, Delaware County, with featured speakers Christman, Monroe, and an official from the

Electrical Workers Union. The large pageant, "under the auspices of the State Historical society took place on Labor Day, 1945, and was followed by a picnic, a parade, and a baseball game," recounted Norman Studer, director of Camp Woodland. Studer and others from the camp observed the day's activities as part of their immersion in the folklore of the Catskills. "Descendants of the 'Calico Indians' gathered to reenact one of the most sensational events of the protracted struggle, the killing of Sheriff Osman Steele" on the Earle farm. Studer would eventually dramatize these same events on Dingle Hill in a short story and musical play, as we will see. The works were a response to the depth of feeling he encountered. "The anti-rent war is a living democratic tradition among the folk of the Catskills," he observed.[46] "The people of the area still feel very close to these events, and know that it was a significant engagement in the struggle to throw off old forms of servitude."[47] The residents of Andes perpetuated the spirit of the Anti-Rent movement with another commemoration in 1976 in conjunction with the United States' bicentennial.[48] Twenty years later, the Andes Society for History and Culture presented "Confrontation on Dingle Hill" to mark the event's 150th anniversary.[49] Studer had correctly predicted that the Anti-Rent movement would persist as living memory in Delaware County.

Cultural Front Centennial: National Notice

The most notable examples of Anti-Rent-inspired aesthetic work to reach beyond a regional audience at its centennial are Anya Seton's 1944 novel *Dragonwyck* and the eponymous Hollywood film that followed on its success. *Dragonwyck* and *My Theodosia*, a fictional biography of Aaron Burr's daughter, were Seton's first major bestsellers. Her lasting reputation as a major author of carefully researched historical fiction was sealed by the 1954 novel *Katherine*. In *Dragonwyck*, Seton made clever use of the manor system to create a gothic horror romance set in the American Northeast. The patroon of Dragonwyck, Nicholas Van Ryn, is desperate to produce a male heir to perpetuate the family estate.[50] The story is told largely through the eyes of Miranda, the naïve young woman he recruits, seduces, and marries in pursuit of this desire. Most of the action takes place at Van Ryn's grand upstate residence. In a prefatory note to the novel, Seton assures readers that manor houses like Dragonwyck did exist at one time in the American Northeast. "Gothic magnificence and eerie manifestations" were not limited to "English castles or Southern plantations!"[51] The author's assiduous research and imaginative narrative illuminates both the splendor of New York's aristocracy and the forces challenging that social class.

Dragonwyck begins in late spring 1844 with Miranda's move to the manor amidst mounting tension between the patroons and tenant farmers. At the rent day delivery of goods on the manor grounds (which Seton slyly reschedules to the Fourth of July), one farmer refuses to remove his hat in Van Ryn's presence. "I take my hat off to no man. I'm a free American citizen," he retorts.[52] Neither has he brought the expected rent. The farmer's open defiance leads to his family being evicted and his suicide. The patroons' power over life is one of the novel's central themes, as is the injustice of their authority and concentrated wealth. "The Van Ryns can mince in silks and velvets while I and my children go hungry," comments a farmwoman at an Anti-Rent meeting.[53]

Seton incorporated many actual people and events associated with the movement into the fanciful world of *Dragonwyck*. The Van Ryns hear "Big Bill Snyder" sung to the tune of "Old Dan Tucker" after a frightening chance encounter with "masked figures in lurid calico costumes." A man with tin horn shouts, "We're Indians! We've banded together on the warpath to right a grievous wrong!"[54] Doctor Smith Boughton appears as a close friend of the fictional young doctor who becomes Miranda's alternative love interest. A grand dinner party hosted by Van Ryn has James Fenimore Cooper inveighing against Boughton, "who skulks about preaching rebellion and defiance of the law."[55] The events that led to Boughton's arrest in December 1844 are vividly described; his two trials, life sentence, and pardon are recounted as *Dragonwyck*'s plot unfolds.

Ultimately, Van Ryn's invulnerability and cruel superiority give way to self-delusion and folly. The tenant farmers' success in ending the manor system—represented by Governor Young's election and the revised state constitution—has its corollary in Miranda's growing autonomy and independence. After the patroon's demise by steamboat race, his young widow makes the surprising decision to give away most of the possessions she has inherited.[56] "The land shall go to the farmers, the workers. It's only the workers who have a right to things," Miranda explains.[57] *Dragonwyck* consistently evokes cultural front themes such as the rights of laborers and the dignity of ordinary people and weaves them into a compelling *bildungsroman* of the heroine's moral and emotional development. This was not unusual for Seton, whose many novels posed alternatives to conventional happily-ever-after endings.[58]

The Hollywood studio Twentieth Century Fox quickly bought the film rights from Seton, releasing an adaptation of *Dragonwyck* in 1946. The screenplay was written by Joseph Mankiewicz, who also made his directorial debut with the film. Top billing went to Gene Tierney as Miranda and Walter Huston as her father. The budding villain Vincent Price inhabited the role of Nicholas Van Ryn with haunting arrogance. Alfred Newman composed the lush, melodramatic score.

Although much of the novel's specific Anti-Rent content is inevitably diluted or omitted, the setting and many of its key issues and elements are preserved. For example, the New England freeholder's self-sufficiency is contrasted with the Hudson Valley tenants' dependency early in the film. Miranda's father, who embodies Yankee independence, is appalled to learn of the patroon system. In a close paraphrase of the novel, he declares, "As a farmer I'd rather own one half-acre of barren rock free and clear than work the richest land in the world for someone else" (12:20).[59] Other elements are enhanced in the film through their visualization or narrative reworking. One man's unwillingness to remove his hat "in the presence of the patroon" on rent day foreshadows a parallel scene at the film's climax. A crowd is once again gathered on the manor grounds. This time, however, the people have assembled to witness the patroon's arrest for murder. A delusional Van Ryn threatens them with drawn pistol. Before he can fire, he's mortally wounded by shots from the crowd. The men begin to take off their hats out of respect for the dying man. With his last breath, Van Ryn sneers, "That's right, take off your hats in the presence of the patroon" (1:38:00–1:40:00). His victory is Pyrrhic; the deference Van Ryn had always demanded is now freely given, but he can no longer savor it. Although the patroon's death in the film is completely different from his demise in the novel, a similar sentiment is conveyed.

Another element enhanced in the film owes its power to Newman's score. In the novel, the spirit of a deceased Van Ryn matriarch haunts Dragonwyck. The unhappy ancestor is said to laugh whenever misfortune comes to "this house of hatred."[60] Outsiders cannot hear the sound, but it haunts the patroon. Newman's several cues for the spirit become progressively more intense. Her presence is represented by a weird mix of sounds from the family harpsichord, soprano vocalise, sustained strings, and effects. Various components were recorded on separate channels then mixed slightly out-of-sync, producing strange timbres.[61] Major cues end with the lingering dissonant resonance of struck piano strings. The spirit's audible manifestations, which contribute to Van Ryn's demise in both novel and film, are significantly elaborated in the latter. No doubt, Newman's score helped make *Dragonwyck* the thirty-seventh top-grossing film of 1946.[62] New editions of both book and movie have appeared in recent years, extending the Anti-Rent movement's legacy of aesthetic works into the twenty-first century.[63]

The culminating non-fiction work of Anti-Rent's centennial phase was *Tin Horns and Calico*. Henry Christman was immediately recognized for bringing eloquence, remarkable insight, and "careful investigation of the sources" to his subject by the *New York Times*.[64] Granville Hicks observed that in providing the first "adequate history" of the Anti-Rent movement, *Tin Horns and Calico* made a more accurate understanding of the period's literature possible, and of Cooper's Littlepage trilogy in particular.[65] Carl Carmer anticipated such responses in his introduction while emphasizing Anti-Rent's larger and lasting implications in populist terms. He lauded Christman for showing that the movement's goals were accomplished not by great men but by "earnest citizens of less than average means whose chief weapon was a burning belief in the rightness of their cause." *Tin Horns and Calico*'s tale of the democratic spirit's triumph "over the unjustified pretensions of aristocracy," was timely because "to this day our country is far from free" from similar claims.[66] Carmer's hope that the book would inspire another era of aesthetic expression was realized in numerous regional productions and works. One of the most sustained efforts was linked to another populist initiative, folksong advocacy.

Upstate Folk Spirit

As early as 1941, participants at Camp Woodland in Phoenicia, New York, created theatrical works inspired by the Anti-Rent movement. Their efforts led to the presentation of a full-length musical play, *On Dingle Hill*, in 1958. The play, written by Norman Studer and with music by Norman Cazden, was featured at the Eighteenth Annual Folk Festival of the Catskills. The yearly festivals were sponsored by Camp Woodland until its dissolution in 1962. In keeping with the camp's goals, they often featured "a cantata based on local materials, with a camper chorus of a hundred voices and an orchestral accompaniment."[67]

Studer was a cofounder of Camp Woodland and its director for more than twenty years. The not-for-profit summer retreat had a progressive mission: to immerse New York City children of all backgrounds in the "rich ecology of the Catskill region for two months each summer. The curriculum and experience of Camp Woodland were deeply rooted in the folklore and folk culture of the Catskill Mountains."[68] From the start, Studer organized field trips that brought campers into contact with local culture-bearers. Folksong collection was a major initiative under camp music directors Herbert Haufrecht and Norman Cazden. They both incorporated elements of folk music into their original compositions, and Cazden published collections of traditional songs and dances. The three men's shared interests led to their monumental *Folk Songs of the Catskills*, "an annotated documentation of the traditional ballads and songs collected under the auspices of Camp Woodland."[69]

Inevitably, Studer and his colleagues learned of the patroon system. The property deed to Camp Woodland showed it occupied "Great Lot No. 8 of the Hardenbergh patent," which was originally granted by Queen Anne "to a group of favorites in a transaction that reeked of corruption and set the stage for generations of bickering over titles."[70] The folklorists and campers heard about the Anti-Renters directly from the current generation. "The fathers and mothers of many of the old men and women whom we interviewed in the Catskills had been involved in the struggle, and they gave their children an eye witness account." Camp Woodland sponsored short plays that shared the title "Down Rent" in the early 1940s. An early effort was based on "materials gathered from people . . . in the Woodstock area, and was presented at the Grange Hall at Mt. Tremper." With the 1945 pageant at Andes, Studer became focused on the episode at the Earle farm. "We spent many summers ferreting out this story" in the vicinity, he recalled. "Each year we took a group of campers to the Hubble farm, where Mrs. Harry Hubble brought out an old calico Indian costume her grandfather wore that day on Dingle Hill."[71] Studer's fieldwork included interviews, site visits, and artifacts. He wrote a short story and musical play that put Parthenia Davis, an adult member of the Earle household, at the center of events.[72] The musical play, *On Dingle Hill*, debuted at the Phoenicia Playhouse on August 17, 1958, with "some of the songs that grew out of the struggle."[73]

Unfortunately, none of Norman Cazden's music for the play is available. However, we can get a sense of how music was used from Studer's typed script.[74] Most of the songs are incorporated

Table 4.1. Songs of *On Dingle Hill* by Norman Studer, et al. Norman Studer Papers, M. E. Grenander Special Collections and Archives, University at Albany, SUNY.

Title, first line, or refrain	Performers
Act 1	
"Ballad of Dingle Hill"	Narrator, soloist, chorus
"Hungry for Earth We Came to These Hills"	Moses Earle, soloists, chorus
"Freedom We Asked of the Hemlocked Hills"	Moses Earle, chorus
"How Can I Keep From Thinking"	Parthenia, girls chorus
"What a Wonderful Spot for a Picnic"	Parthenia, Warren
"Fourth of July Song"	Chorus
*"Big Bill Snyder"	Chorus
*"Haste to Delhi"	(Spoken) voice
Act 2	
"What Do You Hear on Dingle Hill?"	Narrator, soloist, chorus
"Warren Scudder's Song"	Soloist
"Make Haste to the Polls"	Female trio, chorus
"March Winds Crust the Melting Snow . . ."	
"What Do You Hear on Dingle Hill?"	Narrator, soloist, chorus
"The Clarion of Freedom"	Unspecified
"Freedom We Asked of the Hemlocked Hills" (short reprise)	Chorus, narrator 2, all

*Anti-Rent period contrafactum

into the twenty-seven-page script; additional numbers and details are appended on another seven pages. My table combines all this information, indicating the songs' titles, performing forces, and sequence. All but two—the Anti-Rent period contrafacta—have original lyrics by Studer. In addition to the sung numbers, music sometimes accompanies spoken word, an underscoring technique used in mid-twentieth-century American cantatas of the period. Studer's play opens with "The Ballad of Dingle Hill" for chorus and unspecified soloist, followed by a scene at the Earle home. A Fourth of July gathering in a local grove allows for speeches by several of the movement's leading figures. "Big Bill Snyder" is incorporated into the confrontation with Osman Steele. The first act ends with "Haste to Delhi" outside Judge Parker's courtroom, where the Anti-Renters are sentenced harshly. The second act follows fugitive Anti-Renter Warren Scudder into his hiding place in a nearby cave and locals' preparations for a political rally. Time passes, the pardoned prisoners are welcomed home, and Scudder emerges with a marriage proposal for Parthenia. (In Studer's short story, she holds progressive opinions about women's equality and anticipates living independently as a teacher.) After Scudder assures her that they won't need to live in a cave, Parthenia accepts his proposal. The chorus concludes with, "Our winter of terror is over at last."

> We'll plow the hillside fields again,
> Plant the seed and harvest the hay;
> Walk in freedom on land of our own,
> The promise of Amerikay.

As far as I have ascertained, *On Dingle Hill* had only one performance. Studer and the other author-editors of *Folksongs of the Catskills* acknowledge the Anti-Rent movement's importance but give scant attention to its songs. Readers are instead referred to Christman's collection of lyrics, many of which "continue to be sung in the Catskill region, if only in snatches."[75]

From Child's Play to Tactical Performance

Camp Woodland was at the vanguard of the folksong movement's focus on youth. Advocates such as Pete Seeger increasingly directed their efforts toward young people in the face of political harassment during the 1950s.[76] One outcome was the incorporation of folksong and "people's history" into progressive education, as is evident in the next phase of Anti-Rent-inspired works: productions with school-age children. In the mid-1970s, schoolteacher Richard Weeks developed a play with students titled *When the Bough Breaks*. Henry Christman assisted with the research, and Arthur Gregg "lent a tin horn" for the show, which was developed at the Heldeberg Workshop [*sic*] in Voorheesville.[77] Participants sang "The Helderberg War Song," which was based on a poem reprinted in *Tin Horns and Calico*.[78] "Hark in the mountains I hear a great roar / Those Helderberg farmers are at it once more," it begins. Several performances took place at the Voorheesville high school in August 1974 and May 1975. Weeks expanded the play to include adults, leading to a half-dozen performances at Five Rivers Environmental Education Center's outdoor amphitheater in Albany County, August–September 1975. Five Rivers hosted another half-dozen performances for the US bicentennial in July 1976.[79]

Fifteen years later, another Anti-Rent play for schoolchildren, *Until Our Rightful Day*, was developed by Voorheesville village historian Dennis Sullivan. The author wanted "kids to get involved in history" by creating a work for the 150th anniversary of the Helderberg conflict. The production came together in May 1991 with about fifty fourth-graders from the Voorheesville Elementary School, a hired director, and the contributions of teachers, parents, and community theater volunteers. Students also performed *Until Our Rightful Day* at neighboring schools "so the hill and valley towns would learn about our common cultural experience," said Sullivan.[80] Among the adult participants was the folksinger George Ward, who wrote and performed an original song at the shows. Its title is the first line of the song's chorus.

Old Horns, Proud Horns,
Songs of long ago;
Stand up for what is right and true,
Hear the tin horns blow.[81]

The message and catchy tune of "Old Horns, Proud Horns" were a good fit for both Until Our Rightful Day and the future theatrical productions, . . . *of the People and Down with the Rent!*

A different type of commemoration was held amidst the educational activities at Hoags Corners in the town of Nassau, Rensselaer County. From 1984 to 1994, locals deemed the Fourth of July "Big Thunder Day." The annual community festival was named for Doctor Smith Boughton, who addressed the Anti-Renters at Hoags Corners on July 4, 1844. With input from New York State Museum historians Philip Lord and Ed Winslow, residents reenacted the historic confrontation. Rensselaer County's current sheriff good-naturedly represented the law, and the defiant tenant farmers were rescued by Calico Indians. The day-long celebration on Diane Maguire's farm included a parade, militia drills, and live music. According to the Albany *Times Union*, hundreds attended every year. As one enthusiastic parent described, "it gives the kids a sense of history, about how this land became a part of the people.[82]

A few years later, Rensselaerville was the site of a more formal "costumed reenactment." An original Anti-Rent musical, . . . *of the People* was performed a half-dozen times in summer 1997. Written and directed by Richard Creamer of Impulse Theatre and Dance, the show featured a cast of twenty-one children, teens, and adults and was partially funded by the New York State Council on the Arts. George Ward arranged the music, performed on a variety of instruments, and sang with the cast. A live recording of the show's musical numbers was made during a performance and later sold to benefit Impulse Theatre and Dance.[83] The repertory included Ward's "Old Horns, Proud Horns," four period Anti-Rent songs, and five new settings of Anti-Rent poetry created by Ward. Seventeen years later, these songs would form the musical foundation of Old Songs' *Down with the Rent!*

Andy Spence, the creator of *Down with the Rent!*, described its genesis in an interview just prior to the pandemic shutdown. Like me, she first learned about the Anti-Rent movement after moving to the region. By the time Spence began developing the show, she had collaboratively created and produced two works of musical folk theater with Old Songs members. Those shows focused on the Adirondack Mountains and Civil War Era, respectively.[84] Various colleagues—especially the environmental activist Louis Ismay—urged Spence to create a similar work about the Anti-Renters.

With the generous assistance of several people involved in the 1990s productions, Spence gathered materials, undertook extensive research, and developed a script. She also constructed face masks with genuine antlers and a cloth backdrop depicting a Helderberg sunset for the stage.

Spence's script eloquently tells the Anti-Rent story, from its seventeenth-century origins in Dutch and English land appropriations to the death of Stephen Van Rensselaer III and the tenant farmers' subsequent rent strike. The narration succinctly describes all the high points of the struggle—from the Anti-Renters' initial organization in 1839 through the revision of the state constitution in 1846—and briefly touches on some of its lasting consequences. Each narrative segment leads to one or more songs delivered by varying instrumental and vocal forces. Some of these segments are acted out in short sketches with costumes and props.

Four period Anti-Rent songs shared with . . . *of the People* were incorporated into *Down with the Rent!*: "The End of Bill Snyder," "We Will Be Free," "Haste to Delhi," and "The Landlord's Lament." "The Halderbarak Quick Step" served as an overture, and George Ward closed the Old Songs' show with his composition, "Old Horns, Proud Horns." These six titles will already be familiar to readers. Ward wrote new music for another three songs, and four of the songs using preexisting tunes that he created for . . . *of the People* were repurposed. Six of those seven texts were drawn from the collection of songs and ballads in Christman's *Tin Horns and Calico*. Ward's three original tunes are settings of "Lay Down the Murderous Musket," "Come All True Anti-Renters," and "The Brave Indian" (plate 6). The poems he set to traditional tunes include "A Great Revolution," "Native's Enquiry," and "The Prisoners in Jail" (plate 20).[85] For the fourth, "On Reidsville Hill," Ward used the Anglo-American folksong "The Girl I Left Behind." He was apparently unaware of the poem's association with "True Thomas" when it appeared in the *New York Herald* in 1839 (plates 1a–c). To sum up, George Ward composed or arranged eight of the twenty-one different songs performed in *Down with the Rent!* These were interspersed with the five period Anti-Rent works and additional numbers appropriate to the era.[86]

Andy Spence and her collaborators are well-aware that their show was unique in many ways. The all-adult cast and target audience allowed a complex narrative that "encompassed the history recorded in local newspapers of the time and kept alive with stories and lore," Spence told the *Altamont Enterprise* in 2014. "We'd like to be able to perform it around. We'd like to bring history alive, again."[87] Old Songs realized that goal with a dozen performances at nine venues throughout the region. For me, the most thrilling moment in *Down with the Rent!* was when the stately Greg Clarke, in top hat and elegant jacket, delivered "The Landlord's Lament" (plate 30). Clarke haughtily snorted and stomped his gentleman's cane to emphasize the landlord's indignation through the song's satirical verses, which he sang a cappella. In retrospect, this was a gestic moment: the frivolity of a children's song is juxtaposed with the seriousness of the patroon's grievances, underscoring his fading power. Clarke's rich baritone and exaggerated movements embodied the unsustainable social relations that precipitated the Anti-Rent movement. The contrast of tune and text perfectly encapsulates the story conveyed in *Down with the Rent!* The playful show was about people compelled to play for high stakes.

"The Landlord's Lament" can also be understood in terms of what L. M. Bogad calls "tactical performance," the use of theatrical elements for political protest. One of the strengths of *Down with the Rent!* is that it vividly conveys the Anti-Renters' pioneering use of "sociodrama" for the purpose of effecting change.[88] The masks, calico gowns, and tin horns had the immediate, practical use of warning and camouflage. But they were also tools for staging disruptive actions, such as distress auctions where no one bid, the ritualized seizing and burning of writs, and other acts of living theater. Music was part of the play, providing mood and commentary—rallying spirits, recounting genealogies, taunting antagonists, mourning losses. The songs and sounds of the Anti-Renters, their allies, on-lookers—and even detractors—were the aesthetic expressions of one of the great nineteenth-century reform movements. We would do well to listen closely.

Part 2

Musical and Lyrical Works

List of Works

Plates

1a. "The Route of Reidsville." *New York Herald*, December 14, 1839.

1b. "True Thomas." *Minstrelsy of the Scottish Border*, in Walter Scott and John Gibson Lockhart, *The Poetical Works of Sir Walter Scott* (Philadelphia: E. L. Carey and A. Hart, 1839), 195.

1c. "The Route of Reidsville" set to "True Thomas."

2. "The Dutchman's Dirge over His Dead Pig" and "Barthram's Dirge" (abridged), compared. *New York Herald*, December 16, 1839; and Walter Scott, *Minstrelsy of the Scottish Border*, 85.

3a. "The Bloody Battle at Clarksville Ale House" and "The Battle of Pentland Hills," compared. *New York Herald*, December 16, 1839; and Walter Scott, *Minstrelsy of the Scottish Border*, 100.

3b. "Pentlend Hills." James Oswald, *The Caledonian Pocket Companion* (London: Straight & Skillern, [1770?]), 12:157. Image reused under the Creative Commons Attribution 4.0 International License and reproduced with the permission of the National Library of Scotland, NLS shelf-mark: Ing.75.

3c. "The Bloody Battle at Clarksville Ale House" set to "Pentland Hills."

4a. "Marcy's March" and "Lesly's March," compared. *New York Herald*, December 16, 1839; and Walter Scott, *Minstrelsy of the Scottish Border*, 93–94.

4b. "Lasly's March." James Oswald, *The Caledonian Pocket Companion*, 6 vols. (London: printed for the author, [1747?]), 36. Image reused under the Creative Commons Attribution 4.0 International License and reproduced with the permission of the National Library of Scotland, NLS shelf-mark: Glen 223.

4c. "Marcy's March" set to "Lasly's March."

5. "Halderbarak Quick Step." Composed and respectfully dedicated to the Ladies of Rensellear Ville [*sic*] by a member of the Troy Citizens Corps (New York: Hewitt & Jaques, 1840). Courtesy of the American Antiquarian Society.

6. "The Brave Indian." As transcribed in Christman, *Tin Horns and Calico*, 328–29.

7a. "The Horrible Murder of Bill Snyder." Broadside, figure 2.1.

7b. "Old Dan Tucker." Words by Old Dan D. Emmit, as sung by the Virginia Minstrels (Boston: C. H. Keith, 1843). Courtesy of the Lester S. Levy Collection of Sheet Music, Sheridan Libraries, Johns Hopkins University.

7c. "Bill Snyder" set to "Old Dan Tucker."

8a. "The Working Men's League." *Working Man's Advocate*, May 25, 1844.

8b. "The Working Men's League" set to "Old Dan Tucker."

9a. "The Agrarian Ball." *Working Man's Advocate*, June 8, 1844.

9b. "Old Rosin the Beau." Arranged by J. C. Beckell (Philadelphia: Osbourn's Music Saloon, 1838). Courtesy of the Lester S. Levy Collection of Sheet Music, Sheridan Libraries, Johns Hopkins University.

9c. "The Agrarian Ball" set to "Rosin the Beau."

10a. "We Are True Anti-Renters." Broadside, figure 2.2.

10b. "The Teetotallers Are Coming." William Bradbury, ed., *Temperance Chimes* (New York: National Temperance Society, 1867).

10c. "We Are True Anti-Renters" set to "The Teetotallers Are Coming."

11. Lyric No. 1, "Ye Sons of Tuscarora." Broadside, figure 2.3.

12a. Lyric No. 2, "With His Mask upon His Brow" and "With Helmet on His Brow," compared. Broadside, figure 2.3; and J. R. Planché, *The Posie . . .* Part 3 (Glasgow: Francis Orr and Sons, 1830), 37.

12b. "Le petit tambour." *The Sky-Lark: A Collection of Songs Set to Music* (London: Thomas Tegg, 1825), 188. Image reused under the Creative Commons Attribution 4.0 International License and reproduced with the permission of the National Library of Scotland, NLS shelf-mark: Glen.110.

12c. "With His Mask upon His Brow" set to "Le petit tambour."

13a. "Downfall of Feudalism." *Working Man's Advocate*, May 31, 1845.

13b. "Blue Eyed Mary," a favorite song for the piano forte (Philadelphia: G. Willig's Musical Magazine, ca. 1817).

13c. "Downfall of Feudalism" set to "Blue Eyed Mary."

14a. "The Native's Enquiry." *Albany Freeholder*, July 2, 1845.

14b. "Bruce's Address to His Army," a favorite Scotch song (Philadelphia: G. Willig's Musical Magazine, n.d). Courtesy of the Lester S. Levy Collection of Sheet Music, Sheridan Libraries, Johns Hopkins University.

14c. "The Native's Enquiry" set to "Bruce's Address."

15a. "Hail to the Glorious Birth-day of the Nation." *Albany Freeholder*, July 2, 1845.

15b. "Hail to the Chief," Chorus, *Lady of the Lake*. Composed by James Sanderson (New York: Wm. Dubois, 1817 or 1818).

15c. "Hail to the Glorious Birth-day of the Nation" set to "Hail to the Chief."

16a. "Hardy Tillers of the Soil." *Albany Freeholder*, July 2, 1845.

16b. "Hardy Tillers of the Soil" set to "Bruce's Address."

17a. "The Farmer's Song." *Young America*, July 5, 1845.

17b. "A Life on the Ocean Wave." Composed by Henry Russell, words by Epes Sargent (New York: Hewitt & Jaques, 1838), 1–4.

17c. "The Farmer's Song" set to "A Life on the Ocean Wave."

18. "In Days of Yore." *Albany Freeholder*, July 9, 1845.

19a. "We Will Be Free." *Albany Freeholder*, July 9, 1845.

19b. "De Boatmen's Dance." An original banjo melody by Old Dan. D. Emmit, leader of the Virginia Minstrels (Boston: C. H. Keith, 1843). Courtesy of the Lester S. Levy Collection of Sheet Music, Sheridan Libraries, Johns Hopkins University.

19c. "We Will Be Free" set to "De Boatmen's Dance."

20. "The Prisoners in Jail." *Albany Freeholder*, July 9, 1845.

21a. "An Anti-Rent Song." *Albany Freeholder*, July 9, 1845.

21b. "Caroline and Her Brisk Young Sailor Boy." Transcription by F. L. Guyer, in the George Gardiner Manuscript Collection, Vaughan Williams Memorial Library. Licensed from the English Folk Dance and Song Society.

21c. "An Anti-Rent Song" set to "Bold Caroline."

22a. "The Contest." *Albany Freeholder*, August 6, 1845.

22b. "The Contest" set to "Bruce's Address."

23. "Dere vos a Time," transliteration. *Albany Freeholder*, October 8, 1845.

24a. "Haste to Delhi." *Young America*, November 22, 1845.

24b. "Haste to Delhi" set to "Bruce's Address."

25. "Come Join the Anti-Renters." *Albany Freeholder*, May 20, 1846.

26a. Anti-Rent Song, "This Great Commotion." Broadside, figure 3.2.

26b. "Tippecanoe and Tyler Too!" A Comic Glee, excerpt (Philadelphia: G. E. Blake, 1840). Music for the Nation, American Sheet Music, 1820–1860, Library of Congress, Music Division.

26c. "The Little Pigs." A Favorite Comic Glee. Composed by Alexander Lee (Boston: C. Bradlee, ca. 1835). Courtesy of the Lester S. Levy Collection of Sheet Music, Sheridan Libraries, Johns Hopkins University.

26d. "This Great Commotion" set to "Tippecanoe and Tyler Too!"

27a. "Keep Thy Spirit, Swell Thy Faith." *Albany Freeholder*, October 28, 1846.

27b. "Salt River Chorus." George Washington Clark, arr., *The Free Soil Minstrel* (New York: Martyn & Ely, 1848), 19–20.

27c. "Keep Thy Spirit" set to "Cheer Up My Lively Lads."

28a. "Rouse, Ye Anti-Renters, Wake!" *Albany Freeholder*, October 28, 1846.

28b. "Rouse, Ye Anti-Renters, Wake!" set to "Bruce's Address."

29a. "Anti-Rent Song of Triumph." *Albany Freeholder*, December 9, 1846.

29b. "Anti-Rent Song of Triumph" set to "Old Dan Tucker."

30a. "The Land Lord's Lament." *Albany Freeholder*, December 30, 1846.

30b. "Oh Dear, What Can the Matter Be" (New York: E. Riley, ca. 1823).

30c. "The Land Lord's Lament" set to "Oh Dear, What Can the Matter Be."

In accordance with the suggestion of our correspondent,
we here give a border ballad, illustrative of the late onslaught
of the sheriff in the Hilderbarrack hills.

On Reidsville hill a fray began,
    At Clark's Ale House it ended,
The Dutch out o'er the soldiers ran,
    Sae merrily they bended.

The sheriff from the city came,
    Wi' young Prince John came he,
The young, the old, the blind, the lame,
    They bore him good company.

They reached the Helderbarrack hill,
    Said the sheriff, "I see one farm
Where I must seize, for good or ill,
    Therefore we'll sing a psalm."

When they came to the Reidsville hill,
    As daylight did appear,
The[y] spied an aged Dutchman,
    And he did draw them near.

"Come hither, aged Dutchman,"
    The sheriff he did cry.
"And tell where are your stout men
    With all their great army?"

"But virst you moust gum dell do me
    If vrends or voes you be;
I hear you be de shorief's moin,
    Gum up from Albany."

"But first you must come tell to me
    If friends or foes you be;
I hear you be the sheriff's men,
    Come up from Albany."

"And hif you be de shorief,
    As I do dink you be,
Hoim sorre you has bring'd so vew,
    Mid your bad gompanee."

"And if you be the sheriff,
    As I do think you be,
I'm sorry you have brought so few,
    With your bad company."

"Dere's joist den dousend Dutchmen,
    Stand vast upon de hill,
Dey'll make kold jhunks of all your men
    Dey won't dere bellies fill."

"There's just ten thousand Dutchmen,
    Stand fast upon the hill,
They'll make cold chunks [?] of all your men
    They want their bellies full."

97

Then up spoke Marcy sadly,
    "For the Dutchmen I'm a match,
I've tore my breeches badly;
    They must give me a patch."

Then up spoke Prince John after,
    "The Dutch girls to me hight"—*
(He spoke midst shouts of laughter,)
    "To sleep with them this night."

"O march men," cried the sheriff,
    "And mind not all this rain;
If the Dutch do not surrender,
    We'll all march back again."

The Dutchmen dared them all to shoot,
    And threatened them to kill,
They ran, and stopt but at the foot,
    Of Helderbarrack hill.

And there Prince John did take a drink
    And Marcy, he drank too;
And said, "Good troth, I truly think,
    We'll ne'er reach Westerloo."

"To Small Potatoes we will send
    For troops these Dutch to fight,
And then I will my breeches mend,
    And sleep away the night."

Now let us all for Prince John pray,
    And Marcy, long live he;
Although they had the worst that day
    With that Dutch company.

---

*"Promised"

TRUE THOMAS.

THE ANCIENT TUNE.

99

Plate 1c. "The Route of Reidsville" set to "True Thomas."

On Reids - ville hill a - fray be - gan, At

Clark's Ale House _____ it end - ed, The

Dutch out o'er the _____ sol - diers ran, Sae _____

mer - ri - ly they _____ bend - ed.

Plate 2. "The Dutchman's Dirge over His Dead Pig" and "Barthram's Dirge" (abridged), compared.

"The Dutchman's Dirge over His Dead Pig"
(after the manner of "Bartham's Dirge")

"Barthram's Dirge" (abridged)

Dey shot him dead at the Hel'burgh hill,
Vere de Reidsville roads do cross,
And dey leave him lay dare mid his blood,
And never pay for de loss.

They shot him dead at the Nine Stone Rig
Beside the Headless Cross
And they left him lying in his blood,
Upon the moor and moss
***

Dey made a bier of de broken bough,
De pine and de birch tree gray:
And dey bore him to de old pig trough,
And leave him dere all day.

They made a bier of the broken bough,
The sauch and the aspen gray,
And they bore him to the Lady Chapel,
And waked him there all day.

A sow pig came to dat old trough,
And throw'd her ears aside,
She grunted all day, did dat same old sow,
And she laid by the boar pig's side.

A lady came to that lonely bower,
And threw her robes aside,
She tore her ling (long) yellow hair,
And knelt at Barthram's side.

But ve laid dat pig in de vater hot,
From his skin scraped the bristles, free,
Ve boil'd his ears in de iron pot,
And good lard of his fat mad ve.

She bathed him in the Lady-Well,
His wounds so deep and sair,
And she plaited a garland for his breast,
And a garland for his hair.

Ve roasted a spare rib and pickled his feet,
And his sides ve salted down,
And de vrow she made some sausage meat,
Of de scraps 'twix his tail and his crown.

They rowed him in a lily-sheet,
And bare him to his earth,
(And the Gray Friars sung the dead man's mass,
As they pass'd the Chapel Garth.)
[Two verses omitted]

And dat pig's meat in de chimney hung,
And it lasted for many a day,
And long shall dat pig's merits be sung,
Who fell in de Reidsville fray.

A Gray Friar staid upon the grave,
And sang till the morning tide,
And a friar shall sing for Barthram's soul,
While the Headless Cross shall bide.

Plate 3a. "The Bloody Battle at Clarksville Ale House" and "The Battle of Pentland Hills," compared.

"The Bloody Battle at Clarksville Ale House"

"The Battle of Pentland Hills"

This celebrated ballad, like Scott's ballad, the battle of Pentland Hills, is "copied verbatim from an old woman's recitation."

This Ballad is copied verbatim from the old Woman's Recitation

Oh! The gallant troops came from New York,
To steal our chickens and eat our pork,
The New York lads they marched slow,
To be at the Clarksville ale house row.

The gallant Grahams cam from the west,
Wi' their horses black as ony craw;
The Lothian lads they marched fast,
To be at the Rhyns o' Gallows.

'Twixt Helderbergh and New York town,
The lads marched on but their heads hung down.
Coblers and tailors unto them drew,
Their covenants for to renew.

Betwixt Dumfries town and Argyle,
The lads they marched many a mile;
Souters and tailors unto them drew,
Their covenants for to renew.

The locos they wi' their merry crack,
Gar'd the poor soldiers to turn their back,
But aye sinsyn [since long] they do repent,
The renewing o' their covenant.

The Whigs, they, wi' their merry cracks,
Gar'd the poor pedlars lay down their pack
But aye sinsyne they do repent
The renewing o' their Covenant.

In New York Park, where they were reviewed,
Two thousand men in broad cloth shew'd;
But ere they came in the Dutchmen's sight,
The half o' them ran back in fright.

At the Mauchline muir, where they were review'd,
Ten thousand men in armour show'd;
But, ere they came to the Brockie's burn.
The half of them did back return.

General Sandford, as I hear tell,
Was their great Major General;
And General Morris, with wit and skill,
Was to guide them over the Held'burgh hill.

General Dalyell as I hear tell,
Was our lieutenant-general;
And Captain Welsh, wi' his wit and skill,
Was to guide them on to the Pentland hill.

They met the Dutchmen on the hill,
And asked them what was their will;
And who gave them this protestation
To rise in arms against the nation.

General Dalyell held to the hill,
Asking at them what was their will;
And who gave them this protestation,
To rise in arms against the nation?

"Aldough we all dus drawn up be,
Dis not aging de law's majesty;
Nor yoit do shbill our neighbor's blade,
But mid de Bateroon we'll konkluée."*

"Although we all in armour be,
It's not against his majesty;
Nor yet to spill our neighbour's bluid,
But wi' the country we ll conclude"—

102

"Surrender," says Sandford, "in the Sheriff's name,
And ye shall a'gang safely hame,"
But they all cried out with one consent
"Ve'll fight before ve pay back rent."

"O well," says Morris, "since it is so,
A wilfu' man e'er wanted wo;"
He gave a sign to the New York lads,
And they drew up wi' their brigades.

The Dutch horns blew, and the stones they flew,
And the New York soldiers ran too;
And Morris was never so much aghast,
As to find his little legs run so fast.

The National Greys stood in the van,
But Sandford took to his heels and ran,
Nor he, nor Morris, once "drew rein"
Till they reached Clark's tavern once again.

There were three pigs killed, and four fowls stole,
And in many a breech there was many a hole;
And the troops that night, in that little inn,
Drowned their sorrows in good Dutch gin.

Oh! many a Dutch girl, many a day,
Will remember, who saw, the Clarksville fray!
For such raking and running never was seen,
As the raking and running of Clarksville Green.

"Lay down your arms, in the King's name,
And ye shall a' gae safely hame;"—
But they a' cried out wi' ae consent,
"We'll fight for a broken Covenant."—

"O well," says he, "since it is so,
A wilfu' man never wanted wo."
He then gave a sign unto his lads,
And they drew up in their brigades.

The trumpets blew, and the colours flew,
And every man to his armour drew;
The Whigs were never so much aghast,
As to see their saddles toom+ sae fast.

The cleverest men stood in the van,
The Whigs they took their heels and ran;
But such a raking was never seen
As the raking o' the Rullien Green.

_____

+Toom = empty
*Transliteration:
"Although we all thus drawn up be,
It's not against the law's majesty;
Nor yet to spill our neighbor's blade,
But with the Patroon we'll concluded be."

103

Pentlend Hills

157

Slow

Plate 3c. "The Bloody Battle at Clarksville Ale House" set to "Pentland Hills."

Oh! The gallant troops came from New York, To steal our

chieckens and eat our pork, The New York lads they marched

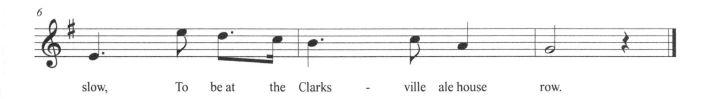

slow, To be at the Clarks - ville ale house row.

Plate 4a. "Marcy's March" and "Lesly's March," compared.

"Marcy's March"	"Lesly's March"

March! March!
   Why the devil do ye na march!
Stand to your broomsticks, lads,
Fight in disorder;
   Front about, do not play,
   Never say, "Well a day,"
   None of you run away,
Till you come to the Helderbergher.

   Stand still and look like men
   The sheriff to maintain
The Dutchmen are frightened to see us a'coming;
   The pigs and poultry seize
Kiss the girls, pocket the cheese,
Too much time has been spent now in running and dunning.
   When to the farms we come,
   We'll levy on every room,
And in the Dutch petticoats make innovation;
That a' the world may see,
There's none i' the right but we
Of the American nation.

   I'll get a Dutch girl's shift
   Prince John he will lift*
Petticoats, sarks, or whate'er he can gather;
   We will flog
   Every Dutch hog,
   Kiss their vrows
   Kill their sows,
Knock down the one and knock up the other.

The fowls so braw,
We'll hae them a'
Whatever come on it;
So come my boys,
Make a noise
And kiss the dear Dutch girls beneath their sma' bonnets.

March! March!
   Why the devil do ye na march?
Stand to your arms, my lads,
Fight in good order;
   Front about, ye musketeers all,

Till ye come to the English Border;

   Stand till't and fight like men,
   True gospel to maintain.
The parliament's blythe to see us a-coming.

   When to the kirk we come,
   We'll purge it ilka room,
Frae popish relics, and a' sic innovation,
That a' the world may see,
There's nane in the right but we,
Of the auld Scottish nation.

   Jenny shall wear the hood,
   Jocky the sark of God;
And the kist-fou of whistles,
That mak sic a cleiro,

Our pipers braw
Shall hae them a,'
Whate'er come on it:
Busk up your plaids, my lads!

Cock up your bonnets!
Da Capo.

---

*A [–] word for plundering or carrying off.

Plate 4b. "Lasly's March."

Plate 4c. "Marcy's March" set to "Lasly's March."

March! March! Why the dev-il do ye __ na march! _____ Stand to your

broom-sticks lads, __ Fight in dis-or-der; _____ Front a-bout, do not play,

_____ Ne-ver say, "well a day," _____ None of you run a-way,

Till _____ you come to the Hel-der-bergh-er. _____ Stand still and

look like men The sher-iff to main-tain _____ The Dutch-men are

fright-ened to see us a' com-ing; _____ The pigs and the poul-try seize

_____ Kiss the girls [kiss the girls], pock-et the cheese, Too much time has been spent

now __ in run-ning and dun-ning. _____

108

Plate 5. "Halderbarak Quick Step."

109

Plate 5. Continued.

The Gathering.

Tin Horn Solo.   Tutti. *f*

Tin Horn Solo.   *ff* Tutti.

G.W. Quidor Eng.ʳ

110

Plate 6. "The Brave Indian."

From rocky mountains we are come
To free our lands from slavery,
Never again to see our home
Till we execute our bravery.

CHORUS: A brave Indian ne'er despise,
           Nor count him as a stranger,
           Remember he your country stays
           In the day and hour of danger.

Your pleasant homes you shall enjoy,
We boldly have avowed it,
Your peace the tyrants would destroy,
But we will not allow it.
                    CHORUS: A brave Indian, etc.

Our tawny arm is stretched out still,
To shield you and protect you,
Our dearest blood we'll freely spill,
We never will neglect you.
                    CHORUS: A brave Indian, etc.

Fatiguing marches we'll endure,
That you may dwell in quiet;
Your lands from rent we will secure,
At least we mean to try it.
                    CHORUS: A brave Indian, etc.

At night in peace you need lie down,
Upon your beds to rest you,
But we must wander through the town,
To see that none molest you.
                    CHORUS: A brave Indian, etc.

Don't drive poor Indian from your door,
Nor with disdain reject him,
But give him of your plenties' store,
How cruel to neglect him.
                    CHORUS: A brave Indian, etc.

Plate 7a. "The Horrible Murder of Bill Snyder."
Air—"Old Dan Tucker"

The moon was shining silver bright;
The sheriff came at dead of night;
High on a hill sat an Indian true,
And on his horn, this blast he blew—
        Keep out of the way—big Bill Snyder—
        We'll tar your coat and feather your hide, sir!

The Indians gathered at the sound,
Bill cocked his pistol—looked around—
Their painted faces, by the moon,
He saw, and heard the same old tune—
        Keep out of the way—&c.

Says Bill, "this music's not so sweet
As I have heard—I think my feet
Had better be used," and he started to run,
But the tin horn still kept sounding on
        Keep out of the way—&c.

"Legs! do your duty now," says Bill,
"There's a thousand Indians on the hill—
When they catch tories they tar their coats,
And feather their hides, and I hear the notes"—
        Keep out of the way—&c.

He ran, and he ran, till he reached the wood,
And there, with horror, still he stood;
For he saw a savage, tall and grim,
And he heard a horn, not a rod from him;
        Keep out of the way—&c.

And he thought that he heard the sound of a gun,
And he cried, in his fright, "Oh! my race is run!
Better had it been, had I never been born,
Than to come within the sound of that tin horn,"
        Keep out of the way—&c.

And the news flew round, and gained belief,
That Bill was murdered by an Indian chief,
And no one mourned that Bill was slain,
But the horn sounded on, again and again—
        Keep out of the way—&c.

Next day the body of Bill was found,
His writs were scattered on the ground,
And by his side a jug of rum,
Told how he to his end had come;
    Keep out of the way—&c.

Plate 7b. "Old Dan Tucker."

The Original
OLD DAN TUCKER.

As sung by the

Virginia Minstrels.

Words by Old Dan. D. Emmit.

Boston: Published by C. H. Keith, 67 & 69 Court St.

I come to town de ud-der night, I hear de noise an

saw de fight, De watch-man was a run-nin roun, cry-in Old Dan Tuck-er's

Gran' Chorus.

come to town, So get out de way!   get out de way!

Ent'd according to act of Congress in the year 1843 by C H Keith in the Clerks office of the Dist Court of Mass.
123

114

get out de way! Old Dan Tuck-er your to late to come to sup-per.

2

Tucker is a nice old man,

He use to ride our darby ram;

He sent him whizzen down de hill,

If he had'nt got up he'd lay dar still.

Get out, &c.

3

Here's my razor in good order

Magnum bonum — jis hab bought 'er;

Sheep shell oats, Tucker shell de corn,

I'll shabe you soon as de water get warm.

Get out &c.

4

Ole Dan Tucker an I got drunk,

He fell in de fire an kick up a chunk,

De charcoal got inside he shoe

Lor bless you honey how de ashes flew

Get out &c.

5

Down de road foremost de stump,

Massa make me work de pump;

I pump so hard I broke de sucker,

Dar was work for ole Dan Tucker.

Get out, &c.

6

I went to town to buy some goods

I lost myself in a piece of woods,

De night was dark I had to suffer,

It froze de heel of Daniel Tucker.

Get out &c.

7

Tucker was a hardened sinner,

He nebber said his grace at dinner;

De ole sow squeel, de pigs did squall

He 'hole hog wid de tail and all.

Get out &c.

Plate 7c. "Bill Snyder" set to "Old Dan Tucker."

The__ moon was shin-ing sil-ver bright; The sher-iff came at dead of night;

High on a hill sat an In - dian true, And on his horn, this blast he blew—

Gran' Chorus

Keep out of the way_____ Keep out of the way_____

Keep out of the way, big Bill Snyder, We'll tar your coat and feather your hide, sir!

116

Come all you who are fond of singing,
Let us set a song a ringing;
Sound the chorus, strong and hearty,
And we'll make a jovial party.
    Get out of the way you speculators,
    You shall no longer be dictators.

Some love *Rents* and speculation,
Some with *Banks* would fill the nation;
In a lump we'll class these *critters*,
And we'll call them speculators.
    Get out of the way, &c.

He who lives by labor only,
Ne'er shall find his fireside lonely;
But his home a happy place is,
Blest with cheerful smiling faces.
    Get out of the way, &c.

Interest steals a man's good feelings,
He's a rogue in all his dealings;
Smirks and smiles until he's found you,
Then, O, crackey! How he's bound you.
    Get out of the way, &c.

All who wish for homes to bless them,
All who wish the girls to kiss them,
Hark! while soberness is o'er us,
Here's a song, and this the chorus,
    Get out of the way, &c.

Once we used to *beg to labor*,
Then to toil was thought a favor;
We'll have a home all smiling, sunny,
Without price and without money.
    Get out of the way, &c.

Time was once when honest workers,
Were put upon a par with porkers,*
But now a new reform's beginning,
Selling land is now a sinning.
    Get out of the way, &c.

See the Agrarian Ball a rolling,
Hark! the knell of Avarice tolling!
Roll the ball to every station,
In our own great Yankee nation.
    Push along and keep it moving,
    The People's Cause is still improving.

Satan saw his trade was falling,
Heard no more the orphans' wailing;
Send his imps about us yelling,
"Don't stop! Don't stop! But keep on selling!"
    Get out of the way you old Land Seller,
    You're a loafing, crafty *feller*.

True you once did *price* demand,
For what was Nature's gift, *the Land*;
Boast you may that you have done it,
Reform's on foot, and you can't come it.
    Get out of the way, though you have done it,
    Reform's the word, and you can't come it.

Monopolists now just be a thinking,
No more at such great wrong be winking;
Come on and own that you're mistaken,
Sign the Pledge, and save your bacon.
    Push it along and keep it moving,
    The People's Cause is still improving.

---

*"Swinish multitude"

Plate 8b. "The Working Men's League" set to "Old Dan Tucker."

Come ___ all you who are fond of sing - ing, Let us set a song a ring - ing;

Sound the chor - us, strong and heart - y, ___ And we'll make a jov - ial par - ty.

Gran' Chorus

Get out of the way _____ Get out of the way _____

Get out of the way you spec - u - la - tors, You shall no longer be dic - ta - tors.

Plate 9a. "The Agrarian Ball."
Tune—"Rosin the Bow"

Come all you true friends of the Nation,
    Attend to humanity's call,
Come aid in your country's salvation,
    And roll on the Agrarian Ball.

Ye Democrats come to the rescue,
    And help on the glorious cause,
And millions hereafter will bless you,
    With heart cheering song of applause.

Come Whigs bid adieu to hard cider,
    And boldly step into the ranks,
To spread the proud banner still wider,
    Upset all the [ras]cally banks.

And when we have form'd the blest union,
    We'll firmly march on, one and all,
We'll shout when we meet in communion,
    And roll on the Agrarian Ball.

The Agrarian army's advancing,
    The Monopoly of Land to destroy,
The glad eye of beauty is dancing,
    Her heart's overflowing with joy.

How can you stand halting while beauty
    Is sweetly appealing to all,
Then come to the standard of duty
    And roll on the Agrarian Ball.

Plate 9b. "Old Rosin the Beau."

121

Plate 9b. Continued.

122

Plate 9b. Continued.

2.

When I'm dead and laid out on the counter,
A voice you will hear from below
Singing some plain whiskey and water
To drink to old Rosin the beau.
To drink &c.

3.

And when I am dead I reckon
The ladies will all want to know
Just lift the lid off of the coffin
And look at old Rosin the beau.
And look &c.

4.

I'll have to be buried I'm thinking
And I would like it done just so
And be sure not to go contrary
To the wish of old Rosin the beau.
To the &c.

5.

You must get some dozen good fellows
And stand them all round in a row
And drink out of half gallon bottles
To the name of old Rosin the beau
To the &c.

6.

Get four or five jovial young fellows
And let them all staggering go
And dig a deep hole in the meadow
And in it toss Rosin the beau.
And in it &c.

7.

Then get you a couple of donocks
Place one at my head and my toe
And do not fail to scratch on it
The name of old Rosin the beau.
The name &c.

8.

I feel the grim tyrant approaching
That cruel implacable foe,
Who spares neither age or condition
Nor even old Rosin the beau.
Nor even &c.

Plate 9c. "The Agrarian Ball" set to "Rosin the Beau."

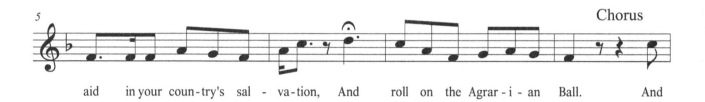

Come all you true friends of the Na-tion, At-tend to hu-man-i-ty's call, Come

Chorus

aid in your coun-try's sal - va-tion, And roll on the Agrar-i-an Ball. And

roll on the Agrar-i-an Ball, _____ And roll on the Agrar-i-an Ball, Come

aid in your coun-try's sal - va-tion, And roll on the Agrar-i-an Ball.

Plate 10a. "We Are True Anti-Renters."
Air—"The Teetotallers Are Coming"

We have met for a convention,
And have many things to mention;
We have met for a convention,
And we'll sound it through the land,
    That we're true anti-renters—
    That we're true anti-renters—
    That we're true anti-renters—
    And we'll sound it through the land.

Unjust rents we have been paying—
So all the world are saying—
To the Patroons for our land;
    But now we're true anti-renters, &c.

But now we mean to stop it,
And Van Rens'laer better drop it;
And we'll sound it through the land,
    For we're true anti-renters, &c.

Our fathers paid their rents in wheat,
And hens, and other things to eat,
For all of their land;
    But we are anti-renters, &c.

Now they want to take our cattle,
With other goods and chattle,
And drive them from our land;
    But they'll find us anti-renters, &c.

Young Stephen thinks it funny,
To make us pay the money;
To have the cash in his hand,
    But we are anti-renters, &c.

But we do not mean to pay it,
And we're not afraid to say it;
And we'll sound it through the land;
    That we're true anti-renters, &c.

We must stick to one another,
As brother should to brother,
All over the land;
    For we're true anti-renters, &c.

Then, surely, we shall beat him,
If like men we do meet him,
Out of all his land;
    For we're anti-renters, &c.

The let us shout, "Down with the rent, my boys!"
And blow our horns and make a noise,
All over the land.
    Then hurra! for the anti-renters, &c.

THE TEETOTALLERS ARE COMING.

1. The tee - to - tal - lers are coming, The tee - to - tal - lers are coming, The tee - to - tal - lers are coming, With the Cold Wa - ter Pledge.

CHORUS.

We're a band of freemen, We're a band of freemen,

Come a band of freemen, We're a band of

freemen, We're a band of freemen, We will sound it thro' the land, Sound it thro' the land.

freemen,

2 We will save our sisters, brothers,
   Our fathers, sons, and mothers,
   Our neighbors and all others,
   With the Cold Water Pledge.

3 We will stop the curse of stilling
   Alcoholic drink for killing,
   And all fermented swilling,

With the Cold Water Pledge.

4 Then come, ye jolly tillers,
   Pedlers, lawyers, doctors, 'stillers,
   Come, jug and bottle fillers,
   Take the Cold Water Pledge.

5 Huzza for reformation
   By all in every station,

Throughout this wide creation,
   With the Cold Water Pledge.

6 May no evil e'er betide us,
   To sever or divide us,
   But the God of mercy guide us,
   With the Cold Water Pledge.

Plate 10c. "We Are True Anti-Renters" set to "The Teetotallers Are Coming."

Plate 11. Lyric No. 1, "Ye Sons of Tuscarora."

Ye sons of Tuscarora, to arms! to arms! advance;
'Tis time to take your guns in hand, and make landholders prance;
    For sixty years our Rents we've paid,
    And not a word against it said,
    Now it's time a settlement's made
        With brave Indian Boys.

We have a gallant chieftain, Tecumseh is his name,
If you are not acquainted you will know him by his fame;
    He is the Indian's joy and pride,
    They'll never be severed from his side,
    But by his fate they will abide
        Like brave Indian Boys.

We never knew the reason these lands could not be sold,
'Till late we found it out, the story soon is told,
    The Deeds they had was to deceive,
    No signer's name could you perceive;
    When this you know you will believe
        The brave Indian Boys.

We advise these British Barons to leave republic land
Before they are surrounded by an angry Indian band,
    For if we get them in our hands
    So closely we will draw their bands
    That they'll be glad to leave their lands
        To brave Indian Boys.

They call us poor rag-muffins, and each disgraceful name;
If we are poor by their oppression I'm sure we're not to blame.
    Our fathers paid their Rents, you see,
    And left their sons in beggary,
    But now we've sworn we will be free,
        Like brave Indian Boys.

We want no treacherous murderers joined to our Indian band,
They always bring destruction when e'er they raise their hand.
    We want brave hearts, that when we try,
    They from our cause will never fly,
    Souls that are not afraid to die,
        Like brave Indian Boys.

Plate 12a. Lyric No. 2, "With His Mask upon His Brow" and "With Helmet on His Brow," compared.
Tune—"With Helmet on His Brow"

"With His Mask upon His Brow"

With his mask upon his brow, and his rifle in his hand,
The Indian marches forth to drive oppression from the
    land;
All English Laws he hates, their tyranny disdains,

Against their never-ending Tax most loudly he
    exclaims.
        Then let the Tin Horn sound 'till hills and vales reply,

    The Indian must for freedom live, or else for
        freedom die.

Old Johnny Bull it seems gave his favourites much
    ground,
But for them a right and title has never yet been
    found;
Likewise he'd ought to know, this generous hearted
    King,
Should not have given lands away that ne'er belong'd
    to him.
        Then let the Tin Horn sound 'till hills give back reply,
        The Indian must be free from Tax, or boldly he must die.

"With Helmet on His Brow"

With helmet on his brow, and sabre on his thigh,
The soldier mounts his gallant steed, to conquer or
    to die!
His plume like a pen[dant] streams on the wanton
    summer wind,
In the path of glory still that white plume shalt thou
    find.
        Then let the trumpet's blast
        To the brazen drum reply,
        "A soldier must with honour live,
        Or at once with honour die!"

O! bright as his own good sword, a soldier's fame
    must be,
And pure as the plume that floats above his helm so
    white and free!
No fear in his heart must dwell, but the dread that
    shame may throw,
One spot on that blade so bright, one stain on that
    plume of snow!
        Then let the trumpet's blast, &c.

Our Country we adore, her Laws are Just and Good,
These would-be-lords of America must cross the raging flood.
Our Freedom, sure it is, the bone and sinew of our hand;
With them we mean to drive these false pretenders from our land.
        Then let the Tin Horn sound, till it reaches o'er the main,
        To tell that monarch we have sent his lordlings home again.

At Boston, we have heard, it was the self-same thing,
That there a few brave Indians dare resist the British King;
Oh! The Taxes came so hard that the Tea went overboard,
From the ships into the ocean, where it had long been stored.
        Then let the Tin Horn sound till it reaches rock and glen,
        The Indian must be free from Tax, or bravely die like them.

Rhode Island too, e'er long, must join the Freedom song,
To break the chain of monarchy that's kept her bound so long,
She has brave hearts and true ones, that e'er long will try
To burst the bands asunder, sworn to conquer or to die.
    Then let the Tin Horn sound till it reaches every brave;
    For Freemen must be free indeed, or find a bloody grave.

America is our boast, and the pretty Squaws our toast,
For their sakes we'd dare to fight a numerous British host.
We cannot marry yet, but if any should survive,
We pray these pretty Squaws to keep a hand for every brave.
    Then let the Old Horn sound till it makes the welkin ring,
    The Indian he is free from Tax, and now he'll shout and sing.

Plate 12b. "Le petit tambour."

THE SKY-LARK,

LE PETIT TAMBOUR.

Je suis le petit Tambour, De la garde natio-

na - le, Faut voir comme j'm'en ré-gale D'rouler l'ta-

pin nuit et jour. L'matin j'commence ma

ron-de, Par monsieur l'sergent major, D'la pour e-

veiller tout le monde, Je me promene en tapant

fort, Eh v'lan rataplan taplan Madam's'é-

veille monsieur gronde, Eh v'lan ra-taplan ta-

plan, C'que c'est qu'd'avoir du talent. Je suis

Plate 12c. "With His Mask upon His Brow" set to "Le petit tambour."

A beacon has been lighted,
    Bright as the noonday sun,
On works [that are] besighted
    Its rays are pouring down.
Full many a shrine of error,
    And many a deed of shame,
Dismayed, has shrunk in terror
    Before the lighted flame.
[Chorus] Victorious, on! victorious!
        Proud beacon, onward haste.
        Till rods of light all glorious
        Illume the social waste.

Base FEUDALISM has foundered,
    The demon grasps for breath,
His rapid march is downward,
    To everlasting death.
Old age and youth united,
    His works have [illegible]—are hurled,
And soon himself, affrighted,
    Shall hurry from this world.
[Chorus] Victorious, on, &c.

DEMOCRACY, untiring,
    Strikes at the monster's heart,
Beneath his blows expiring,
    He dreads the well aimed dart.
His blows, we'll pray "God speed them,"
    The darkness to dispel,
And how we fought for freedom,
    Let future ages tell.
[Chorus] Victorious, on, &c.

friends and for — tune smil'd, but ah! how fortunes va — ry I

now am sorrows child, they call'd me blue ey'd Ma — — ry, when

friends and for — tune smil'd, but ah! how fortunes va — — ry I

now am sor — row's child.

2

Come here I'll buy thy flowers
And ease thy hapless lot.
Still wet with waning showers,
I'll buy, Forget me not.
Kind Sir, then take these Posies,
They're fading like my youth,
But never like these Roses,
Shall wither Mary's truth.

Plate 13c. "Downfall of Feudalism" set to "Blue-Eyed Mary"

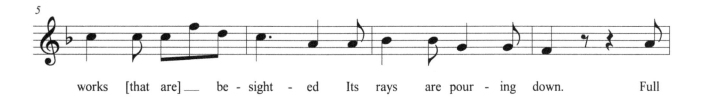

A — bea - con has — been light - ed, — Bright as the noon - day sun, — On

works [that are] — be - sight - ed Its rays are pour - ing down. Full

man - y a shrine of er - ror, And man - y a deed of shame, Dis -

mayed, has shrunk in ter - ror Be - fore the light - ed flame. Vic -

tor - i - ous, on! — Vic - tor - ious! Proud bea - con, on - ward haste. Till

rods of light — all glor - ious Il - lume the so - cial waste.

Plate 14a. "The Native's Enquiry."
Air—"Bruce's Address"

Let strains triumphant rise around—
Let voice to voice responsive sound;
Shall a free People live unbound:
    Or, chained in tyranny?

Shall we dishonor a free soil,
And pamper tyrants with our toil;
Or, be ourselves a tyrant's spoil,
    The slaves of tyranny?

Shall patriots who died to win
Posterity from worlds of sin,
Which tyrant despots bound them in,
    Behold their children free?

Or, shall they see them ground to dust,
The victims of a Patroon's lust,
Like cowards who betray their trust,
    And slave for tyranny?

Shall we ourselves, fill vassals graves,
And our posterity be slaves,
To toil, and toil for patroon knaves,
    The imps of tyranny?

Shall we pervert that sacred trust
Which patriots have sealed to us,
Or, humble lower than the dust
    The imps of tyranny?

A million voices will confess
That feudal tenures need redress,
Amid the general recklessness
    Of vile Patroonery.

A million hands will raise to free
The people from that destiny
Which always follows a tyranny,
    And seal their liberty.

With tyrants we can ne'er possess
Our liberty and happiness;
But always—always stand confess'd,
    The slaves of tyranny.

Let freemen then, with all their might,
Push on the cause of equal rights;
November's ides shall put to flight
    The imps of tyranny.

Now's the day and now's the hour; See the front o' Bat_tle lour;

See approach proud Edward's pow'r, Chains and Sla_ve_rie!

2.

Wha will be a traitor knave?
Wha can fill a coward's grave?
Wha sae base as be a slave?
 Let him turn and flee!
Wha for SCOTLAND's King and law
Freedom's sword will strongly draw,
Freeman stand, or Freeman fa'
 Let him follow me!

3.

By oppression's woes and pains!
By your sons in servile chains!
We will drain our dearest veins,
 But they shall be free!
Lay the proud usurpers low!,
Tyrants fall in every foe!
LIBERTY's in every blow!
 Let us do, or die!

BRUCE'S ADRESS

Plate 14c. "The Native's Enquiry" set to "Bruce's Address."

Let strains tri - um - phant rise a-round, Let voice to voice re-spon - sive sound;

Shall a Peo — ple live un-bound: Or chained in ty - ran-ny?

Shall we dis-hon - or a free soil, And pam - per ty - rants with our toil;

Or, be our-selves a ty - rant's spoil, The slaves of ty - ran-ny?

Plate 15a. "Hail to the Glorious Birth-day of the Nation."
Air—"Hail to the Chief"

Hail to the glorious birth-day of the nation!
Let every freeman rejoice in the sound,
Ever remember the joyful occasion,
And muster and gather, and rally around.
    The time-honored lofty tree
    Sacred to liberty,
Planted by Patriots and watered with gore.
    Deep strike its sturdy roots,
    High upwards mount its shoots,
Till its blessed shadow fall on every shore.

Great were their souls who the vic'try achieved,
Dauntless in spirit, and daring in hand;
Their triumph complete they doubtless believed,
But the grasp of the tyrant was still on the land.
    They left a lordly few,
    Who soon despotic grew,
Claiming our homage by right all divine.
    Edicts of ancient kings,
    Dead and forgotten things,
No longer can the genius of Freedom confine.

Ours is the high and the noble endeavor,
Our country to free from oppression and chains,
Send down to our children unshackled forever,
Our long-cherished hills and our bright sunny plains.
    Here we record the vow,
    Round Freedom's altar now,
Never to yield till our task it be done.
    God give us strength and might,
    As our cause is just and right,
And his be the thanks when the vic'try is won.

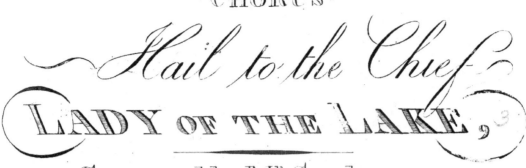

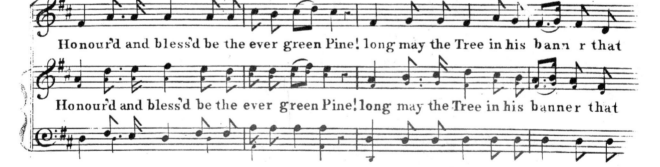

144

2

O irs is no sapling, change _ sown by the fountain,
Blooming at Beltante, in winter to fade;
When the whirlwind has stripp'd ev'ry leaf on the mountain,
The more shall Clan Alpine exult in her shade.
Moor'd in the rifted rock,
Proof to the tempest's shock,
Firmer he roots him the ruder it blow;
Menteith and Breadalbane, the
Echo his praise agen,
"Roderigh Vich Alpine dhu, ho! ieroe!"

3

Row vassals, row, for the pride of the Highlands!
Stretch to your oars, for the ever green pine!
O! that the rose _ bud that graces yon islands,
Were wreathed in a garland around him to twine!
O that some seedling gem,
Worthy such noble stem,
H urd and bless'd in their shadow might grow!
Loud should Clan _ Alpine then,
Ring from her deepmost glen,
"Roderigh Vich Alpine dhu, ho! ieroe!"

Plate 15c. "Hail to the Glorious Birth-day of the Nation" set to "Hail to the Chief."

Plate 16a. "Hardy Tillers of the Soil."
Air—"Bruce's Address"

Hearts to whom your freedom's dear,
Hearts which nought, but Slavery, fear,
Hail ye now, the epoch near,
        Of your liberty.

Hardy tillers of the soil,
Men of sweat, and dust, and toil,
Awake! No longer be the spoil
        Of Patroonery.

Rally, organize, anew;
Old politics keep out of view,
And stand like brothers, firm and true,
        Against Patroonery.

Doubly armed, your cause is just,
In the ballot place your trust,
And triumph, in the end, you must,
        O'er Patroonery.

'Tis no interminable fight,
A few short years secure our right,
Only give the people light,
        On Patroonery.

Fitting is this glorious morn,
On which our country dear was born,
To hurl our mingled hate and scorn,
        At Patroonery.

Helderberg sends forth the strain,
Alps' high hills resound again,
And all the valley shouts amain,
        Down Patroonery.

Plate 16b. "Hardy Tillers of the Soil" set to "Bruce's Address."

Har - dy til - lers of the soil, Men of sweat, and dust, and toil, A -

wake! No long - er be the spoil ___ Of Pa - troon - er - y!

Ral - ly or - gan-ize a - new; Old pol - i - tics keep out of view, And

stand like bro - thers firm and true, A - gainst Pa-troon - er - y!

Plate 17a. "The Farmer's Song."
Air—"A Life on the Ocean Wave"

A life on my native soil—
      A home in a farmer's cot——
I'll never at labor recoil,
      And ask for no happier lot.
The city has not a charm,
      With its turmoil, noise, and strife;
Oh! Give me a snug little farm,
      With a kind and notable wife.
[Chorus]   A life on my native soil—
            A home in a farmer's cot——
            With my three cattle team will I toil,
            And ask for no happier lot.
            Gee up'——gee up!——
            Gee up, gee up, and gee O'

On my native soil I stand,
      Midst blossoming fields around;
While the air is pleasant and bland,
      And the hills with cattle abound!
The river is flowing by;
      The boatman singing we hear;
And the laborers how they ply,
      While echo sends round their cheer!
[Chorus]   A life on my native soil, &c.

How cheerful it is to view
      Whole valleys of waving grain,
And the husbandman's jovial crew
      With sickles prostrating the plain;
Oh! The song of my heart shall be,
      While earth her products shall yield,
The life of a farmer for me,
      A home in the forest and field.
[Chorus]   A life on my native soil—
            A home in a farmer's cot——
            With my three cattle team will I toil,
            And ask for no happier lot.
            Gee up'——gee up!
            Gee up, gee up, and gee O!

Plate 17b. "A Life on the Ocean Wave."

OF COLUMBUS GE?

NEW YORK
Published by HEWITT & JAQUES 239 Broadway.

Plate 17b. Continued.

A LIFE ON THE OCEAN WAVE:

Composed by Henry Russell.

152

Plate 17b. Continued.

Plate 17c. "The Farmer's Song" set to "A Life on the Ocean Wave."

A Life on my na - tive soil,___ A___ home in a far - mer's cot,___ I'll never at labor re -

coil, And___ ask for no hap - pi - er lot. A Life on my na - tive soil,___ A___ home in a far - mer's

cot,___ I'll___ never at labor re - coil,___ And ask for no hap - pi - er lot.___ The

city has not a charm,___ With its tur - moil, noise, and strife;___ Oh! Give me a snug little

farm,___ With a kind and nota - ble wife.___ A life on my na - tive soil,___ A___

home in a far - mer's cot,___ With my three cattle team will I toil, ___ And ask for no hap - pi - er lot. ___ Gee

up'___ gee up!___ Gee up, gee up, and gee O!___ Gee up'___ gee up!___ Gee up, gee up, and gee O!

Plate 18. "In Days of Yore."

In days of yore, as I will relate,
There lived a man in New-York State,
Who claimed an extensive tract of land,
Granted him by a foreign hand.
He gave our sires inducements to come
And make this beautiful tract their home;
And that the terms they easy should be,
As they would have it seven years free.

But when seven years were past and gone,
He ordered our fathers to come on,
And from his hand their leases receive,
Or else their home and improvements leave.
A dilemma this, now what should they do—
The best they could—and so would you.
But the wheat rent now, we mean to destroy,
Declare our freedom, and rout the Old Boy.

Such leases as these might do for a land,
That's governed and ruled by a despot hand;
But in our land where freedom doth reign,
They will ne'er be suffered long to remain.
What! pay him high rent, fowls and day's ride.
He, have all the mines, and water beside
O'erflow your beautiful verdant vales,
To cap the climax, claim the quarter sales.

And if this man has a title that's good,
Why, let him show it, as an honest man would
But if he will not, why, all you can do,
Be firm, united, and all prove true.
Should he ask the quarter sale and day's ride,
The rent, mines, water, and fowls beside,
Tell him to get them where they are due;
For with such fellows you have nothing to do.

Plate 19a. "We Will Be Free."
Air—"The Boatman Dance"

Hail—patriots hail the sacred day!
Our fathers broke the tyrant's sway—
Let earth resound with notes of glee!
It is our nation's jubilee!
    Then shout brothers shout!
    Oh shout brothers shout!
    Loud sound the horn,
    Upon the morn,
    Of Independence day!

(*Repeat*)—Huzza! Huzza! We will be free!
    From Feudal rents and tyranny!

Our feudal lords in coaches ride,
Puffed up with vanity and pride,
Their boasted wealth, they do forget,
Was purchased by the tenant's sweat.
    But shout, &c.

They ne'er remember that the bread
Upon their tables daily spread,
And the rich viands which they eat,
Are products of the farmer's wheat.
    But shout, &c.

Their wives and daughters richly dressed
For nought but "golden charms" caressed,
Oft treat one far more fair with scorn,
Because—forsooth—she's cottage born.
    But shout, &c.

Proud haughty barons—ye may spy,
The tempest gathering in the sky—
The storm ye once thought would not last,
Ye may discern has not yet passed.
    Then shout, &c.

We sons of patriot sires, now swear—
Your loads we will no longer bear;
A thousand hearts now beat as one,
To finish what we have begun.
    Then shout, &c.

157

The time is past, when we'll consent
To pay for land, a yearly rent,
To you, whose title is at best,
One which you dare not now contest.
    Then shout, &c.

No longer o'er the fields and roads,
Our teams shall drag your heavy loads,
We'll bring your tables to adorn—
Not one "fat hen," nor "pepper corn."
    Then shout, &c.

Of lands, o'er which the waters run,
We can consent to spare you—none;
For in those streams, we fear a drought,
If you should take the bottoms out.
    Then shout, &c.

Then hoppy [*sic*] days, return once more!
No sheriff knocking at the door,
With food enough upon our shelves—
We'll spend the "Quarter Sales" ourselves.
    Then shout, &c.

DE BOATMEN'S DANCE.

An original Banjo Melody, by Old Dan. D. Emmit;

Leader of the VIRGINIA MINSTRELS.

Boston: Pub. by C.H.Keith, 67 & 69 Court Street.

Ent'd according to act of Congress in the year 1843 by C.H.Keith in the Clk office of the District Court of Massachusetts.

159

dance de boat-men dance, O dance de boat-men dance, O dance all night till

broad day - light, an go home wid de gals in de morn - ing.

2

De oyster boat should keep to de shore,
De fishin smack should venture more,
De schooner sails before de wind,
De steamboat leaves a streak behind.

> O dance, &c.

3

I went on board de odder day
To see what de boatmen had to say;
Dar I let my passion loose
An dey cram me in de callaboose.

> O dance, &c.

4

I've come dis time, I'll come no more,
Let me loose I'll go on shore;
For dey whole hoss, an dey a bully crew
Wid a hoosier mate an a captin too.

> O dance, &c.

5

When you go to de boatmen's ball,
Dance wid my wife, or dont dance at all;
Sky blue jacket an tarpaulin hat,
Look out my boys for de nine tail cat.

> O dance, &c.

6

De boatman is a thrifty man,
Dars none can do as de boatman can;
I neber see a putty gal in my life
But dat she was a boatman's wife.

> O dance, &c.

7

When de boatman blows his horn,
Look out old man your hog is gone;
He cotch my sheep, he cotch my shoat,
Den put em in a bag an toat em to de boat.

> O dance, &c.

Plate 19c. "We Will Be Free" set to "De Boatmen's Dance."

Huzza! Huzza! We will be free! From Feu - dal _ rents and ty - ran - ny.

Huzza! Huzza! We will be free! From Feu - dal _ rents and ty - ran - ny. Hail

pa - triots hail the sa - cred day! Our fa - thers broke the ty - rant's sway— Let

earth re - sound with notes of glee! It is our na - tion's ju - bi - lee! Then

shout _____ bro - thers shout! Oh, shout ____ bro - thers shout! Loud

sound the horn, U - pon the morn, _ of In - de - pen - dence Day!

Plate 20. "The Prisoners in Jail."
"Lines composed by Mortemus C. Belding [sic], while lying in the Columbia County Jail."

There is Boughton, and Belding, and many besides,
They are quite clever fellows, or else they are belied,
For what they are in Jail, I scarcely do know,
But it is base at the best—well, let it go so,
                    In these hard times.

The sheriffs will out with their array of men,
The County will find them, what money they spend;
They will seize upon prisoners, and into the cell—
If there's anything worse, it must be in Hell,
                    In these hard times.

And there they will keep them confined in the Jail,
Without any liberty for to get bail;
They will do as they please in spite of your friends,
And God only knows where this matter will end,
                    In these hard times.

But the Sheriff, and others, who go in the huddle,
I'm fearful are getting themselves into trouble,
For unless they keep themselves somewhere near strait,
They will be twich't at the eye at a hell of a rate,
                    In these hard times.

But we are prisoners in Jail, our cases are hard,
They look all around to keep on their guard,
Their feet fast in irons chained down to the floor,
They are pretty sheriffs what can they do more,
                    In these hard times.

And as for the Jailor he's a man of renown,
He spends all of his time in ironing them down;
He says for their keeping they don't get half pay,
Although he gives them but two poor meals a day,
                    In these hard times.

The Judges and Jurors are a very fine crew,
They take the poor prisoners and drive them right thro';
The sheriffs will falter, all hell they don't fear,
They will bring them in guilty if they prove themselves clear,
                    In these hard times.

They will send them to Jail, and there for to lie,
On bread and cold water, or else they must die;
Or else down to Sing Sing and there for to dwell,
For twenty-five dollars they would send us to hell,
                     In these hard times.

The District Attorney is a handsome young man,
He spends all his time in laying some plans,
And as for the Sheriff he is a man I despise,
He will go to the Governor with his mouth full of lies,
                     In these hard times.

He seizes upon property, and that he will sell,
And drink by the way he can do very well;
He will do anything that will profit himself,
For Uncle Sam has to pay him as well as the rest,
                     In these hard times.

And as for their counsel they seem to be clever,
They tell them fine stories—make all things fair weather;
But it is for money they go as you're all well aware,
And without it they don't care a d—n how we fare,
                     In these hard times.

But there is the Doctor I like to forgot
Still he is the meanest of all the whole lot;
He says he will cure them for half they possess,
And when they are dead he will sue for the rest,
                     In these hard times.

Although he says the old Jail is very filthy,
And the Jailor must clean it—or else he *will* see,
The prisoners are fast declining, and the Jailor is to blame,
If he don't do his duty, he'll report him very soon,
                     In these hard times.

But I think now it is time to finish my song,
I can prove all I have said if you think I've done wrong;
For they are prisoners in Jail without any bail,
And I think they don't like this lying in Jail,
                     In these hard times.

Plate 21a. "An Anti-Rent Song."
Tune—"Bold Caroline"

Suppose you know the reason
Which has always kept us poor,
And the truth we tell to you my Boys,
You can't deny it more.
    Chorus: So be cheerful my Boys
              Let your hearts never fail
              Whilst the Anti-Renters are
              So potent in the land.

'Twas the Landlords my Boys
Who have always had our labor,
And not only from me,
But they have had it from my neighbor.
        So be cheerful &c.

They are worse than any robber
I think you all will say,
For they have had our money
And squandered it away.
        So be cheerful &c.

We hired our farms
From a set of men, you know,
Who could not show a title,
If to the Devil they should go.
        So be cheerful &c.

They charged us heavy rents,
And we had to pay them down,
And if we happened to fail
They would drive us from the ground.
        So be cheerful &c.

They would take all we had,
And then set us out of door,
And that you see my Boys,
Is what has always kept us poor.
        So be cheerful &c.

They robbed us of our rights,
And always had the Laws,
And, therefore, you see my Boys,
We had to hold our jaws.
　　　　So be cheerful &c.

But now we are determined
To be no longer slaves,
And if we can't by fair means,
We will be a set of knaves.
　　　　So be cheerful &c.

They have had this land unjust,
And that is very well known;
So if a man has got a farm,
Just let him call it his own.
　　　　So be cheerful &c.

Let him work his farm, my Boys,
And the Landlords go to hell,
And there to be left with their
Own tribe to dwell.
　　　　So be cheerful &c.

We will send them to the Devil,
There for to yell and groan,
And then they will execrate the day,
They call'd this land their own.
　　　　So be cheerful &c.

We have had to dig and scratch,
Almost night and day,
For to get a heap of money,
So that we our rents could pay.
　　　　So be cheerful &c.

We labored when we were weary,
Half naked and unwell,
And the hardships we endured
No present tongue can tell.
　　　　So be cheerful &c.

To keep those mighty Landlords
A going with their career,
It's nothing have we said,
At the ending of the year.
   So be cheerful &c.

They are the meanest of men,
And whoever takes their part,
We hope an arrow of conviction
Will strike them to their heart.
   So be cheerful &c.

They do gamble and get drunk,
And do every thing that is [w]rong
And I cannot tell you half,
For it would make my song too long.
   So be cheerful &c.

Plate 21c. "An Anti-Rent Song" set to "Bold Caroline."

Sup - pose you know the rea - son Which al - ways kept us poor, — And the

truth we tell to you my Boys, You can't de - ny — it more. — So be

cheer - ful — my Boys, Let your hearts — nev - er fail — Whilst the

An - ti - Rent - ers are — So po - tent in — the land. —

168

Plate 22a. "The Contest."
Air—"Bruce's Address"

Now the Contest is begun,
　　Freemen, Freemen, every one,
Claim the rights your fathers won,
　　From a foreign foe.

Let the haughty Landlord see
　　Independent you will be;
Deeds that come across the sea
　　Should not bind us here.

Raise the stainless standard high,
　　Throw the Feudal Charter by;
Meet them, and their power defy,
　　On our native soil.

Grants bestow'd by English Lords
　　E'er our fathers drew their swords,
Should not here a right afford,
　　To oppress the free.

Independence proudly towers
　　On Columbia's happy shores;
But, the last cap-stone is yours—
　　Boldly put it on.

Light the spark too long represt,
　　Long it smoulder'd in your breast;
Let it flame till well redrest,
　　And your wrongs shall be.

When you hear the trumpet sound,
　　Foremost in your ranks be found;
Crush oppression to the ground—
　　Set the helpless free.

Countless thousands sound your praise,
　　Happy bards in future days;
High shall sound their proudest lays,
　　To proclaim your fame.

Plate 22b. "The Contest" set to "Bruce's Address."

Now the Con - test is be-gun, Free - men, Free - men, eve - ry one,____

Claim the rights your fa - thers won,____ From a for - eign foe.

Let the haugh - ty Land - lord see In - de - pen - dent you will be;

Deeds that come a - cross the sea____ Should not bind us here.

Plate 23. "Dere vos a Time."

There was a time, I know it well, it was when I was young,
Just thirty years ago it was, and then I was among
A merry company, when first my Katy, I did see;
I fell in love with her, and then, she fell in love with me.

We didn't have much trouble then "to make our traces hitch,"
For she was not so very poor, nor I so very rich,
Nor was our courtship very long, for just to have it done,
We sent and got the dominie, and Kate and I were one.

And then our friends they wished us joy, a long and happy life,
That I might be a happy man, and she a happy wife;
And we *were* happy too, we were, for well did we agree,
And I was satisfied with her, and so was she with me.

But then when we were married, we to one conclusion come,
That we would look around us, for we wanted then a home,
And when the landlord heard of that, that we did want to buy,
He said that he had land to sell which wasn't very high.

And then we bought the land, we did, and Kate and I we felt
That we had got it cheap, but then, we didn't have the "gelt,"
But when we scraped together all the money that we had,
And found we didn't have enough, we borrowed some of dad.

The landlord asked us if we'd have a lease, we said we would,
And then he wrote us one he did, and said that it was good,
We told him that we wanted such, we wanted nothing wrong.
He then declared that it was right, and certainly was *strong*.

And then he read it over, but we didn't like it much,
But then you see we couldn't read, for Kate and I were Dutch [Deutsch].
It was so very long it was, and told about "a rent,"
We didn't understand the word, nor what the fellow meant.

There were a hundred other words that were so very long,
If he had not said that they were right, we'd thought that they were wrong;
But Kate and I you see were Dutch, and so we didn't know,
And when he told us they were right, we thought that it was so.

Then Kate and I we moved upon the land that we had bought,
And then we went to work, as all young married people ought,
And then we built for us a house, and barn upon it too,
And though they wasn't very big, we thought that they would do.

171

When we had got it all aright, exactly as we should,
The fences fixed up, all around, and trees a growing good,
We didn't have to work so hard as we had done before,
For we had been there then half a dozen years, or more.

Well then one day a fellow came to tell us he was sent
To ask us "to come right away and pay up the back rent,"
He told us that his master said that he must let us know
That if we didn't pay right up, that we would have to go.

He said that we "had took a lease, and so we did agree."
I looked at Kate inquiringly, and then she looked at me;
We told him we had bought the land, and had no more to pay,
And told him tell his master so, and then he went away.

But soon an officer he came, he said, as he was told,
And levied on our property, and all of it was sold;
And then he sold our farm, he did, and then the fellow read
A paper that he called a "writ"—I don't know all he said;

It was something 'bout "ejectment," and he said we couldn't stay,
And that our lease was forfeited, and we must go away.
We were in trouble then, for what to do we didn't know,
We hadn't anywheres to stay, nor anywheres to go,

Nor we hadn't any money then, nor any thing to sell,
And how to get another home, just then, we couldn't tell.
And so we didn't go away, 'til driven from the door,
And then we did; and ever since, we have been very poor.

Plate 24a. "Haste to Delhi."

Ye who seek your country's wo[e],
See for freedom's overthrow,
Seek to lay her standard low,
    Haste to Delhi.

Ye who love the feudal law,
Wish to keep the poor in awe,
And their chains more tightly draw,
    Haste to Delhi.

Ye who hate reformers' plan,
Hate the Equal Rights of Man,
Wish to lay them under ban,
    Haste to Delhi.

Ye who wish to seize the store,
Of the injur'd lab'ring poor,
Crush them that they rise no more,
    Haste to Delhi.

Those who choose the assassins' trade,
Choose the gloomy midnight shade,
Peaceful dwellings to invade,
    Haste to Delhi.

Jurors who will find a bill,
Be the witness what it will,
Guiltless blood resolve to spill,
    Haste to Delhi.

Ye who for a golden bribe,
Turn your client's right aside,
And against the truth decide,
    Haste to Delhi.

Ye who blast your neighbor's name,
Strive to soil his spotless fame,
Mischief by a law to frame,
    Haste to Delhi.

Ye whose hearts are dark and fell,
Ye who affidavits sell,
Tory Lords will pay you well,
    Haste to Delhi.

Ye who wish to feast your eyes,
When a noble patriot dies,
Victim of malicious lies,
                    Haste to Delhi.

Justice with her blinded sight,
Might have stumbled on the right,
But she's fairly took her flight
                    From old Delhi.

Ye who wish to fill your fob,
Join the "Law and Order" mob,
You may get a dainty job,
                    At old Delhi.

It's for this the Delhi folks,
Wear their "law and order" cloaks,
Make their courts of law a hoax,
                    In old Delhi.

Dominies throughout the land,
Who would lend a helping hand
To secure the prisoners' bands,
                    Haste to Delhi.

If your flocks love Equal Right,
Leave them for the wolf to bite,
From among them take your flight,
                    Straight to Delhi.

But you who would your country save,
Dare to claim what heaven gave,
Dare the Inquisition brave,
                    Fear not Delhi.

Nothing fear, your cause is just,
Better days will come, we trust,
Tyrants yet will bite the dust,
                    In old Delhi.

Plate 24b. "Haste to Delhi" set to "Bruce's Address."

Ye who seek your coun - try's woe, See for free - dom's o - ver - throw,

Seek to lay her stan - dard low, _____ Haste to Del - hi.

Ye who love the feu - dal law, Wish to keep the poor in awe,

And their chains more tight - ly draw, _____ Haste to Del - hi.

Plate 25. "Come Join the Anti-Renters."

Come, join the Anti-Renters!
Ye young men bold and strong,
And with a warm and cheerful zeal,
Come, help the cause along.

Chorus— O, that will be joyful, joyful, joyful,
        O, that will be joyful, when Patroonery is no more—
        When Patroonery is no more, our happy land all o'er,
        'Tis then we will sing, and off'rings bring,
        When Patroonery is no more.

Come, join the Anti-Renters!
Ye men of riper years,
And save your wives and children dear,
From grief and bitter tears.

Chorus— O, that will be joyful, joyful, joyful—

Come, join the Anti-Renters!
Ye men of hoary heads,
And end your days where Liberty
Its peaceful influence spreads.

Chorus— O, that will be joyful, joyful, joyful—

Come, join the Anti-Renters!
Ye dames and maidens fair,
And breathe around us in our path
Affection's hallowed air.

Chorus— O, that will be joyful, joyful, joyful—
        O, that will be joyful, when women cheer us on—
        When women cheer us on
        To conquest not yet won;
        'Tis then we will sing, and off'rings bring,
        When women cheer us on.

Come, join the Anti-Renters!
Ye who the poor enslave,
And hold the father, mother, child,
Continually—Enslaved

Chorus— O, that will be joyful, joyful, joyful—

O, that will be joyful, when deeds are forged no more—
When deeds are forged no more, our happy land all o'er;
'Tis then we will sing, and off'rings bring,
When Anti-Renters win the day.

Come, join the Anti-Renters!
Ye sons and daughters all
Of thy own America
Come at the friendly rail.

Chorus— O, that will be joyful, joyful, joyful—
O, that will be joyful, when all shall proudly say,
This—this is freedom's day,
Oppression flee away;
'Tis then we will sing, and off'rings bring,
When Anti-Renters win the day.

What has caused this great Commotion, motion, motion,
    Our whole State through?
It is the ball that's rolling on,
    For the right of soil and a title true,
    For the right of soil and a title true,
And for them we'll go to a man, man, in spite of MANOR VAN,
    And for them we'll go to a man.

Have you heard from neighb'ring towns, towns, towns,
    This district through?
The people all are wide awake,
    For the right of soil and a title true,
    For the right of soil and a title true,
And for them we'll go to a man, man, in spite of MANOR VAN,
    And for them we'll go to a man.

Who shall we have for Governors, Governors, Governors,
    Our will to do?
Oh, Young and Gardiner are the men,
    For the right of soil and a title true,
    For the right of soil and a title true,
And for them we'll vote to a man, man, in spite of MANOR VAN,
    And for them we'll vote to a man.

Who shall we have for Senator, Senator, Senator,
    Who's strong and true?
Oh, Harris is the man of men,
    For the right of soil and a title true,
    For the right of soil and a title true,
And for him we'll vote to a man, man, in spite of MANOR VAN,
    And for him we'll vote to a man.

Hark! I hear the voice of Harris, Harris, Harris,
    I see him too;
He stands erect, he's clinching the nail,
    For the right of soil and a title true,
    For the right of soil and a title true,
And for him we'll vote to a man, man, in spite of MANOR VAN,
    And for him we'll vote to a man.

Who shall we send to Congress, Congress, Congress,
    Who tell us who?

Why Johnny I. would fight or die
    For the right of soil and a title true,
    For the right of soil and a title true,
And for him we'll vote to a man, man, in spite of MANOR VAN,
    And for him we'll vote to a man.

Who must we have for Sheriff, Sheriff, Sheriff,
    Who'll justice do?
Oh, Oscar Tyler would "burst his biler"
    For the right of soil and a title true,
    For the right of soil and a title true,
And for him we'll vote to a man, man, in spite of MANOR VAN,
    And for him we'll vote to a man.

Who shall we have for County Clerk, Clerk, Clerk,
    Who'll recording do?
Why, Lawrence Deusen is the man
    For the right of soil and a title true,
    For the right of soil and a title true,
And for him we'll vote to a man, man, in spite of MANOR VAN,
    And for him we'll vote to a man.

Have you heard of Watson, Treadwell, Fuller & Co.,
    Our friends "true blue"?
They're just the ones to wield our guns,
    For the right of soil and a title true,
    For the right of soil and a title true,
And for them we'll vote to a man, man, in spite of MANOR VAN,
    And for them we'll vote to a man.

Awake, Awake, ye Anti-Renters, Renters, Renters,
    Your aim pursue;
Let every soul go up to the poll,
    For the right of soil and a title true,
    For the right of soil and a title true,
And for them we'll vote to a man, man, in spite of MANOR VAN,
    And for them we'll vote to a man.

Philadelphia, G. E. Blake, 13 S⁰ Fifth Street.

What has caused this great com__mo__tion, motion, motion, Our Country through? It

What has caused this great com__mo__tion, motion, motion, Our Country through? It

What has caused this great com__mo__tion, motion, motion, Our Country through? It

Blake's Log Cabin Music__Copy right secured 1840.

181

Plate 26d. "This Great Commotion" set to "Tippecanoe and Tyler Too!"

What has caused this great Com - mo-tion, mo-tion, mo-tion, Our whole State through? It

Chorus

is   the ball that's rol - ling on, For the   right   of soil   and a   ti - tle true, For the

right   of soil   and a   ti - tle true,   And for   them   we'll go   to   a   man,   man,

[man],   in spite of Man - or Van,   And   for   them we'll go   to   a   man.____

Plate 27a. "Keep Thy Spirit, Swell Thy Faith."
Tune—"Cheer Up My Lively Lads"

Keep thy spirit, swell thy faith
    Let hope be even stronger;
Songs of triumph soon we'll sing,
    In louder tones and longer!

CHORUS: Cheer up my lively lads,
    In spite of wind and weather,—
Cheer up my lively lads,
    We'll triumph altogether!

Let your watch-word action be,
    Nor flag nor give up never;
Stem the tide and roll the ball,
    Till your chains shall sever!
        Cheer up, &c.

Raise your standard, raise it high,
    And set your colors flying;
Show the world the hue it wears,—
    Its aspect how defying.
        Cheer up, &c.

Read on it your candidates,
    Nor in your purpose waver;
Save the ticket one and all
    In spite of fear or favor!
        Cheer up, &c.

Watson, Willett, Treadwell too,
    For Fuller and for others,
We'll work and vote with heart and hand,
    And stick to it like brothers!
        Cheer up, &c.

Hail, then the flag which o'er us waves,
    May none of us degrade it,
But wage the war for its success,
    Forgetting not who made it!
        Cheer up, &c.

FREE SOIL MINSTREL.

SALT RIVER CHORUS.

Air, " Cheer up, my lively Lads." Arranged by G. W. C.

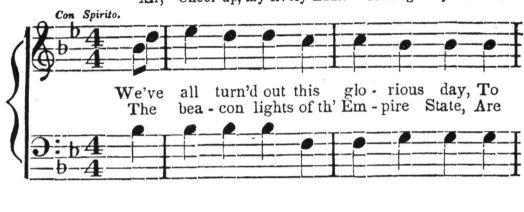

We've all turn'd out this glo - rious day, To
The bea - con lights of th' Em - pire State, Are

join the con - vo - ca - tion—To cheer the friends of
spreading thro' the na - tion, North, east and west are

li - ber - ty, And stop the slave ex - ten - sion. Then,
all on fire, In one great con - fla - gra - tion. Then,

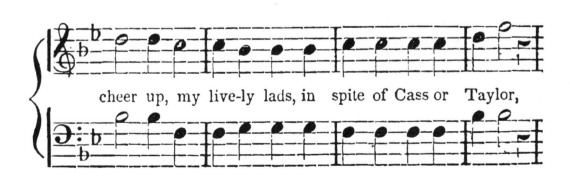

cheer up, my live-ly lads, in spite of Cass or Taylor,

186

FREE SOIL MINSTREL.

Cheer up, we'll stop their craft, and up Salt river sail her.

Our Southern friends are coming on —
   Fraternity 's our motto ;
We welcome them with all our heart,
   As every freeman ought to.
     Then, cheer up my lively lads,
       In spite of Cass or Taylor ;
     Cheer up, we'll stop their craft,
       And up Salt river sail her.

We'll sing " free soil, free soil," my boys,
   Nor sing for Cass or Taylor ;
For Taylor rhymes are growing stale,
   And hunker songs grow staler.
     Then, cheer up, &c.

Now slavery's craft is floating by,
   Containing Cass and Taylor,
Aboard, my boys, and seize the helm,
   And up Salt river sail her.
     Then, cheer up, &c.

For conscience whigs, and liberty men,
   And every true barnburner,
Here join to stay proud slavery's curse,
   And from free soil to spurn her.
     Then, cheer up, &c.

Our flag is floating on the breeze,
   Though not for Cass or Taylor,
'Tis for FREE SOIL, FREE SOIL, my boys,
   And to the MAST we'll nail her.
     Then, cheer up, &c.

Plate 27c. "Keep Thy Spirit" set to "Cheer Up My Lively Lads."

Keep thy spir - it, swell thy faith Let hope be ev - en strong-er;____

Songs of tri - umph soon we'll sing, In loud - er tones and long - er!____

Cheer up my live - ly lads, In spite of wind and wea - ther,

Cheer up my live - ly lads, We'll tri - umph al - to - ge - ther!

Plate 28a. "Rouse, Ye Anti-Renters, Wake!"
Air—"Bruce's Address"

Rouse, ye Anti-Renters, wake!
Press the aim that you've at stake
Nerve your arms a conquest make,—
    Strike for Liberty!

Save your soil and save your friends,
Stand by those who'll gain your ends,
Seal your hopes while time attends,—
    Be among the free!

Spurn the wight who yonder stands,—
Base at heart with bloody hands,
Thinking how he'll burst our bands,
    Kill our cause and aim!

Shun the Ice-berg's blasting breeze,
Scorn the Monster—slave to fees—
Let him fly where'er he please,
    Stained with guilt and shame!

Hail, oh hail the joyous day,—
Haste its speed all freemen pray,—
Day when justice has its sway,
    Rides o'er Tyranny!

Happy moments then we'll see,
Freed from thralldom then are we,—
"Quarter sales" no more will be,—
    Source of Misery!

Plate 28b. "Rouse, Ye Anti-Renters, Wake!" set to "Bruce's Address."

Rouse, ye An - ti - Rent - ers wake! Press the aim that you've at stake

Nerve your arms a con - quest make, Strike for Lib - er - ty!

Save your soil and save your friends, Stand by those who'll gain your ends,

Seal your hopes while time at - tends, Be a - mong the free!

190

Plate 29a. "Anti-Rent Song of Triumph."
Air—"Dan Tucker"

As I've got time I'll tell you all
The Counties that go no rent this fall,
'Tis easy told and thus 'tis done
They all did go for *Johnny Young*.

Chorus—*Then*, Silas Wright get out of Chair sir,
    Make room now for honest men sir
    Get out the way you Silas Wright sir,
    Make room now for JOHNNY YOUNG sir.

Old Albany began the dance,
And woke dear Silas from his trance;
'Tis hard for him the boys to beat,
Who on the Heldeberg do eat.
Chorus—Then, Silas, &c.

Next come the news from Rensselaer—
'Tis mighty bad for me says *Van* sir;
For *Silas* too, it is a roarer,
And speaks in louder tones than thunder.
Chorus—Then, Silas, &c.

More news has come from Columbia's shore,
It makes Van Buren grit once more,
And Old Schoharie in the distance rolls,
A mighty sound to all the four's.
Chorus—Then, Silas, &c.

Old Delaware too, did her best,
To put the winded nag at rest;
Of *Anti-Rent* votes she has to *lotts*,
"Long time ago," she had the Botts.
Chorus—Then, Silas, &c.

To all good men conjoin'd I say,
Be up and dress'd and swear to *day*,
T' remove afar this crying sin,
To "pick your flints and try again."
Chorus—Then, Silas, &c.

Plate 29b. "Anti-Rent Song of Triumph" set to "Old Dan Tucker."

As__ I've got time I'll tell you all, The Coun-ties that go no rent this fall,

'Tis easy told and thus 'tis done, They all did go for John - ny Young.

Gran' Chorus

Then Si - las Wright get out of Chair sir, Make room__ now for hon - est men sir.

Get out the way you Si - las Wright sir Make room now for John - ny Young sir.

Plate 30a. "The Land Lord's Lament."
Air—"Oh Dear, What Can the Matter Be"

Chorus—Oh dear, dear, what can the matter be?
       Dear, dear, what can the matter be?
       What shall I do with my tenants?
       How shall I get all my *rents*?

The Helderberg *boys* are playing the dickens!
The night of confusion around me now thickens,
Unless the *Rent* business with some of us quickens,
We'll all have to live without Rents.
       Oh dear, &c.

I used to get rich through the *poor* toiling tenants,
And I spent all their earnings in pleasures satanic,
But now I confess I'm in a great panic,
Because I can get no more *Rent*.
       Oh dear, &c.

My tenants once to my office were flocking,
Some without a coat, or a shoe, or a stocking,
But now I declare it is really shocking,
To know I shall get no more *Rent*.
       Oh dear, &c.

I must give up this business I *vow* it's no use to me,
It's been a continual source of abuse to me;
The friends of *equal rights* give no peace to me,
Until they get clear of the *Rent*.
       Oh dear, &c.

Plate 30b. "Oh Dear, What Can the Matter Be."

O DEAR WHAT CAN THE MATTER BE.

NEW YORK Engrav'd Printed & Sold by E RILEY Nº 29 Chatham Street.

O dear! what can the matter be! Dear! dear! what can the matter be! O dear! what can the matter be, Johny's so long at the fair? He promis'd to bring me a fairing would please me, And then for a kifs O! he vow'd he would tease me; He promis'd to bring me a bunch of blue rib-bons To tie up my bonny brown hair.

O dear! what can the matter be!
Dear! dear. what can the matter be!
O dear! what can the matter be!
 Johny's so long at the fair?
He promis'd to bring me a fairing would please me,
And then for a kifs, O! he vow'd he would tease me;
He promis'd to bring me a bunch of blue ribbons
 To tie up my bonny brown hair.

O dear! what can the matter be.
Dear! dear! what can the matter be!
O dear! what can the matter be,
 Johny's so long at the fair?
He promis'd to bring me a basket of posies,
A garland of lilies, a garland of roses;
A little straw hat to set off the blue ribbons
 That tie up my bonnie brown hair.

194

Plate 30c. "The Land Lord's Lament" set to "Oh Dear, What Can the Matter Be."

Oh dear, dear, what can the mat-ter be? Dear, dear, what can the mat-ter be?

What shall I do with my ten-ants? How shall I get all my rents? The Hel-der-berg boys are

play-ing the dick-ens! The night of con-fu-sion a-round me now thick-ens, Un-

less the Rent busi-ness with some of us quick-ens, We'll all have to live with-out Rents.

Notes

Prelude

1. "Attorney General James Applauds Repeal of Law Criminalizing Group Mask Use in Public," press release, Office of the New York State Attorney General, May 28, 2020, https://ag.ny.gov/press-release/2020/attorney-general-james-applauds-repeal-law-criminalizing-group-mask-use-public.

2. Max Maretzek, *Crotchets and Quavers, or, Revelations of an Opera Manager in America* (New York: S. French, 1855), 95. In the same chapter, Maretzek describes obtaining stage scenery for upcoming productions by outwitting the sheriff and agents leading a distress sale. The scenery originally belonged to Edward Fry's opera company, which had failed financially. As we will see, resisting distress sales was one of the Anti-Renters' major activities.

3. L. M. Bogad, "Facial Insufficiency: Political Street Performance in New York City and the Selective Enforcement of the 1845 Mask Law," *The Drama Review* 47, no. 4 (Winter 2003): 75–84. For an overview of New York's anti-mask legislation since 1845, see Ruthann Robson, *Dressing Constitutionally: Hierarchy, Sexuality, and Democracy from Our Hairstyles to Our Shoes* (New York: Cambridge University Press, 2013), 125–27.

Introduction

1. Facsimile indenture, in Mary Fisher Torrance, *The Story of Old Rensselaerville* (New York: privately printed, 1939), insert facing p. 14. The old Dutch scheppel is roughly equivalent to 0.75 bushels.

2. *Down with the Rent!: The Anti-Rent Rebellion in New York*, presented by Old Songs at their base in Voorheesville, New York, November 21–22, 2014; program pamphlet in author's collection.

3. Indenture in Torrance, *Story of Old Rensselaerville*.

Chapter 1

1. Henry Rowe Schoolcraft, *Helderbergia: Or the Apotheosis of the Heroes of the Antirent War* (Albany: J. Munsell, 1855), canto 1, stanza 2.

2. Howard Zinn, *A People's History of the United States* (New York: HarperCollins, 2003), 48.

3. Other terms include *durable lease* and *perpetual lease*.

4. Reeve Huston, *Land and Freedom: Rural Society, Popular Protest, and Party Politics in Antebellum New York* (New York: Oxford University Press, 2000), 5. *Wyck* is a general Dutch term for "district."

5. Zinn, *A People's History*, 211.

6. Historical sources contain many different spellings for the escarpment today known as Helderberg, including Hilderburgh and Hallebarreck. The name originated from the Dutch terms for bright or clear (*helder*) and mountain (*bergh*). On variants, see Arthur Gregg, *Old Hellerbergh: Historical Sketches of the West Manor of Rensselaerwyck*, foreword by Alexander Flick (1936; repr., Guilderland Center, NY: Guilderland Historical Society, 1975), 104.

7. Henry Christman, *Tin Horns and Calico: A Decisive Episode in the Emergence of Democracy*, introduction by Carl Carmer (1945; bicentennial ed., Cornwallville, NY: Hope Farm Press, 1978).

8. Roger Hecht, " 'Rouse Ye Anti-Renters': Poetry and Politics in the Anti-Rent Press," *The Hudson River Valley Review* 28, no. 2 (Spring 2012): 3–21; here, 4. Hecht derived the concept of an "Anti-Rent imaginary" from Chartist scholarship, which adopts Louis Althusser's "definition of ideology: the imaginary relationship of individuals to their real conditions" (p. 20, nt. 3). Chartism's relevance to the Anti-Renters is addressed in chapter 3.

9. Emelyn Gardner, *Folklore from the Schoharie Hills, New York* (Ann Arbor: University of Michigan Press, 1937), 32.

10. "Bill Snyder" is discussed in chapter 2. Albany-area musician Justin Friello arranged and recorded the "Anti-Rent Song," a political campaign song that begins, "What has caused this great Commotion?" (plate 26). I recorded the piano part of "Halderbarak Quick Step" with Matt Malsky on tin horn (plate 5). These performances, along with audio files for the sixteen Anti-Rent contrafacta tunes, can be accessed on my SoundCloud page, https://soundcloud.com/user-373664407.

11. Although it is beyond the scope of this volume, much poetry was created that does not have musical associations. For examples, see Christman, *Tin Horns and Calico*, 321–43, and Roger Hecht, *Freemen Awake! Rally Songs and Poems from New York's Anti-Rent Movement* (N.p.: Delaware County Historical Association, 2017).

12. Ruth Crawford Seeger, *The Music of American Folk Song and Selected Other Writings on American Folk Music*, ed. Larry Polansky with Judith Tick (Rochester, NY: University of Rochester Press, 2003), 23–30; here, 26 and 30.

13. Charles McCurdy, *The Anti-Rent Era in New York Law and Politics* (Chapel Hill: University of North Carolina Press, 2001).

14. Christman, *Tin Horns and Calico*, xv and 321.

15. David Maldwyn Ellis, *Landlords and Farmers in the Hudson-Mohawk Region, 1790–1850* (Ithaca, NY: Cornell University Press, 1946), 245.

16. Ellis, *Landlords and Farmers*, 295.

17. McCurdy, *The Anti-Rent Era*, 330.

18. Ellis, *Landlords and Farmers*, 2.

19. See, for example, Gustavus Myers, *History of the Supreme Court of the United States* (Chicago: Charles H. Kerr, 1912), especially 135–50.

20. For Hamilton's draft of the notice he advised Stephen III to send, see Hamilton Papers, "Stephen Van Rensselaer to the Tenants of Rensselaerwyck (July–August 1786)," Founders Online, National Archives, https://founders.archives.gov/documents/Hamilton/01-26-02-0002-0122. Original source: *The Papers of Alexander Hamilton*, vol. 26, *1 May 1802–23 October 1804, Additional Documents 1774–1799, Addenda and Errata*, ed. Harold C. Syrett (New York: Columbia University Press, 1979), 467.

21. Ron Chernow, *Alexander Hamilton* (New York: Penguin Press, 2004), 13.

22. "An Act Concerning Tenures (1787)," in *Laws of the State of New-York* (Albany: Websters and Skinner, 1807), 1:66.

23. Ellis, *Landlords and Farmers*, 38. Ellis puts the number of Rensselaerwyck tenants when Stephen III assumed control at fewer than three hundred; McCurdy says it was about six hundred (cf. *The Anti-Rent Era*, 12).

24. The 1790 census records approximately 76,000 residents of Albany County, including 4,000 enslaved people (i.e., about 5 percent) and 26 free Blacks. Historian Oscar Williams observes that enslaved people in the

region supplied extensive labor for the Rensselaer, Livingston, and Schuyler families' manors and industries; see "Slavery in Albany, New York, 1624–1827," *Afro-Americans in New York Life and History* 34, no. 2 (July 2010): 154–68.

25. Torrance, *The Story of Old Rensselaerville*, indenture.

26. David Murray, "The Antirent Episode in the State of New York," in *Annual Report of the American Historical Association for 1896* (N.p.: US Government Printing Office, 1897), 1:139–73. With prices in flux, calculating the cash value of rent and land became another arena of conflict between landlords and tenants.

27. Devyr, *The Odd Book of the Nineteenth Century*, American Section (Greenpoint, NY: published by the author, 1882), 49.

28. Huston, *Land and Freedom*, 26, 28.

29. Cooper, *The Redskins, or Indian and Injin* (New York: Burgess, Stringer, 1846), xiv.

30. McCurdy, *The Anti-Rent Era*, 9–15. Reports of the exact amount of Stephen III's debt vary, but Murray was certain of its cause. "In consequence of his mistaken kindness toward his tenants, as well as his personal liberality and bountifulness in his home life, he was involved in debts almost equal to the arrears in rent on his domain" ("The Antirent Episode," 147).

31. Ellis, *Landlords and Farmers*, 34–36; on tenant rebellions during British colonial administration, see pp. 10–12. For a contrasting view, see Sung Bok Kim, *Landlord and Tenant in Colonial New York: Manorial Society, 1664–1775* (Chapel Hill: University of North Carolina Press, 1978).

32. Huston, *Land and Freedom*, 101.

33. "An Act Concerning Tenures" in *Laws of the State of New-York*, 66.

34. McCurdy, *The Anti-Rent Era*, 28. The Anti-Renters were also beholden to common law doctrine, which held that by assuming the premises and paying the rent, tenants acknowledged the landlord's title (101).

35. McCurdy, *The Anti-Rent Era*, 304–8.

36. McCurdy, *The Anti-Rent Era*, 29.

37. "The Anti-Rent Question," from the *Albany Evening Journal*, reprinted in *The Harbinger*, July 24, 1847, 105.

38. As quoted in McCurdy, *The Anti-Rent Era*, 28. The Dutchess County case was brought by Livingston and Beekman family members.

39. Samuel Rezneck, "The Social History of an American Depression, 1837–1843," *The American Historical Review* 40, no. 4 (July 1935): 662–87; here, 662.

40. Norma Basch, *In the Eyes of the Law: Women, Marriage, and Property in Nineteenth-Century New York* (Ithaca, NY: Cornell University Press, 1982), 17, 122.

41. Murray, "The Antirent Episode," 151.

42. McCurdy, *The Anti-Rent Era*, 194–99.

43. McCurdy, *The Anti-Rent Era*, 305.

44. Article 1, section 12, New York Constitution of 1846, as quoted in Murray, "The Antirent Episode," 165.

45. McCurdy, *The Anti-Rent Era*, xiv.

Chapter 2

1. Schoolcraft, *Helderbergia*, canto 1, stanza 7.

2. McCurdy, *The Anti-Rent Era*, 15. Stephen III's widow, Cornelia Paterson, received a life estate in the family mansion and an annuity; their other adult children received cash, commercial buildings, city lots, securities, and other assets.

3. Christman, *Tin Horns and Calico*, 16–19.

4. *Albany Daily Argus*, December 3, 1839, as reprinted in Philip Foner, ed., *We, the Other People: Alternative Declarations of Independence, 1829–1975* (Urbana: University of Illinois Press, 1976), 59–63.

5. McCurdy, *The Anti-Rent Era*, 19; on the developments of autumn 1839, see Christman, *Tin Horns and Calico*, 20–38.

6. William H. Seward, "'A Proclamation,' by William H. Seward, Governor of the State of N. York," *New York Herald*, December 12, 1839. The next day, the *Herald* printed the names of thirty "ringleaders" from the six dissenting Helderberg townships.

7. As quoted in Edward Potts Cheyney, *The Anti-Rent Agitation in the State of New York, 1839–1846* (Philadelphia: Porter and Coates, 1887), 35. My summary of the state's intervention is based on pp. 30–35.

8. "The Revolt of the Helderburgh!!! War!! War!!!" *Albany Microscope Extra*, December 10, 1839. The image and lengthy report are available through the New York State Library Digital Collections (BRO1508+), https://nysl.ptfs.com/data/Library5/108871.PDF.

9. James Crouthamel, *Bennett's* New York Herald *and the Rise of the Popular Press* (Syracuse, NY: Syracuse University Press, 1989), 105–6.

10. James Gordon Bennett, "'A Proclamation,' by James Gordon Bennett, Governor of the State of Good Sense," *New York Herald*, December 12, 1839.

11. A decade after its establishment, the *Herald's* circulation of twelve thousand made it "the most popular and profitable daily newspaper in the United States" (Crouthamel, *Bennett's* New York Herald, 4).

12. James Johnson, "King Robert the Bruce's Address to His Army," in *The Scotish Musical Museum*, with notes by William Stenhouse (Edinburgh: William Blackwood and Sons, 1839), 495–96.

13. Crouthamel, *Bennett's* New York Herald, 6.

14. Although the more modern spelling would be *rout* rather than *route*, I use the original here. In *Tin Horns and Calico*, Christman discusses the *Herald's* satire (37–38) and transcribes it (322–23) but does not mention a corresponding tune.

15. Walter Scott and J. G. Lockhart, *The Poetical Works of Sir Walter Scott, Comprising Minstrelsy of the Scottish Border . . .* (Philadelphia: E. L. Carey and A. Hart, 1839), 195. "Thomas the Rhymer" is discussed on pp. 194–203.

16. Francis James Child, *The English and Scottish Popular Ballads*, vol. 1, part 2 (Boston: Houghton Mifflin, 1884), 317–29.

17. Bertrand Bronson, *The Traditional Tunes of the Child Ballads* (Princeton, NJ: Princeton University Press, 1959), 1:324–25.

18. Bertrand Bronson, "Some Observations about Melodic Variation in British-American Folk Tunes," *Journal of the American Musicological Society* 3, no. 2 (Summer 1950): 120–34; here 127.

19. Marcy served three terms as New York governor, 1833–1838. "Prince" John's appellation was initially occasioned by his 1837 trip to England for Victoria's coronation, where he danced with the young queen. See Pierre Van Buren Hoes, "Van Buren's Lindenwold," *New York Times*, July 30, 1898.

20. Scott, *Minstrelsy of the Scottish Border*, 85; Grove Music Online, s.v. "Scotland, Traditional Music," by Kenneth Elliott, Francis Collinson, and Peggy Duesenberry, January 20, 2001, https://doi.org/10.1093/gmo/9781561592630.article.40113.

21. Scott, *Minstrelsy of the Scottish Border*, 99–100.

22. James Oswald, *The Caledonian Pocket Companion, Containing a Favorite Collection of Scots Tunes with Variations for the German Flute or Violin*, book 12 (London: Straight & Skillern, [1770?]), 157.

23. Franz Joseph Haydn, "Pentland Hills," Hoboken XXXIa:33, in *A Selection of Original Scots Songs*, ed. William Napier, vol. 2, no. 34 (London: William Napier, 1792).

24. James Hogg, *The Jacobite Relics of Scotland; Being the Songs, Airs and Legends of the Adherents to the House of Stuart* (Edinburgh: William Blackwood, 1819), 163–65. The two versions of "Lesley's March" appear

on pp. 5–8. In 1810, Hogg published a volume of songs and poems called *The Forest Minstrel*. This phrase was used as a nom-de-plume by the Anti-Renter who wrote "The Contest" (plate 22) and "Haste to Delhi" (plate 24), as discussed in chapter 3.

25. Scott does not include a melody; see *Minstrelsy of the Scottish Border*, 92–94. Sources use several spellings of Lesley's surname interchangeably.

26. *Vrow* is dialect for the Dutch "vrouw" (i.e., *woman* in English; cf. the German *Frau*).

27. Oswald, "Lasly's March," in *The Caledonian Pocket Companion, in Six Volumes* (London: printed for the author, [1747?]), 36.

28. See, for example, the essays in Mark Slobin, James Kimball, Katherine Preston, and Deane Root, eds., *Emily's Songbook: Music in 1850s Albany* (Middleton, WI: A-R Editions, 2011).

29. Henry Jones Ford, *The Scotch-Irish in America* (Princeton, NJ: Princeton University Press, 1915), 249–58. Also, see *The Encyclopedia of New York State* (Syracuse, NY: Syracuse University Press, 2005), s.vv. "immigration," "Scots."

30. Charles Hamm, *Yesterdays: Popular Song in America* (New York: W. W. Norton, 1979), 59–61. The Scotch snap is a rhythm in which a short, accented note is followed by a longer note; it is often notated as a sixteenth on the beat followed by a dotted eighth.

31. McCurdy, *The Anti-Rent Era*, 37–55.

32. My rendition—with Matt Malsky on tin horn—can be heard on SoundCloud: https://soundcloud.com/user-373664407/halderbarak-quickstep.

33. Lester S. Levy, *Picture the Songs: Lithographs from the Sheet Music of Nineteenth-Century America* (Baltimore: Johns Hopkins University Press, 1976), 42.

34. Harry Judson, *A History of the Troy Citizen Corps, Troy, N. Y.* (Troy, NY: Troy Times Printing House, 1884), 155–56; New York State Library catalog entry for "Halderbarak Quick Step" (SCO12564). The entry speculates that the dedication's "ladies" may be the dress-wearing Calico Indians. However, the Anti-Renters' adoption of such disguises began the following year, 1841.

35. *Albany Argus*, December 16, 1840, quoted in Judson, *History of the Troy Citizen Corps*, 22. On the Helderberg campaign, see 17–23.

36. Jewel Smith, *Transforming Women's Education: Liberal Arts and Music in Female Seminaries* (Urbana: University of Illinois Press, 2019), 158.

37. John Andrews, "Troy Citizens Corps Grand March" (Troy, NY: Troy Music Saloon, n.d.), https://levysheetmusic.mse.jhu.edu/collection/180/097. This work is available through the Lester S. Levy Collection of Sheet Music (hereafter, Levy Collection). I wish to thank curator Sam Bessen for providing information on the physical imprint.

38. Judson, *A History of the Troy Citizen Corps*, 156.

39. Andrews's "Firemans Quick March" is available through the Levy Collection. Editions were published by Andrews in Troy, and by Firth & Hall and J. L. Hewit in New York. None include a publication date.

40. Christman, *Tin Horns and Calico*, 41.

41. As quoted in McCurdy, *The Anti-Rent Era*, 69.

42. "A Helderberg farmer," as quoted in Christman, *Tin Horns and Calico*, 43.

43. The title was included in a long list of works published by Atwill in the *New York Tribune*, September 4, 1841; Atwill advertised the title again in the *New York Herald*, May 4 and 16, 1842.

44. C. L. Underner, "The Van Rensselaer Guards Grand March and Quickstep," arranged for pianoforte by W. L. Reston (Albany: 1837). The only known imprint of this work is in volume 3 of the "Collection of Sheet Music for Piano Assembled by Ursula Jane Boyd in the 19th Century," held by Special Collections, Mitchell Memorial Library, Mississippi State University. Boyd was the mother of John Boyd Thacher, whose widow

donated the land for John Boyd Thacher (NY) State Park (encompassing much of the Helderberg Escarpment). Underner's "Governor Seward's Quick Step" (Albany, NY: Wm. G. Boardman, 1839) is available through the Levy Collection.

45. *New-York Military Magazine* 1, no. 11 (August 21, 1841): 175.

46. Deloria, *Playing Indian* (New Haven, CT: Yale University Press, 1998), 2.

47. As quoted by Huston, *Land and Freedom*, 116.

48. Several of the alleged perpetrators of Cornelius Hogeboom's death fled to Canada; another dozen were tried and acquitted in New York (Ellis, *Landlords and Farmers*, 34–35).

49. Ellis, *Landlords and Farmers*, 12; Myers, *History of the Supreme Court*, 109–11. Within the next few years, the Seneca lost more than two million acres in the Phelps and Gorham Purchase. Robert Morris acquired another four million acres, which he promptly sold to the Holland Land Company.

50. Deloria, *Playing Indian*, 64.

51. Calvin Pepper, *Manor of Rensselaerwyck* (Albany, NY: Albany and Rensselaer Anti-Rent Associations, 1846), 6–8. Pepper's thirty-five-page pamphlet was a compilation of articles he published in the *Albany Freeholder* in 1845.

52. Huston, *Land and Freedom*, 103–11.

53. Albert Champlin Mayham, *The Anti-Rent War on Blenheim Hill* (Jefferson, NY: Frederick Frazee, 1906), 33.

54. Christman, *Tin Horns and Calico*, 328–29.

55. Huston, *Land and Freedom*, 123–24; representative tabulations of the age, occupation, and property of those who identified as "Indians" appear on pp. 226–27.

56. Gardner, *Folklore from the Schoharie Hills*, 31–32.

57. Gardner, *Folklore from the Schoharie Hills*, 31; Thomas Wermuth, "Charivari on the Hudson: Misrule, Disorder, and Festive Play in the Countryside, 1750–1900," *The Hudson River Valley Review* 32, no. 2 (Spring 2016): 27–52. Also, see Roger Abraham, "Calico Indians: Festive Play in Acts of Resistance," *Voices: The Journal of New York Folklore* 32, nos. 3–4 (Fall–Winter 2006): 35–41.

58. Huston, *Land and Freedom*, 121–22; Deloria, *Playing Indian*, 3.

59. Broadside, Stephen Foster Collection, Center for American Music, University of Pittsburgh Library System. The only other known imprint is held by Special Collections, New York State Library (SCO BD1633). Unfortunately, the full titles of both "Bill Snyder" and its companion broadside ("We Are True Anti-Renters") are missing from the latter's tattered copies. Both sets of broadsides can be viewed online through the respective libraries' digital collections.

60. Richard Crawford casts doubt on Emmett's having composed the music of "Dan Tucker" for several reasons, including the sheet music's attribution of the lyrics alone to him. See *America's Musical Life: A History* (New York: W. W. Norton, 2001), 202–12.

61. Playbill of March 20–21, 1843, in William Mahar, *Behind the Burnt Cork Mask: Early Blackface Minstrelsy and Antebellum Popular Culture* (Urbana: University of Illinois Press, 1999), 42.

62. According to Kathryn Haines, head of the Center for American Music, University of Pittsburgh, there is no known connection between Stephen Collins Foster and S. H. Foster (email of January 2, 2024). On Solomon H. Foster, see Donna Lagoy and Donna Seldman, *The Underground Railroad in the Adirondack Town of Chester* (Charleston, SC: History Press, 2016), 115–16.

63. Sheriff Batterman was tarred and feathered, and his several assistants were compelled to jump three times while shouting "Down with the Rent!" See "Anti-Rent Insurrection in Albany—Outrage on the Sheriff," *Illustrated London News*, October 5, 1844, 211 and ff.

64. Gardner, following Mayham, attributed the song to "the Franklin Brothers of South Jefferson"; see *Folklore from the Schoharie Hills*, 32; Mayham, *Anti-Rent War on Blenheim Hill*, 38.

65. "The End of Bill Snyder," in Christman, *Tin Horns and Calico*, 321.

66. Seeger and Renehan's rendition is available through Smithsonian Folkways (FH5257). Seeger first released "Old Dan Tucker" in 1957 on *American Favorite Ballads* (Smithsonian Folkways FW02320_207).

67. Edward Renehan, ed., *The Clearwater Songbook* (New York: G. Schirmer, 1980), 58–59. Jerry Silverman's setting appears in *New York Sings: 400 Years of the Empire State in Song* (Albany: State University of New York Press: 2009), 230–31.

68. Silverman, *New York Sings*, 231. Renehan describes the typical confrontation between farmers and deputies as follows: "the farmers would waylay him, burn his writs of eviction, tar and feather and (most often) kill him" (*The Clearwater Songbook*, 58). Pete Seeger and Paul Du Bois Jacobs claim not only that Snyder was killed but also that the incident took place in Greene (rather than Albany) County. See Pete Seeger and Paul Du Bois Jacobs, *Pete Seeger's Storytelling Book* (San Diego: Harcourt, 2001), 195–98.

69. Ralph Frasca, "The *Helderberg Advocate*: A Public-Nuisance Prosecution a Century before *Near v. Minnesota*," *Journal of Supreme Court History* 26, no. 3 (November 2001): 215–30, here 218 and 219. As Frasca laments, just two issues of the biweekly are extant. The last known full run, held by Rutgers University Library, has disappeared.

70. McCurdy, *The Anti-Rent Era*, 95.

71. Frasca, "The *Helderberg Advocate*," 220.

72. Frasca, "The *Helderberg Advocate*," 221–22; also see Thomas Summerhill, *Harvest of Dissent: Agrarianism in Nineteenth Century New York* (Urbana: University of Illinois Press, 2005), 67–69.

73. Reeve Huston, "Multiple Crossings: Thomas Ainge Devyr and Transatlantic Land Reform," in *Transatlantic Rebels: Agrarian Radicalism in Comparative Context*, ed. Thomas Summerhill and James Scott (East Lansing: Michigan State University Press, 2004), 137–66.

74. Devyr included an excerpt from his third letter to the *Helderberg Advocate* in his *Odd Book of the Nineteenth Century*, American Section, 42–43.

75. As characterized in Christman, *Tin Horns and Calico*, 57–58.

76. Mayham, *The Anti-Rent War on Blenheim Hill*, 31–32. A large cloth banner with this phrase (probably made in Grafton circa 1845) can be viewed through the Albany Institute of History and Art digital exhibit, "50 Objects: New York's Capital Region in 50 Objects," https://www.albanyinstitute.org/online-exhibition/50-objects/section/anti-rent-movement.

77. As quoted in Christman, *Tin Horns and Calico*, 62.

78. Huston, *Land and Freedom*, 103.

79. Huston, "Multiple Crossings: Thomas Ainge Devyr," 151; Devyr, *Our Natural Rights* (Williamsburg, NY: published by the author, 1842).

80. As quoted in Daniel Mandell, *The Lost Tradition of Economic Equality in America, 1600–1870* (Baltimore: Johns Hopkins University Press, 2020), 193. Although this was usually expressed as the right of "man," the NRA generally supported equal rights for women.

81. Helene Zahler, *Eastern Workingmen and National Land Policy, 1829–1862* (1941; repr., New York: Greenwood Press, 1969), 22.

82. Zahler, *Eastern Workingmen*, 41.

83. *Working Man's Advocate*, March 30, 1844, as quoted in Jamie Bronstein, "'Under Their Own Vine and Fig Tree': Land Reform and Working-Class Experience in Britain and America, 1830–1860" (PhD diss., Stanford University, 1996), 11.

84. Reprinted in Foner, *We, the Other People*, 47–50; emphasis in the original.

85. As quoted by Christman, *Tin Horns and Calico*, 20.

86. Sean Wilentz, *The Rise of American Democracy: Jefferson to Lincoln* (New York: W. W. Norton, 2006), 506. Also, see Derek Scott, "The US Presidential Campaign Songster, 1840–1900," in *Cheap Print and Popular Song*

in the Nineteenth Century: A Cultural History of the Songster, ed. Paul Watt, Derek Scott, and Patrick Spedding (Cambridge: Cambridge University Press, 2017), 73–90.

87. Greeley, as quoted by McCurdy, *The Anti-Rent Era*, 55.

88. A. B. Norton, ed., *Tippecanoe Songs of the Log Cabin Boys and Girls of 1840* (Mt. Vernon, OH: A. B. Norton, 1888).

89. Ray Browne, *The Alabama Folk Lyric: A Study in Origins and Media of Dissemination* (Bowling Green, OH: Bowling Green University Popular Press, 1979), 404.

90. "The Liberty Ball" appeared in George Washington Clark's *The Liberty Minstrel*, discussed in chapter 3. Additionally, "Rosin the Beau" was the basis for the shape-note hymn "Sawyer's Exit," published in the 1850 collection *The Sacred Harp*. It became associated with the Seattle area as the "Old Settlers Song" and "Acres of Clams." "Down in the Willow Garden" (sometimes called "Rose Connelly") "is invariably sung" to "Rosin the Beau"; see D. K. Wilgus, "'Rose Connoley': An Irish Ballad," *Journal of American Folklore* 92, no. 364 (April–June 1979): 172–95; here 172–73.

91. Edward Bunting, *The Ancient Music of Ireland* (Dublin: Hodges and Smith, 1796–1840; repr. Dublin: Waltons' Piano and Musical Instrument Galleries, 1969), 14. Bunting claims an emphasis on the submediant (scale degree 6) is also a "Scotic" trait, "for we Irish are the original Scoti" (14).

92. On song at the NRA's New York meetings, see Jamie Bronstein, *Land Reform and Working-Class Experience in Britain and the United States, 1800–1862* (Stanford, CA: Stanford University Press, 1999), 144–46. Lyrics for "The Working Man's League" and "The Agrarian Ball" are included in Philip Foner, *American Labor Songs of the Nineteenth Century* (Urbana: University of Illinois Press, 1975), 47–49.

93. Zahler, *Eastern Workingmen*, 43; for additional details, see Mark Lause, *Young America: Land, Labor, and the Republican Community* (Urbana: University of Illinois Press, 2005), 36–39.

94. Zahler, *Eastern Workingmen*, 47; John Pickering, *Working Man's Political Economy* (Cincinnati: Thomas Varney, 1847), concludes with poems and songs on pp. 194–206 (note that "The Agrarian Ball" is titled "Freeman's Song").

95. Huston, *Land and Freedom*, 108.

96. McCurdy, *The Anti-Rent Era*, 149–51. The activist Sojourner Truth and her parents were enslaved by Hardenbergh descendants at the time of her birth (circa 1800) in Ulster County.

97. Hecht, "Poetry and Politics in the Anti-Rent Press," 10.

98. Dale Cockrell, ed., *Excelsior: Journals of the Hutchinson Family Singers, 1842–1846* (Stuyvesant, NY: Pendragon Press, 1989), 96–97.

99. The Hutchinson Family, "The Old Granite State" (Boston: Oliver Ditson, 1843), https://levysheetmusic. mse.jhu.edu/collection/020/102. Scott Gac notes that the Hutchinsons' appearance in Albany was the "defining moment" of their early career. See *Singing for Freedom: The Hutchinson Family Singers and the Nineteenth-Century Culture of Reform* (New Haven, CT: Yale University Press, 2008), 142–43.

100. On the spread of voluntary and faith-based associations devoted to issues such as temperance, abolition, and community reform in the leasehold districts, see Huston, *Land and Freedom*, 61–64. For an overview of "Temperance songs" in the United States, see my entry in *Grove Music Online*, July 1, 2014, https:// doi.org/10.1093/gmo/9781561592630.article.A2263236.

101. William Bradbury, ed., *Temperance Chimes* (New York: National Temperance Society, 1867). Lyrics (but not music) for "The Teetotallers Are Coming" were published in the *New Temperance Melodist* (Boston: Oliver Ditson, 1839). It is worth noting that *Hewlett's Temperance Songster*, published in 1844 in nearby Cooperstown, indicated that "The Teetotallers Are Coming" should be sung to Air–"Granite State."

102. The Albany printer of "We Are True Anti-Renters" seems to have economized on space by omitting repetition of the first line of text in verses 2–9 (ABC). Presumably, that line was repeated in performance so that each verse would resemble the first verse (ABAC).

103. The tune and text for "Old Church Yard," which appeared in Joshua Himes's *Millennial Harp; Designed for Meetings on the Second Coming of Christ* (Boston, 1843), is reprinted in Cockrell's edition of the Hutchinson journals, *Excelsior* (99).

104. As quoted in Ellie Hisama, "The Ruth Crawford Seeger Sessions," *Daedalus* 142, no. 4 (Fall 2013): 51–63; here, 56. Also, see Ruth Crawford Seeger's 1951 essay, "Keep the Song Going!" in her collection, *The Music of American Folk Song*, 137–43.

105. Christman, *Tin Horns and Calico*, 82–83.

106. Jay Gould, *History of Delaware County and Border Wars of New York, Containing a Sketch of the Late Anti-Rent Difficulties in Delaware* (Roxbury, NY: Keeny & Gould, 1856), 255, 260–63. These pages include a vibrant description of "Indian" disguises.

107. On spreading the news, see Zahler, *Eastern Workingmen*, 43–46.

108. Huston, "Multiple Crossings: Thomas Ainge Devyr," 149, emphasis original. The classic study of the worker who reads is Jacques Ranciere, *Nights of Labor: The Workers' Dream in Nineteenth Century France*, trans. John Drury (Philadelphia: Temple University Press, 1989).

109. Imprints are held by four archives, including the American Antiquarian Society and the Clements Library, University of Michigan.

110. The head and cap are not unlike the bust in the 1825 Society of Red Men poster reproduced in Deloria, *Playing Indian*, 61.

111. After graduating from Union College in Schenectady, Morgan founded two such groups, the Gordian Knot and the New Confederacy, that actively aided the Iroquois (Deloria, *Playing Indian*, 72–73).

112. A neat additional syncretism is that the figure's short skirt could allude to the Scots Highlander kilt.

113. Mayham, *The Anti-Rent War on Blenheim Hill*, 33, 40–41.

114. Planché's several influences on theater include the introduction of historically accurate costumes. His libretto for *Oberon* became Carl Maria von Weber's last opera.

115. *The Posie; An Elegant Selection of the Most Popular Songs, Duets, and Glees*, part 3 (Glasgow: Francis Orr and Sons, 1830), 37. Planché's authorship is not acknowledged in this edition. In *Hadaway's Select Songster*, a Mr. Walton is credited with singing "With Helmet on His Brow." Neither author nor tune is named. *Hadaway's Select Songster* was edited by T. H. Hadaway, comedian (Philadelphia: Gihon and Kucher, 1840), 70.

116. Hathitrust has digitized several American versions, including John Hill Hewitt's "A Soldier's the Lad I Adore" (Baltimore: George Willig, 1828). The violinist Joseph Mayseder popularized variations on the tune.

117. *The Sky-Lark: A Collection of Songs Set to Music* (London: Thomas Tegg, 1825), 188–90; available through the National Library of Scotland: https://digital.nls.uk/special-collections-of-printed-music/archive/87683584.

118. Zahler, *Eastern Workingmen*, 46, 101; Huston, *Land and Freedom*, 164. Bovay moved to Wisconsin in 1850 and soon cofounded Ripon College.

119. Gould, *History of Delaware County*, 254–55; Devyr, *Odd Book of the Nineteenth Century*, Irish and English Section, 161–62.

120. Christman, *Tin Horns and Calico*, 97. A fundraising letter issued by the "Freeholders Committee of Safety" is held by the American Antiquarian Society (BDSDS, February 20, 1845). The committee name recalls patriots' organizations preceding the American Revolution.

121. Christman, *Tin Horns and Calico*, 109.

122. Ellis, *Landlords and Farmers*, 247.

123. As quoted in McCurdy, *The Anti-Rent Era*, 166.

Chapter 3

1. Schoolcraft, *Helderbergia*, canto 4, stanza 83.

2. Silas Wright, "Message to the Legislature—1845," New York State Government Documents, New York State Library, OCLC/NY ID 4671459 (January 7, 1845).

3. The act, which was approved January 28, 1845, is reproduced in Gould, *History of Delaware County*, 263–66. As I noted in the prelude, the core of New York's mask law would remain in effect until summer 2020, when the COVID-19 pandemic necessitated its repeal.

4. McCurdy, *The Anti-Rent Era*, 175–76.

5. Ellis, *Landlords and Farmers*, 272.

6. Christman, *Tin Horns and Calico*, 144–45; cf. McCurdy, *The Anti-Rent Era*, 177–78.

7. "The Spring Campaign, or, The Tory Exploits," transcribed in Dorothy Kubik, *A Free Soil—A Free People: The Anti-Rent War in Delaware County, New York* (Fleischmanns, NY: Purple Mountain Press, 1997), 139–41; also Christman, *Tin Horns and Calico*, 329–32. Kubik's source is a broadside at the Delaware County Historical Association; Christman says the poem was supplied by a Delaware County resident "from Anti-Rent material gathered by his mother."

8. Gould, *History of Delaware County*, 266–72. It's worth noting that Gould and Mayham (*Anti-Rent War on Blenheim Hill*, 44) identify Squires as "Big Thunder," the pseudonym Boughton was alleged to have used.

9. Christman, *Tin Horns and Calico*, 164. Boughton's homecoming was celebrated by an open-air dinner and ball at the tavern in Alps.

10. *The Working Man's Advocate*, March 15, 1845, reprinted in Zahler, *Eastern Workingmen*, 207–8 (appendix 2); emphasis added.

11. I wish to thank Martha Rozett for this observation.

12. Richard J. Wolfe, *Secular Music in America, 1801–25: A Bibliography* (New York: New York Public Library, 1964), 1:92–93.

13. "Blue Eyed Mary" (Philadelphia: G. Willig's Musical Magazine [1817?]); available at HathiTrust (https://hdl.handle.net/2027/mdp.39015096477008). Helen Kendrick Johnson, *Our Familiar Songs and Those Who Made Them: Three Hundred Standard Songs* (New York: Henry Holt, 1881), 275–76.

14. William Cullen Bryant, "Letter of February 4, 1821 (#65)," in *The Letters of William Cullen Bryant*, vol. 1, *1809–1836*, eds. William Cullen Bryant II and Thomas Voss (New York: Fordham University Press, 1975), 100–101. Bryant was living in Great Barrington, Massachusetts, at the time; presumably, "Blue Eyed Mary" was purchased in nearby Albany. Wolfe does not list any Albany publications in *Secular Music in America*.

15. John Howson, "Edward Rushton (1856–1914): Radical Liverpool Poet and Ballad Maker," *Folk Music Journal* 12, no. 2 (2022): 36–59. Rushton's 1799 illustrated broadside, with the complete poem, appears on p. 43. The abolitionist Rushton established Liverpool's first school for the blind.

16. *The American Poetical Miscellany, Original and Selected* (Philadelphia: Robert Johnson, C. & A. Conrad, and Mathew Carey, 1809), 13–15; emphasis original.

17. Greeley began the *Tribune* in 1841 as an outgrowth of his work on the Whig party organ, *Log Cabin*; see Adam-Max Tuchinsky, *Horace Greeley's New-York Tribune: Civil War–Era Socialism and the Crisis of Free Labor* (Ithaca, NY: Cornell University Press, 2009), 5–6, 129–39.

18. Douglas Jerrold, *The Rent Day*, 2nd ed. (London: C. Chapple, 1832), 65.

19. "The Park Theatre," *New-York Mirror*, September 22, 1832, 95. Although her first name is not given, it is likely that the young Miss Turnbull commended for the premiere was Julia Turnbull, who performed in conjunction with the 1845 production of *The Rent Day* in Albany.

20. "Theatrical," *Albany Argus*, June 1, 1841. The play was so popular at mid-century that sources often refer to it metonymically through the main character's name, Martin Heywood.

21. Carl Carmer, *The Hudson* (New York: Farrar and Rinehart, 1939), 269. Unfortunately, Carmer does not identify his sources.

22. Jerrold, *The Rent Day*, 7.

23. Advertisement, *Albany Evening Atlas*, June 10, 1845; Carmer, *The Hudson*, 270.

24. Digital images of David Wilkie's painting *Distraining for Rent* (1815) and an engraving (by Abraham Raimbach) of his *Rent Day* (1807) can be viewed on the National Galleries of Scotland website (https://www.nationalgalleries.org).

25. Frank Rahill, *The World of Melodrama* (University Park: Pennsylvania State University Press, 1967), 162. Jerrold, who considered himself the inventor of British domestic melodrama, also authored the comic *Mrs. Caudle's Curtain Lectures*, which was serialized in the London *Punch* and reprinted in the *Albany Freeholder* and *Young America* during the summer of 1845.

26. Carmer, *The Hudson*, 270.

27. Nancy Fredricks, *Melville's Art of Democracy* (Athens: University of Georgia Press, 1995), 13; on Melville and Jerrold's mutual admiration, see 142n9.

28. Huston, *Land and Freedom*, 108.

29. Hecht, "Poetry and Politics in the Anti-Rent Press," 5.

30. Hecht, "Poetry and Politics in the Anti-Rent Press," 9.

31. Thomas Devyr, "Original Poetry," *Albany Freeholder*, July 2, 1845.

32. As quoted by William Stenhouse in James Johnson, *The Scotish Musical Museum* (Edinburgh: William Blackwood and Sons, 1839), 493. This publication reprinted—with supplemental material by Stenhouse—*The Scots Musical Museum*, compiled by James Johnson and published in six volumes from 1787 to 1803.

33. In a neat symmetry, Delaware County historian John Duncan Monroe dedicated his account of the movement to a past family member "who, as a boy of fifteen, saw the War Chief of the Anti-Renters as another Rob Roy." See John Duncan Monroe, *The Anti-Rent War in Delaware County, New York: The Revolt Against the Rent System* (privately printed, 1940). Thanks to Joe Festa, Special Collections Librarian, Fenimore Art Museum, for making this text available.

34. Stenhouse, in Johnson, *Scotish Musical Museum*, 494.

35. Wolfe, *Secular Music in America*, 138–39. Wolfe lists more than a dozen distinct publications, not including reissues, encompassing several different instrumental and vocal arrangements.

36. "Bruce's Address to His Army" (Philadelphia: G. Willig's Musical Magazine, n.d.), https://levysheetmusic.mse.jhu.edu/collection/063/018. George Odell, *Annals of the New York Stage*, vol. 2, *1798–1821* (New York: Columbia University Press, 1927), 507–8.

37. Johnson, *Scotish Musical Museum*, 495–96. Stenhouse substitutes a different arrangement of "Bruce's Address" for the one that appeared in Johnson's collection. The editor's goal was to restore the work's "original simplicity, according to the first intention of the bard," Robert Burns.

38. From *The New England Psalm Singer* (1770), reprinted in Richard Crawford, *An Introduction to America's Music* (New York: W. W. Norton, 2001), 30–31.

39. Hecht, "Poetry and Politics in the Anti-Rent Press," 11.

40. Socrates, "(*For the Albany Freeholder*) . . . [dated May 10]," *Albany Freeholder*, June 11, 1845.

41. James Sanderson, "Hail to the Chief" (New York: William Dubois, 1817 or 1818); available through HathiTrust, https://hdl.handle.net/2027/mdp.39015096438398. Elise Kirk, " 'Hail to the Chief': The Origins and Legacies of an American Ceremonial Tune," *American Music* 15, no. 2 (Summer 1997): 123–36; here, 127–28.

42. Kirk, " 'Hail to the Chief,' " 131.

43. Although Christman indicates that this song (like "Bill Snyder") also appeared on a "handbill," no such broadside seems extant; see *Tin Horns and Calico*, 332–33.

44. Related 1843 publications include "Boatman's Dance," issued by G. Willig and A. Fiot (Philadelphia) and William Dubois (New York); also, "Boatman's Song" (G. P. Reed, Boston).

45. E. Brown, "Anti-Rent Celebration," *Albany Freeholder*, July 16, 1845; Christman, *Tin Horns and Calico*, 159–60. Hecht claims that "Hardy Tillers" closed the celebration at Peter's Grove ("Poetry and Politics in the Anti-Rent Press," 3–4). Christman and Hecht's transcriptions omit the first stanza.

46. "Middleburgh Anti-Rent Celebration," *Albany Freeholder*, July 9, 1845.

47. "Anti-Rent Celebration," *Albany Freeholder*, July 2, 1845; "Anti-Rent Celebration at Bloomville," *Albany Freeholder*, July 16, 1845.

48. Hecht, "Poetry and Politics in the Anti-Rent Press," 14. The entire poem is reprinted in his collection, *Freemen Awake*, 43–46.

49. Huston, *Land and Freedom*, 113.

50. Hogg's collection was published without musical notation. However, a modern critical edition of James Hogg's *The Forest Minstrel*, edited by P. D. Garside and Richard Jackson, includes musical notation prepared by Peter Horsfall and a CD (Edinburgh University Press, 2006); on Carey's edition, see p. xlix. Carey was also the American publisher of Rushton's "Blue Eyed Mary."

51. James Hogg and S. DeWitt Bloodgood, *Familiar Anecdotes of Sir Walter Scott* (New York: Harper and Brothers, 1834), 22.

52. A slightly different version of the third verse—said to be "composed by a woman over in 'Batahvy' . . . to the tune of 'Bannockburn'"—appears in Dr. Clara Barrus's biography, *John Burroughs: Boy and Man* (New York: Doubleday, Page, 1920), 129. The future naturalist Burroughs, like his schoolmate Jay Gould, was an eyewitness to Anti-Rent activities in Delaware County (123–33).

53. Christman, *Tin Horns and Calico*, 158–59; "Prisoners in Jail" is reprinted on pp. 340–41. The July 9 *Freeholder* reproduced a short item from the *Hudson Gazette* complaining about Little Thunder's violin playing in jail.

54. The poem does not appear to be related to Stephen Foster's song "Hard Times," which was published in 1854.

55. The town, part of the 160,000-acre Livingston Manor, was named for the family's place of origin in Scotland.

56. Steve Roud, *The New Penguin Book of English Folk Songs* (London: Penguin Classics, 2012), 432. The seven verses of "Caroline and Her Young Sailor Bold" appear with a representative tune variant on pp. 157–59. Additional versions of the lyrics are available through Broadside Ballads Online, Bodleian Library, Oxford University. For an exemplary performance, see Joe Heaney's 1964 recording on *The Road from Connemara*, rereleased on CD by Topic Records Ltd. in 2000.

57. Moses Blake's melody and five verses are preserved in the entry: J. F. Guyer, "Caroline and Her Brisk Young Sailor Boy," June 1906 (?), George Gardiner Manuscript Collection, Vaughan Williams Memorial Library, https://www.vwml.org/record/GG/1/5/278.

58. Devyr, *Odd Book of the Nineteenth Century*, American Section, 43; also, see Christman, *Tin Horns and Calico*, 155–57. On Anti-Rentism and contemporary party politics, see Thomas Summerhill, *Harvest of Dissent: Agrarianism in Nineteenth Century New York* (Urbana: University of Illinois Press, 2005), 60–88.

59. Huston, "Multiple Crossings: Thomas Ainge Devyr," 157–58.

60. Russell lived in North America from the early 1830s until 1842, when he made his London debut. Charles Hamm considers him one of the most important mid-century composers of American song for his mixing of ethnic and classical styles; see *Yesterdays*, 176–84.

61. Hamm, *Yesterdays*, 182. "A Life on the Ocean Wave" has been a regimental march of Her Majesty's Royal Marines since the late nineteenth century.

62. Henry Russell and Epes Sargent, "A Life on the Ocean Wave," (New York: Hewitt & Jaques, 1838). The complete score is available from HathiTrust, https://hdl.handle.net/2027/mdp.39015096394237.

63. Ego, "For the Freeholder," *Albany Freeholder*, October 8, 1845.

64. On German Palatinate immigrants to the region and their early entanglements with the Livingstons, see Hudson Gazette, ed., *Columbia County at the End of the Century* (Hudson, NY: Hudson Gazette, 1900), 23–27.

65. Azar Nafisi, "An Iranian American Writer Makes a Case against Censorship and for Rushdie," interview by Steve Inskeep, *Morning Edition*, NPR, August 23, 2022, audio, 7:00, https://www.npr.org/2022/08/23/1118959407/an-iranian-american-writer-makes-a-case-against-censorship-and-for-rushdie.

66. Christman, *Tin Horns and Calico*, 220.

67. McCurdy, *Anti-Rent Era*, 216. Detailed accounts of the confrontation appear in Christman, *Tin Horns and Calico*, 175–84; Monroe, *Anti-Rent War in Delaware County*, 22–34; and Cheyney, *The Anti-Rent Agitation*, 44–47.

68. McCurdy, *Anti-Rent Era*, 219; on the "Delhi Bastille," see 369n25. I have approximated the number of individuals charged, held, and tried because contemporary and scholarly accounts vary.

69. *Young America* printed Edward O'Conner's farewell poem to his fiancée and friends directly above "Haste to Delhi" (November 22, 1845).

70. Huston, *Land and Freedom*, 150; George Henry Evans quoted in McCurdy, *Anti-Rent Era*, 221.

71. "The Inhuman Anti Rent Murder" is available through the American Antiquarian Society Digital Image Archive, https://gigi.mwa.org/imagearchive/fileName/535569_0001.tif. "The Death of Osman N. Steele" is available through the Smithsonian Institution National Museum of American History, https://americanhistory.si.edu/collections/search/object/nmah_324900.

72. Christman, *Tin Horns and Calico*, 183; no tune is indicated.

73. Gould, *History of Delaware County*, 272–82.

74. For a good account of the confrontation and its resonance for Delaware County residents to the mid-1990s, see Kubik, *A Free Soil*, 96–137.

75. "Anti-Rent War," site marker erected by the New York State Education Department in 1932.

76. Steele quoted in Christman, *Tin Horns and Calico*, 178.

77. Isabel Thompson Kelsay, "The Trial of Big Thunder," *New York History* 16, no. 3 (Cooperstown, NY: Fenimore Art Museum, July 1935): 266–77; Christman, *Tin Horns and Calico*, 204–19. Jordan succeeded Van Buren as the New York State attorney general. On the practice of inmates providing undercompensated labor under harsh conditions, which began in Auburn, NY, see Robin Bernstein, *Freeman's Challenge: The Murder That Shook America's Original Prison for Profit* (Chicago: University of Chicago Press, 2024).

78. McCurdy, *Anti-Rent Era*, 223–28.

79. Huston, *Land and Freedom*, 150.

80. McCurdy, *Anti-Rent Era*, 256–58.

81. Huston, *Land and Freedom*, 125–29.

82. Devyr, *Odd Book of the Nineteenth Century*, American Section, 46–50; Christman, *Tin Horns and Calico*, 261–64.

83. Kubik, *A Free Soil*, 120; General Root quoted on 121.

84. McCurdy, *Anti-Rent Era*, 256–57; Thurlow Weed's *Evening Journal* editorial is quoted on 260.

85. Basch, *In the Eyes of the Law*, 149–56; here, 155.

86. Quoted from the New York State Library catalog entry for Broadside SCO BD1398. Endorsement of the Democrat Gardiner was a surprise and disappointment to Whig party operatives; see McCurdy, *Anti-Rent Era*, 266.

87. [Alexander Coffman Ross], "Tippecanoe and Tyler Too!" (Philadelphia: G. E. Blake, 1840). The full score is available online in "Music for the Nation, 1820–1860," Library of Congress, Music Division, https://lccn.loc.gov/2023797862.

88. Alexander Lee, "Little Pigs" (Boston: Charles Bradlee, n.d.), https://levysheetmusic.mse.jhu.edu/collection/047/116. The publisher was located at the address indicated (107 Washington Street) from 1834; see

Christine Ayars, *Contributions to the Art of Music in America by the Music Industries of Boston, 1640–1936* (New York: H. W. Wilson, 1937), 10–11.

89. Not completely obscure: Richard Dyer-Bennet's rendition can be heard on his self-titled 1958 LP, "Songs with Young People in Mind," reissued on CD in 2000 on Smithsonian Folkways (SFW45053). In the liner notes, Dyer-Bennet describes learning the song as a Scottish lullaby in 1934.

90. Some secondary sources associate "Little Pigs" with American minstrelsy. I suspect that the association, if correct, is from blackface performers taking up the glee as it gained popularity in the United States.

91. Johnson, *Our Familiar Songs*, 473–76. A jeweler by trade, the multifaceted Ross also pioneered the daguerreotype in the US. See C. B. Galbreath, "Song Writers of Ohio" in *Ohio Archaeological and Historical Publications* 14, no. 1 (Columbus: Ohio Archaeological and Historical Society, 1905): 62–87.

92. "This Great Commotion," arranged, performed, and recorded by Justin Friello; mixed and mastered by Olivia Canavan, available on SoundCloud (https://soundcloud.com/user-373664407/great-commotion). On the ramifications of the election, see Reeve Huston, "The Parties and 'The People': The New York Anti-Rent Wars and the Contours of Jacksonian Politics," *Journal of the Early Republic* 20, no. 2 (Summer 2000): 241–71.

93. Hecht, "Poetry and Politics in the Anti-Rent Press," 13.

94. Anonymous, "The Devil-Tavern," *The Knickerbocker*, July 1843, 32–44.

95. Joseph Waugh, *The Temperance Muse* (Providence, RI: H. H. Brown, 1842), 62–63.

96. George Washington Clark, *The Free Soil Minstrel* (New York: Martyn & Ely, 1848), 19–20. Although much of the material in this collection was reprinted from Clark's *The Liberty Minstrel*, "Salt River Chorus" was a new addition containing topical references. For more on Clark and his three antislavery and political song collections, see Jon Michael Spencer, *Protest and Praise: Sacred Music of Black Religion* (Minneapolis, MN: Fortress Press, 1990), 42–46.

97. See, for example, the broadside reprinted in Huston, *Land and Freedom*, 109.

98. For example, see G. H. Evans, "To Gerrit Smith," *Working Man's Advocate*, July 6, 1844.

99. Paul Miller's 2021 documentary *Searching for Timbuctoo* chronicles recent archaeological excavation of the community in the context of Smith's biography (https://www.timbuctoofilm.com/). Also see Amy Godine, *The Black Woods: Pursuing Racial Justice on the Adirondack Frontier* (Ithaca, NY: Cornell University Press, 2023).

100. New York Constitution of 1846, article 1, sections 12–15; as quoted in Murray, "The Anti-Rent Episode," 165.

101. McCurdy, *Anti-Rent Era*, 261.

102. An entirely different poem called "The Landlord's Lament" (and without a musical association) was published in the *Albany Freeholder*, October 29, 1845. See Hecht's transcription in *Freemen Awake* (70–71) and discussion in "Poetry and Politics in the Anti-Rent Press," 17–18.

103. William Chappell and George Alexander Macfarren, *The Ballad Literature and Popular Music of the Olden Time* (London: Chappell, 1855), 2:732. Chappell speculates that "Oh Dear" was probably created "not many years" before its theatrical debut circa 1790.

104. "Oh Dear, What Can the Matter Be" (New York: E. Riley, ca. 1823); available online through HathiTrust, https://hdl.handle.net/2027/mdp.39015096435980.

105. On the debate over pardon at the 1846 constitutional convention and its ramifications for the Anti-Renters and Governor Young, see Carolyn Strange, *Discretionary Justice: Pardon and Parole in New York from the Revolution to the Depression* (New York: New York University Press, 2016), 82–87.

106. Christman, *Tin Horns and Calico*, 281–90.

107. James Boughton, "Dr. Smith Azer Boughton," in *Bouton–Boughton Family* (Albany: Joel Munsell's Sons, 1890), 185–91.

108. "The Case of Smith Boughton," *New York Times*, February 23, 1896. After characterizing the "Anti-Rent League" as "immoral and demoralizing," the article abruptly concludes, "In fine, Boughton's conception of the 'institutions of his country' was wholly and absolutely evil."

109. "Home of Big Thunder," "Big Thunder" (at Hoags Corners), and "Sand Lake Union" (cemetery) can be viewed online at the Historical Marker Database, https://www.hmdb.org/.

110. See Mayham, *Anti-Rent War on Blenheim Hill*, 74–76, for a letter containing the "probable terms" of sale and signed by numerous tenant-purchasers.

111. McCurdy, *Anti-Rent Era*, 273.

112. McCurdy, *Anti-Rent Era*, 282–83 and 304–8. The title-test resolution revived the argument of *Quia Emptores*, according to which no new manors could be created after 1290. Quarter reservations were invalidated in *De Peyster v. Michael*.

113. Ellis, *Landlords and Farmers*, 302–3.

114. Simon Rosendale, "Closing Phases of the Manorial System in Albany," *Proceedings of the New York State Historical Association* 8 (1909): 234–45; here, 245.

115. Rosendale, "Closing Phases," 238–39.

Chapter 4

1. H. R. Schoolcraft, *Helderbergia*, canto IV, stanza 93. *Yclept* means to name or call.

2. The Albany Manor was occupied by Stephen IV until his death in 1868. In the early 1890s, much of the building was transported to Williams College, where it housed a fraternity until 1963. The building was demolished in 1973. Beverwyck Manor was home to the St. Anthony-on-Hudson Franciscan Seminary from 1912 to 1989 and is currently associated with the Roman Catholic Diocese of Albany.

3. William Van Rensselaer to Thomas Cole, July 18, 1839, as quoted in William Lavine Coleman, "Something of an Architect: Thomas Cole and the Country House Ideal" (PhD diss., University of California, Berkeley, 2015), 69.

4. Coleman, "Something of an Architect," 30, 71.

5. Stephen Van Rensselaer III became president of the Albany Institute in 1824 and was its "primary benefactor" until his death in 1839; see Christine Miles, "History of the AIHA Collections," introduction to *Albany Institute of History and Art: 200 Years of Collecting*, ed. Tammis Groft and Mary Alice Mackay (New York: Hudson Hills Press, 1998), 17–22.

6. Oliver J. Shaw, "The Rensselaer Grand Waltz" (Boston: W. H. Oakes, n.d.); available online through the New York State Library Digital Collections, Special Collections (SCO141).

7. Stephen and William's parents had been similarly honored by W. Van Deusen's pianoforte composition: "General Stephen Van Renselaer's March and Lady Van Renselaer Waltz" [*sic*] (Albany: published by the author, n.d.). A rare imprint is included in volume 3 of the *Collection of Sheet Music for Piano Assembled by Ursula Jane Boyd in the 19th Century*, held by Special Collections, Mitchell Memorial Library, Mississippi State University.

8. Oliver J. Shaw's many compositions are a rich source of information. He lived in Albany for about a decade, relocating to Utica, New York, in 1852; see Slobin et al., *Emily's Songbook*, 12.

9. Oliver J. Shaw's compositions, "Governor Bouck's Grand Quick Step" (Albany: Boardman & Gray, 1842); "Governor Wright's Grand March" (Boston: Wm. H. Oakes, 1844); and "Mansion Hall, Waltz Brilliante" (New York: A. A. Van Gelder, 1848), are available online through the Levy Collection. Contrary to the sheet music's caption, the building occupied by Mansion Hall was erected in the early eighteenth century, not 1680.

It is the legendary place where "Yankee Doodle" was written; today it houses New York's Crailo State Historic Site.

10. Otsego Hall was completed in 1799. A few years later, Fenimore Cooper was sent to school in Albany, where he became friends with Stephen IV. Wayne Franklin, *James Fenimore Cooper: The Early Years* (New Haven, CT: Yale University Press, 2007), 32–45. On the DeLanceys, see pp. 145–46.

11. David Maldwyn Ellis, "The Coopers and New York State Landholding Systems," *New York History* 35, no. 4 (1954): 412–22; here, 412. Also, see Alan Taylor, *William Cooper's Town: Power and Persuasion on the Frontier of the Early American Republic* (New York: A. A. Knopf, 1995).

12. James Fenimore Cooper, preface to *Satanstoe* (New York: Burgess, Stringer, 1845), vi.

13. Granville Hicks, "Landlord Cooper and the Anti-Renters," *The Antioch Review* 5, no. 1 (Spring 1945): 95–109; here 98. For a different interpretation, see Wayne Franklin, *James Fenimore Cooper: The Later Years* (New Haven, CT: Yale University Press, 2017), 361–84.

14. Deloria, *Playing Indian*, 40.

15. Cooper, *Redskins*, 506.

16. James Fenimore Cooper, *The Chainbearer. Or, The Littlepage Manuscripts*, ed. Lance Schachterle and James P. Elliott (Albany: State University of New York Press, 2020), 1–3.

17. Hugh Egan, historical introduction to *The Redskins*, by James Fenimore Cooper (Albany: State University of New York Press, 2024). My thanks to Hugh Egan and the press for allowing me to see an advance copy of the introduction.

18. Franklin, *Cooper: The Later Years*, 377.

19. Although Melville's reading of *The Redskins* has not yet been documented, many parallels exist between Cooper's novel and *Pierre*. See Roger Hecht, "Rents in the Landscape: The Anti-Rent War in Melville's *Pierre*," *American Transcendental Quarterly* 19, no. 1 (March 2005): 37–50.

20. Herman Melville, *Pierre: Or, The Ambiguities*, ed. Robert Levine and Cindy Weinstein (1852; repr., New York: W. W. Norton, 2017), 15.

21. Roger Hecht, " 'Mighty Lordships in the Heart of the Republic': The Anti-Rent Subtext in *Pierre*," in *A Political Companion to Herman Melville*, ed. Jason Frank (Lexington: University Press of Kentucky, 2013): 141–61; here, 143.

22. Melville, *Pierre*, 274.

23. Fredricks, *Melville's Art of Democracy*, 100.

24. Melville, *Pierre*, 275.

25. Hecht, "Rents in the Landscape," 39.

26. Melville, *Pierre*, 16.

27. The most comprehensive biography is Richard Bremer's *Indian Agent and Wilderness Scholar: The Life of Henry Rowe Schoolcraft* (Mount Pleasant, MI: Clarke Historical Library, Central Michigan University, 1987). For a regional perspective on this native son, see Gregg, *Old Hellebergh*, 185–88.

28. On métis culture and the Johnston family, see *The Sound the Stars Make Rushing Through the Sky: The Writings of Jane Johnston Schoolcraft*, edited and with an introduction by Robert Dale Parker (Philadelphia: University of Pennsylvania Press, 2007), 1–28; and Kelly Wisecup, *Assembled for Use: Indigenous Compilation and the Archives of Early Native American Literatures* (New Haven, CT: Yale University Press, 2021), 99–136. I wish to thank Kelly for her insightful observations on the Johnston-Schoolcraft legacy.

29. Bremer, *Indian Agent*, 162–71. Anishinaabe refers to a major group of culturally related Indigenous peoples in the Great Lakes region that includes the Ojibwe (Chippewa) and Odawa (Ottawa). The two tribes' respective languages are part of the Algonquian linguistic family. Henry Schoolcraft coined the neologism *Algic* as a general designation for the Anishinaabe and other Native Americans who resided between the northern Atlantic coast and the Mississippi River.

30. Bremer, *Indian Agent*, 275–81. This work led to Schoolcraft's final major project, the six-volume *Historical and Statistical Information Regarding the History, Conditions, and Prospects of the Indian Tribes of the United States* (Philadelphia: J. B. Lippincott, 1851–1857).

31. Guilderland's glass manufacture and pine barrens assume a mythological aura in the next stanza (II:37):

Place—once renowned for furnaces, that threw
Their rolling volumes to the amber skies,
Where reeking glassmen their bright fabrics blew
'Neath roofs that shamed the piny hills for size.

32. Lewis Henry Morgan's New Confederacy, which required Indian costume for its white fraternal members, literally hailed Schoolcraft with an invitation to address their annual meeting so garbed. Schoolcraft gave the address in summer 1845, but whether he donned Indian apparel is unclear; see Deloria, *Playing Indian*, 85–88.

33. Parker, in Jane Schoolcraft, *The Sound the Stars Make*, 45.

34. Mary Howard Schoolcraft was a slaveowner and author of the notorious novel *The Black Gauntlet*. On her work as Henry's amanuensis, see Debra Lindsay, "Intimate Inmates: Wives, Households, and Science in Nineteenth-Century America," *Isis* 89, no. 4 (December 1998): 631–52.

35. Parker, in Jane Schoolcraft, *The Sound the Stars Make*, 58.

36. The Schoolcrafts produced fifteen issues of a monthly journal, *The Muzzeniegun, or Literary Voyager*, from 1826 to 1827; see Parker, in Jane Schoolcraft, *The Sound the Stars Make*, 34–36.

37. In his pioneering work on this period, Michael Denning describes the "cultural front" as "the extraordinary flowering of arts, entertainment and thought based on the broad social movement that came to be known as the Popular Front"; see *The Cultural Front: The Laboring of American Culture in the Twentieth Century* (London: Verso, 1997), xvi.

38. Alexander Flick, foreword to Gregg, *Old Hellerbergh*, viii.

39. Gregg, *Old Hellerbergh*, 153–54.

40. Monroe, *The Anti-Rent War*, vii.

41. Monroe, *Chapters in the History of Delaware County, New York* (N.p.: Delaware County Historical Association, 1949), title page. Curiously, the Anti-Rent episode is not discussed in this book.

42. New York State does not maintain a list of markers; the best source for information is the Historical Marker Database (https://www.hmdb.org/).

43. Lithgow created fourteen murals depicting regional history for the library of the Milne School, a progressive high school teacher training program of the State Normal College. The Milne building now houses University at Albany's Rockefeller College. A digital reproduction of *"An Incident of Anti-Rentism" Milne 200 Mural, 1935* can be viewed online at the M. E. Grenander Department of Special Collections and Archives, University Libraries, University at Albany, State University of New York (https://archives.albany.edu/).

44. A photograph of the installed mural can be viewed online at https://livingnewdeal.org/. Earley's preliminary study for the mural, *Down Rent War, around 1845* (oil on canvas), can be viewed online at the Smithsonian American Art Museum, https://americanart.si.edu/artist/mary-earley-7365.

45. John Martin, "The Dance: In the Offing," *New York Times*, December 14, 1941; Judith Cody, *Vivian Fine: A Bio-Bibliography* (Westport, CT: Greenwood Press, 2002).

46. Undated typescript, p. 15, series 9, box 1, folder 10, Norman Studer Papers, 1817–2012, M. E. Grenander Special Collections and Archives, University at Albany, State University of New York (hereafter referred to as the Studer Papers).

47. Undated typescript, p. 32, series 4.2, box 2, folder 1, the Studer Papers.

48. The program cover for the August 1976 "Andes Anti-Rent War Celebration" included a photo of an original Calico Indian costume—gown, mask, and tin horn—preserved by local families; reproduced in Rachelle Saltzman, "Calico Indians and Pistol Pills: Traditional Drama, Historical Symbols, and Political Actions in Upstate New York," *New York Folklore* 20, nos. 3–4 (1994): 1–17; here, 6.

49. A photo from the August 1995 commemoration is reproduced in Kubik, *A Free Soil*, 137.

50. It seems more than coincidental that the same name—spelled *Van Rhijn*—is used for one of the principal "old money" families in Julian Fallowes's current HBO series, *The Gilded Age*.

51. Anya Seton, *Dragonwyck*, reprint ed. (Garden City, NY: The Sun Dial Press, 1945). The novel was serialized in *Ladies Home Journal* during summer 1943. I wish to thank Pamela Barrie for sharing her many insights on the author, novel, and film.

52. Seton, *Dragonwyck*, 64.

53. Seton, *Dragonwyck*, 99.

54. Seton, *Dragonwyck*, 104–6. Seton would have recognized something of her father in the Anti-Renters' "playing Indian." Ernest Thompson Seton was the founder of the Woodcraft Indians, an organization devoted to introducing Anglo-American youth to Native American practices. Seton brought this idea to the Boy Scouts, which he cofounded; see Deloria, *Playing Indian*, 95–115.

55. Seton, *Dragonwyck*, 72–73.

56. Seton's account of Hudson River steamboat races led to an entanglement with Carl Carmer, who had published on historical disasters in *The Hudson*; see Lucinda MacKethan, *Anya Seton: A Writing Life* (Chicago: Chicago Review Press, 2020), 92–94.

57. Seton, *Dragonwyck*, 312.

58. MacKethan, *Anya Seton*, 97.

59. Film timings refer to the DVD, *Dragonwyck*, dir. Joseph Mankiewicz, issued with the boxed set, *Fox Horror Classics*, vol. 2 (Twentieth Century Fox, 2008). In the novel, Miranda's father says, "I would rather own one half-acre of barren stony land myself free and clear, than work the richest farm in the country for someone else" (Seton, *Dragonwyck*, 27).

60. Seton, *Dragonwyck*, 90.

61. Commentary by Steve Haberman at 51:15–52:15, special features, *Dragonwyck* DVD.

62. "60 Top Grossers of 1946," *Variety* 165, no. 5 (January 8, 1947): 8. *Dragonwyck* earned $3 million in the first nine months after its release.

63. Seton's novel was reissued by Houghton Mifflin Harcourt in 2013; a limited edition DVD of the remastered film was released in the UK by Powerhouse Films in 2017.

64. Review by John Krout, "The Patroon Meets His Waterloo," *New York Times*, March 18, 1945.

65. Hicks, "Landlord Cooper and the Anti-Renters," 95.

66. Carmer, introduction to *Tin Horns and Calico*, by Christman, xviii–xix.

67. Norman Studer, "Folk Festival of the Catskills," *New York Folklore Quarterly* 16, no. 1 (1960): 6–10; here, 8. I wish to thank Meara McTague for sharing her research on Camp Woodland with me.

68. Online catalog description, "Summary: Biographical/Historical," the Studer Papers, https://archives.albany.edu/description/catalog/apap116#background.

69. Norman Cazden, Herbert Haufrecht, and Norman Studer, eds., *Folk Songs of the Catskills* (Albany: State University of New York Press, 1982), xiii.

70. Undated, unnumbered typescript, series 4.2, box 2, folder 1, the Studer Papers.

71. Undated typescript, pp. 31–33, series 4.2, box 2, folder 1; and "Plays, 'Down Rent,' 1941, 1945," series 4.2, box 2, folder 5, the Studer Papers. Presumably, the costume described by Studer is the same one pictured on the cover of Kubik, *A Free Soil*.

72. For Studer's story, "Action on Dingle Hill," see the undated, fifty-five-page typescript in series 8, box 1, folder 3, the Studer Papers; also available online. According to the Andes Society for History and Culture

president, Joanne Kosuda-Warner, Parthenia Davis's local family sent her to live with and help the Earles at about age twelve. She became an informal family member and remained with the Earles for many years (private communication with author, July 19, 2023).

73. Undated typescript, p. 33, series 4.2, box 2, folder 1, the Studer Papers.

74. For Studer's musical play, see the undated, thirty-four-page typed script in series 4.2, box 2, folder 1, the Studer Papers.

75. Cazden et al., *Folksongs of the Catskills*, 583.

76. Robert Cantwell, *When We Were Good: The Folk Revival* (Cambridge, MA: Harvard University Press, 1996), 269–310; on Camp Woodland, see 275–76. On Norman Studer's lifelong work in progressive education, see the online catalogue description, "Summary: Biographical/Historical," the Studer Papers.

77. "Anti-Rent Wars Remembered in Art, Literature, and Drama," *Altamont Enterprise*, May 24, 2018. Weeks began the education center's theater program in 1962; see "Heldeberg Workshop Dedicating New Theatre Building to Influential Teacher," *Altamont Enterprise*, August 2, 2023.

78. Christman, *Tin Horns and Calico*, 336–38. Christman's source for "The Helderberg War" was *The Working Man's Advocate*, January 4, 1845.

79. "VCH Schedules Drama," *Altamont Enterprise*, May 16, 1975; and "List of New Scotland Bicentennial Events," *Altamont Enterprise*, April 23, 1976.

80. Sullivan, as quoted by Melissa Hale-Spencer, "Getting Kids Involved in History," *Altamont Enterprise*, April 4, 1991. I wish to thank Dennis Sullivan, Voorheesville historian since the mid-1980s, for sharing information about the production with me.

81. I wish to thank George Ward for permission to quote the lyrics of "Old Horns, Proud Horns."

82. Elizabeth Schwartz, "Hey, Nay, We Won't Pay! Hoag Corners' Big Thunder Day," *Times Union* (Albany, NY), July 5, 1989. Thanks to Caroline Leising of the Nassau Free Library, home of the Hoags Corners Association collection, for assistance finding information on this event. Big Thunder Day is described by Saltzman in conjunction with a photo of several flyers announcing the 1992 and 1993 celebrations; see "Calico Indians and Pistol Pills," 12–13.

83. "Anti-Rent Song is Available," *Altamont Enterprise*, October 2, 1997. The recording, "Songs and Ballads of the Anti-Rent Rebellion in New York State, 1839–1889," was produced by the Rensselaerville Historical Society.

84. Information on "The Visitors: The History, Music and Songs of the Adirondacks," and "Four Seasons, Four Years—The Civil War, a Musical Journey," is available on Old Songs' website, https://oldsongs.org/.

85. Note that "Come All True Anti-Renters," which appears in Christman (*Tin Horns and Calico*, 342) is a different text than "We Are True Anti-Renters" (plate 10). Also, Ward's "Native's Enquiry" is different from that of plate 14 despite their nearly identical titles. His source was Devyr's Albany newspaper, *The Anti-Renter* (April 4, 1846). Ward set the poem to the traditional Irish jig "Larry O'Gaff."

86. My summary is based on the program for the November 2014 premiere of *Down with the Rent!* (author's collection). Old Songs produced a DVD of a 2015 production with a slight reordering and a few substitutions of musical works.

87. Spence, as quoted in "Singing Songs That Raised a Rebellion," *Altamont Enterprise*, November 12, 2014.

88. L. M. Bogad, *Tactical Performance: The Theory and Practice of Serious Play* (New York: Routledge, 2016), 5–10.

Bibliography

Newspapers and Serials

Albany Argus
Albany Freeholder
Altamont Enterprise (Albany County, New York)
Anti-Renter
New York Herald
Working Man's Advocate
Young America: Organ of the National Reform Association

Books, Articles, and Primary Sources

Abraham, Roger. "Calico Indians: Festive Play in Acts of Resistance." *Voices: The Journal of New York Folklore* 32, nos. 3–4 (Fall–Winter 2006): 35–41.

The American Poetical Miscellany, Original and Selected. Philadelphia: Robert Johnson, C. & A. Conrad, and Mathew Carey, 1809.

"An Act Concerning Tenures (1787)." In *Laws of the State of New-York*. Vol. 1: 64–66. Albany, NY: Websters and Skinner, 1807.

Ayars, Christine. *Contributions to the Art of Music in America by the Music Industries of Boston, 1640–1936*. New York: H. W. Wilson, 1937.

Barrus, Clara. *John Burroughs: Boy and Man*. New York: Doubleday, Page, 1920.

Basch, Norma. *In the Eyes of the Law: Women, Marriage, and Property in Nineteenth-Century New York*. Ithaca, NY: Cornell University Press, 1982.

Bernstein, Robin. *Freeman's Challenge: The Murder That Shook America's Original Prison for Profit*. Chicago: University of Chicago Press, 2024.

Bogad, L. M. "Facial Insufficiency: Political Street Performance in New York City and the Selective Enforcement of the 1845 Mask Law." *The Drama Review* 47, no. 4 (Winter 2003): 75–84.

———. *Tactical Performance: The Theory and Practice of Serious Play*. New York: Routledge, 2016.

Boughton, James. *Bouton–Boughton Family*. Albany: Joel Munsell's Sons, 1890.

Bradbury, William, ed. *Temperance Chimes*. New York: National Temperance Society, 1867.

Bremer, Richard. *Indian Agent and Wilderness Scholar: The Life of Henry Rowe Schoolcraft*. Mount Pleasant, MI: Clarke Historical Library, Central Michigan University, 1987.

Bronson, Bertrand. "Some Observations about Melodic Variation in British-American Folk Tunes." *Journal of the American Musicological Society* 3, no. 2 (Summer 1950): 120–34.

———. *The Traditional Tunes of the Child Ballads*. Vol. 1, *Ballads 1 to 53*. Princeton, NJ: Princeton University Press, 1959.

Bronstein, Jamie. *Land Reform and Working-Class Experience in Britain and the United States, 1800–1862*. Stanford, CA: Stanford University Press, 1999.

———. "'Under Their Own Vine and Fig Tree': Land Reform and Working-Class Experience in Britain and America, 1830–1860." PhD diss., Stanford University, 1996.

Browne, Ray. *The Alabama Folk Lyric: A Study in Origins and Media of Dissemination*. Bowling Green, OH: Bowling Green University Popular Press, 1979.

Bryant, William Cullen. *The Letters of William Cullen Bryant*. Vol. 1, *1809–1836*, edited by William Cullen Bryant II and Thomas Voss. New York: Fordham University Press, 1975.

Bunting, Edward. *The Ancient Music of Ireland*. 3 vols. Dublin: Hodges and Smith, 1796–1840. Reprint, Dublin: Waltons' Piano and Musical Instrument Galleries, 1969.

Cantwell, Robert. *When We Were Good: The Folk Revival*. Cambridge, MA: Harvard University Press, 1996.

Carmer, Carl. *The Hudson*. New York: Farrar and Rinehart, 1939.

Cazden, Norman, Herbert Haufrecht, and Norman Studer, eds. *Folk Songs of the Catskills*. Albany: State University of New York Press, 1982.

Chappell, William, and George Alexander Macfarren. *The Ballad Literature and Popular Music of the Olden Time*. Vol. 2. London: Chappell, 1859.

Chernow, Ron. *Alexander Hamilton*. New York: Penguin Press, 2004.

Cheyney, Edward Potts. *The Anti-Rent Agitation in the State of New York, 1839–1846*. Philadelphia: Porter and Coates, 1887.

Child, Francis James. *The English and Scottish Popular Ballads*. 5 vols. (1882–1898). Vol. 1, Part 2. Boston: Houghton Mifflin, 1884.

Christman, Henry. *Tin Horns and Calico: A Decisive Episode in the Emergence of Democracy*. Introduction by Carl Carmer. Bicentennial Edition. Cornwallville, NY: Hope Farm Press, 1978. First published 1945 by Henry Holt.

Clark, George Washington. *The Free Soil Minstrel*. New York: Martyn & Ely, 1848.

Cockrell, Dale, ed. *Excelsior: Journals of the Hutchinson Family Singers, 1842–1846*. Stuyvesant, NY: Pendragon Press, 1989.

Cody, Judith. *Vivian Fine: A Bio-Bibiography*. Westport, CT: Greenwood Press, 2002.

Coleman, William Lavine. "Something of an Architect: Thomas Cole and the Country House Ideal." PhD diss., University of California, Berkeley, 2015.

Cooper, James Femimore. *The Chainbearer. Or, The Littlepage Manuscripts*. Edited by Lance Schachterle and James P. Elliott. Introduction by Lance Schachterle, Wesley Mott, and John P. McWilliams. Albany: State University of New York Press, 2020.

———. *The Redskins*. Historical introduction, notes, and text by Hugh Egan. Albany: State University of New York Press, 2024.

———. *The Redskins, or Indian and Injin*. New York: Burgess, Stringer, 1846.

———. *Satanstoe*. New York: Burgess, Stringer, 1845.

Crawford, Richard. *America's Musical Life: A History*. New York: W. W. Norton, 2001.

———. *An Introduction to America's Music*. New York: W. W. Norton, 2001.

Crawford Seeger, Ruth. *The Music of American Folk Song and Selected Other Writings on American Folk Music*. Edited by Larry Polansky and Judith Tick. Rochester, NY: University of Rochester Press, 2003.

Crouthamel, James. *Bennett's* New York Herald *and the Rise of the Popular Press*. Syracuse, NY: Syracuse University Press, 1989.

Deloria, Philip. *Playing Indian*. New Haven, CT: Yale University Press, 1998.

Denning, Michael. *The Cultural Front: The Laboring of American Culture in the Twentieth Century*. London: Verso, 1997.

Devyr, Thomas Aige. *The Odd Book of the Nineteenth Century, or, "Chivalry" in Modern Days, A Personal Record of Reform—Chiefly Land Reform, for the Last Fifty Years*. Greenpoint, NY: Published by the author, 1882.

———. *Our Natural Rights*. Williamsburg, NY: published by the author, 1842.

Ellis, David Maldwyn. "The Coopers and New York State Landholding Systems." *New York History* 35, no. 4 (1954): 412–22.

———. *Landlords and Farmers in the Hudson-Mohawk Region, 1790–1850*. Ithaca, NY: Cornell University Press, 1946.

Foner, Philip, ed. *American Labor Songs of the Nineteenth Century*. Urbana: University of Illinois Press, 1975.

———, ed. *We, the Other People: Alternative Declarations of Independence . . . 1829–1975*. Urbana: University of Illinois Press, 1976.

Ford, Henry Jones. *The Scotch-Irish in America*. Princeton, NJ: Princeton University Press, 1915.

Franklin, Wayne. *James Fenimore Cooper: The Early Years*. New Haven, CT: Yale University Press, 2007.

———. *James Fenimore Cooper: The Later Years*. New Haven, CT: Yale University Press, 2017.

Frasca, Ralph. "The *Helderberg Advocate*: A Public-Nuisance Prosecution a Century before *Near v. Minnesota*." *Journal of Supreme Court History* 26, no. 3 (November 2001): 215–30.

Fredricks, Nancy. *Melville's Art of Democracy*. Athens: University of Georgia Press, 1995.

Gac, Scott. *Singing for Freedom: The Hutchinson Family Singers and the Nineteenth-Century Culture of Reform*. New Haven, CT: Yale University Press, 2008.

Galbreath, C. B. "Song Writers of Ohio." *Ohio Archaeological and Historical Publications* 14, no. 1 (1905): 62–87.

Gardner, Emelyn. *Folklore from the Schoharie Hills of New York*. Ann Arbor: University of Michigan Press, 1937.

Godine, Amy. *The Black Woods: Pursuing Racial Justice on the Adirondack Frontier*. Ithaca, NY: Cornell University Press, 2023.

Gould, Jay. *History of Delaware County and Border Wars of New York, Containing a Sketch of the Late Anti-Rent Difficulties in Delaware*. Roxbury, NY: Keeny & Gould, 1856.

Gregg, Arthur. *Old Hellerbergh: Historical Sketches of the West Manor of Rensselaerwyck*. Foreword by Alexander Flick. 1936. Reprint, Guilderland Center, NY: Guilderland Historical Society, 1975.

Hadaway, T. H., ed. *Hadaway's Select Songster*. Philadelphia: Gihon and Kucher, 1840.

Hamilton, Alexander. "Stephen Van Rensselaer to the Tenants of Rensselaerwyck (July–August 1786)." *Founders Online*, National Archives, https://founders.archives.gov/documents/Hamilton/01-26-02-0002-0122.

Hamm, Charles. *Yesterdays: Popular Song in America*. New York: W. W. Norton, 1979.

Hecht, Roger. *Freemen Awake! Rally Songs and Poems from New York's Anti-Rent Movement*. N.p.: Delaware County Historical Association, 2017.

———. " 'Mighty Lordships in the Heart of the Republic': The Anti-Rent Subtext in *Pierre*." In *A Political Companion to Herman Melville*, edited by Jason Frank, 141–61. Lexington: University Press of Kentucky, 2013.

———. "Rents in the Landscape: The Anti-Rent War in Melville's *Pierre*." *American Transcendental Quarterly* 19, no. 1 (March 2005): 37–50.

———. "'Rouse Ye Anti-Renters': Poetry and Politics in the Anti-Rent Press." *The Hudson River Valley Review* 28, no. 2 (Spring 2012): 3–21.

Hewlett's Temperance Songster. Cooperstown, NY: printed for S. M. Hewlett, 1844.

Hicks, Granville. "Landlord Cooper and the Anti-Renters." *Antioch Review* 5, no. 1 (Spring 1945): 95–109.

Hisama, Ellie. "The Ruth Crawford Seeger Sessions." *Daedalus* 142, no. 4 (Fall 2013): 51–63.

Hogg, James. *Familiar Anecdotes of Sir Walter Scott*, with a *Sketch of the Shepherd's Life* by S. DeWitt Bloodgood. New York: Harper and Brothers, 1834.

———. *The Forest Minstrel.* Edited by P. D. Garside and Richard Jackson, musical notation prepared by Peter Horsfall. Edinburgh: Edinburgh University Press, 2006.

———, compiler and illustrator. *The Jacobite Relics of Scotland; Being the Songs, Airs and Legends of the Adherents to the House of Stuart.* Edinburgh: William Blackwood, 1819.

Howson, John. "Edward Rushton (1856–1914): Radical Liverpool Poet and Ballad Maker." *Folk Music Journal* 12, no. 2 (2022): 36–59.

Hudson Gazette, ed. *Columbia County at the End of the Century.* Hudson, NY: Hudson Gazette, 1900.

Huston, Reeve. *Land and Freedom: Rural Society, Popular Protest, and Party Politics in Antebellum New York.* New York: Oxford University Press, 2000.

———. "Multiple Crossings: Thomas Ainge Devyr and Transatlantic Land Reform." In *Transatlantic Rebels: Agrarian Radicalism in Comparative Context*, edited by Thomas Summerhill and James Scott, 137–66. East Lansing: Michigan State University Press, 2004.

———. "The Parties and 'The People': The New York Anti-Rent Wars and the Contours of Jacksonian Politics." *Journal of the Early Republic* 20, no. 2 (Summer 2000): 241–71.

Jerrold, Douglas. *The Rent Day.* 2nd ed. London: C. Chapple, 1832.

Johnson, Helen Kendrick. *Our Familiar Songs and Those Who Made Them: Three Hundred Standard Songs.* New York: Henry Holt, 1881.

Johnson, James. *The Scotish Musical Museum.* Notes by William Stenhouse. 6 vols. Edinburgh: William Blackwood and Sons, 1839.

Judson, Harry. *A History of the Troy Citizen Corps, Troy, N.Y.* Troy, NY: Troy Times Printing House, 1884.

Kelsay, Isabel Thompson. "The Trial of Big Thunder." *New York History* 16, no. 3 (July 1935): 266–77.

Kim, Sung Bok. *Landlord and Tenant in Colonial New York: Manorial Society, 1664–1775.* Chapel Hill: University of North Carolina Press, 1978.

Kirk, Elise. "'Hail to the Chief': The Origins and Legacies of an American Ceremonial Tune." *American Music* 15, no. 2 (Summer 1997): 123–36.

Kubik, Dorothy. *A Free Soil—A Free People: The Anti-Rent War in Delaware County, New York.* Fleischmanns, NY: Purple Mountain Press, 1997.

Lagoy, Donna, and Donna Seldman. *The Underground Railroad in the Adirondack Town of Chester.* Charleston, SC: History Press, 2016.

Lause, Mark. *Young America: Land, Labor, and the Republican Community.* Urbana: University of Illinois Press, 2005.

Levy, Lester. *Picture the Songs: Lithographs from the Sheet Music of Nineteenth-Century America.* Baltimore: Johns Hopkins University Press, 1976.

Lindsay, Debra. "Intimate Inmates: Wives, Households, and Science in Nineteenth-Century America." *Isis* 89, no. 4 (December 1998): 631–52.

MacKethan, Lucinda. *Anya Seton: A Writing Life.* Chicago: Chicago Review Press, 2020.

Mahar, William. *Behind the Burnt Cork Mask: Early Blackface Minstrelsy and Antebellum Popular Culture.* Urbana: University of Illinois Press, 1999.

Mandell, Daniel. *The Lost Tradition of Economic Equality in America, 1600–1870.* Baltimore: Johns Hopkins University Press, 2020.

Mankiewicz, Joseph, dir. *Dragonwyck*. 1946. *Fox Horror Classics*, Vol. 2. Los Angeles, CA: Twentieth Century Fox, 2008. DVD.

Maretzek, Max. *Crotchets and Quavers, or, Revelations of an Opera Manager in America*. New York: S. French, 1855.

Mayham, Albert Champlin. *The Anti-Rent War on Blenheim Hill*. Jefferson, NY: Frederick Frazee, 1906.

McCurdy, Charles. *The Anti-Rent Era in New York Law and Politics*. Chapel Hill: University of North Carolina Press, 2001.

Melville, Herman. *Pierre: Or, The Ambiguities*. Edited by Robert Levine and Cindy Weinstein. New York: W. W. Norton, 2017. First published 1852 by Harper & Bros.

Miles, Christine. "History of the AIHA Collections." Introduction to *Albany Institute of History and Art: 200 Years of Collecting*, edited by Tammis Groft and Mary Alice Mackay. New York: Hudson Hills Press, 1998.

Monroe, John Duncan. *The Anti-Rent War in Delaware County, New York: The Revolt against the Rent System*. Privately printed, 1940.

———. *Chapters in the History of Delaware County, New York*. N.p.: Delaware County Historical Association, 1949.

Murray, David. "The Antirent Episode in the State of New York." *Annual Report of the American Historical Association for 1896*, 1 (1897): 139–73.

Myers, Gustavus. *History of the Supreme Court of the United States*. Chicago: Charles H. Kerr, 1912.

New-York Military Magazine 1, no. 11 (August 21, 1841): 175.

Norman Studer Papers, 1817–2012. M. E. Grenander Special Collections and Archives, University at Albany, State University of New York.

Norton, A. B., ed. *Tippecanoe Songs of the Log Cabin Boys and Girls of 1840*. Mt. Vernon, OH: A. B. Norton, 1888.

Odell, George. *Annals of the New York Stage*. Vol. 2, *1798–1821*. New York: Columbia University Press, 1927.

Oswald, James. *The Caledonian Pocket Companion, Containing a Favorite Collection of Scots Tunes with Variations for the German Flute or Violin*. London: Straight & Skillern, [1770?].

———. *The Caledonian Pocket Companion, in Six Volumes*. London: printed for the author, [1747?].

Pepper, Calvin. *Manor of Rensselaerwyck*. Albany, NY: Albany and Rensselaer Anti-Rent Associations, 1846.

Pickering, John. *Working Man's Political Economy*. Cincinnati: Thomas Varney, 1847.

The Posie; an Elegant Selection of the Most Popular Songs, Duets, and Glees. Part 3. Glasgow: Francis Orr and Sons, 1830.

Rahill, Frank. *The World of Melodrama*. University Park: Pennsylvania State University Press, 1967.

Ranciere, Jacques. *Nights of Labor: The Workers' Dream in Nineteenth Century France*. Translated by John Drury. Philadelphia: Temple University Press, 1989.

Renehan, Edward, ed. *The Clearwater Songbook*. New York: G. Schirmer, 1980.

Rezneck, Samuel. "The Social History of an American Depression, 1837–1843." *The American Historical Review* 40, no. 4 (July 1935): 662–87.

Robson, Ruthann. *Dressing Constitutionally: Hierarchy, Sexuality, and Democracy from Our Hairstyles to Our Shoes*. New York: Cambridge University Press, 2013.

Rosendale, Simon. "Closing Phases of the Manorial System in Albany." *Proceedings of the New York State Historical Association* 8 (1909): 234–45.

Roud, Steve. *The New Penguin Book of English Folk Songs*. London: Penguin Classics, 2012.

Saltzman, Rachelle. "Calico Indians and Pistol Pills: Traditional Drama, Historical Symbols, and Political Actions in Upstate New York." *New York Folklore* 20, nos. 3–4 (1994): 1–17.

Schoolcraft, Henry Rowe. *Helderbergia: Or the Apotheosis of the Heroes of the Antirent War*. Albany, NY: J. Munsell, 1855.

Schoolcraft, Jane Johnston. *The Sound the Stars Make Rushing Through the Sky: The Writings of Jane Johnston Schoolcraft*. Edited and with an introduction by Robert Dale Parker. Philadelphia: University of Pennsylvania Press, 2007.

Scott, Derek. "The US Presidential Campaign Songster, 1840–1900." In *Cheap Print and Popular Song in the Nineteenth Century: A Cultural History of the Songster*, edited by Paul Watt, Derek Scott, and Patrick Spedding, 73–90. Cambridge: Cambridge University Press, 2017.

Scott, Walter, and John Gibson Lockhart. *The Poetical Works of Sir Walter Scott, Comprising Minstrelsy of the Scottish Border*. Philadelphia: E. L. Carey and A. Hart, 1839.

Seeger, Pete, and Paul Du Bois Jacobs. *Pete Seeger's Storytelling Book*. San Diego: Harcourt, 2001.

Seton, Anya. *Dragonwyck*. Reprint, Garden City, NY: The Sun Dial Press, 1945.

Silverman, Jerry. *New York Sings: 400 Years of the Empire State in Song*. Excelsior Editions. Albany: State University of New York Press, 2009.

The Sky-Lark: A Collection of Songs Set to Music. London: Thomas Tegg, 1825.

Slobin, Mark, James Kimball, Katherine Preston, Deane Root, eds. *Emily's Songbook: Music in 1850s Albany*. Middleton, WI: A-R Editions, 2011.

Smith, Jewel. *Transforming Women's Education: Liberal Arts and Music in Female Seminaries*. Urbana: University of Illinois Press, 2019.

Spencer, Jon Michael. *Protest and Praise: Sacred Music of Black Religion*. Minneapolis, MN: Fortress Press, 1990.

Strange, Carolyn. *Discretionary Justice: Pardon and Parole in New York from the Revolution to the Depression*. New York: New York University Press, 2016.

Studer, Norman. "Folk Festival of the Catskills." *New York Folklore Quarterly* 16, no. 1 (1960): 6–10.

Summerhill, Thomas. *Harvest of Dissent: Agrarianism in Nineteenth Century New York*. Urbana: University of Illinois Press, 2005.

Taylor, Alan. *William Cooper's Town: Power and Persuasion on the Frontier of the Early American Republic*. New York: A. A. Knopf, 1995.

Torrance, Mary Fisher. *The Story of Old Rensselaerville*. New York: privately printed, 1939.

Tuchinsky, Adam-Max. *Horace Greeley's* New-York Tribune: *Civil War-Era Socialism and the Crisis of Free Labor*. Ithaca, NY: Cornell University Press, 2009.

Waugh, Joseph. *The Temperance Muse*. Providence, RI: H. H. Brown, 1842.

Wermuth, Thomas. "Charivari on the Hudson: Misrule, Disorder, and Festive Play in the Countryside, 1750–1900." *The Hudson River Valley Review* 32, no. 2 (Spring 2016): 27–52.

Wilentz, Sean. *The Rise of American Democracy: Jefferson to Lincoln*. New York: W. W. Norton, 2006.

Wilgus, D. K. "'Rose Connoley': An Irish Ballad." *Journal of American Folklore* 92, no. 364 (April–June 1979): 172–95.

Williams, Oscar. "Slavery in Albany, New York, 1624–1827." *Afro-Americans in New York Life and History* 34, no. 2 (July 2010): 154–168.

Wisecup, Kelly. *Assembled for Use: Indigenous Compilation and the Archives of Early Native American Literatures*. New Haven, CT: Yale University Press, 2021.

Wolfe, Richard. *Secular Music in America, 1801–25, A Bibliography*. Vol. 1. New York: New York Public Library, 1964.

Wright, Silas. "Message to the Legislature—1845." New York State Government Documents, New York State Library. OCLC/NY ID 4671459. January 7, 1845.

Zahler, Helene. *Eastern Workingmen and National Land Policy, 1829–1862*. New York: Greenwood Press, 1969. First published 1941 by Columbia University Press.

Zinn, Howard. *A People's History of the United States*. New York: HarperCollins, 2003.

Index

Plates are indicated in *italics*.